IMAGES
of America

LOWNDES COUNTY

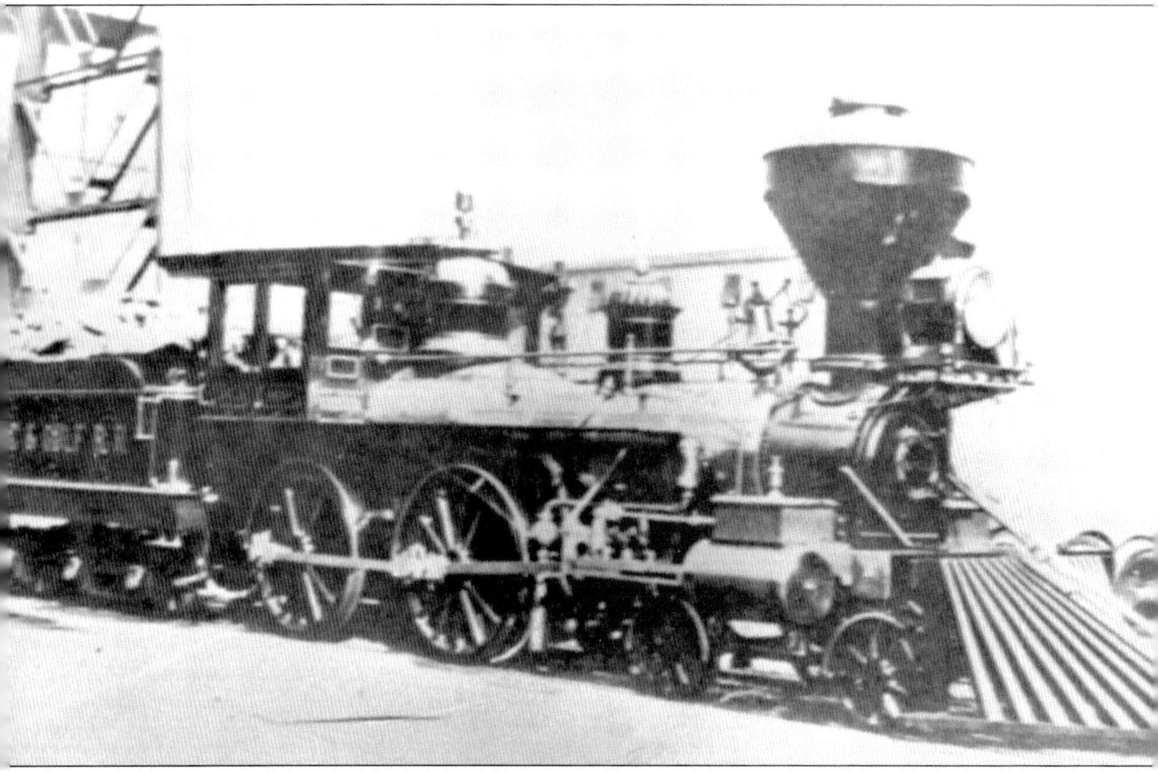

This image—the arrival of the first train on the recently completed railroad tracks from Savannah—symbolizes a development of major historical significance for both Lowndes County and the new county seat of Valdosta. As local historian Louis Schmier wrote, "It was called 'an awesome wonder of nature.' Most residents of the county had never seen 'one of them new-fangled steamers.' Therefore, when the Satilla No. 3, with its train of passenger cars, first rolled into Valdosta in July, 1860, most people had gathered more out of curiosity than to celebrate the linking of the area with Savannah."

ON THE COVER: Historically tobacco was among Lowndes County's most important agricultural products. In this undated photograph, apparently from the 1950s, a fully grown crop of unusually tall tobacco is shown in the field when only the lower leaves have been "cropped." Inspecting the field are James Blanchard, on the left, and Judge Harley Langdale, on the right. (Valdosta–Lowndes County Chamber of Commerce.)

IMAGES
of America

LOWNDES COUNTY

Dr. Joseph A. Tomberlin on behalf of
the Lowndes County Historical Society

ARCADIA
PUBLISHING

ISBN 978-0-7385-4376-5

Published by Arcadia Publishing
Charleston, South Carolina

Printed in the United States of America

Library of Congress Catalog Card Number: 2006932458

For all general information contact Arcadia Publishing at:
Telephone 843-853-2070
Fax 843-853-0044
E-mail sales@arcadiapublishing.com
For customer service and orders:
Toll-Free 1-888-313-2665

Visit us on the Internet at www.arcadiapublishing.com

This book is dedicated to my wife, Norma, who is part of all that I do, and to the late Dr. William M. Gabard, my mentor and longtime friend, who was instrumental in founding the Lowndes County Historical Society almost 40 years ago and served as the society's first president.

Contents

ACKNOWLEDGMENTS

In the nearly 40 years of its existence, the Lowndes County Historical Society has developed an excellent museum of local history that displays artifacts and houses a first-class research library of books, journals, maps, original documents, and photographs. The principle followed in the creation of this book was to include only images selected from the museum's photographic archives. I am indebted to the society for granting total access to all collections and to Myrna Ballard, president of the Valdosta–Lowndes Chamber of Commerce, for permitting me to use pictures from the chamber's collection, which is archived in the museum.

I particularly thank Julie Branch Smith, president of the Lowndes County Historical Society and a gifted historian in her own right, for persisting in her effort to persuade me to assemble this pictorial history and for her encouragement along the way. I extend my gratitude to the museum's staff, including Donald O. Davis, who was helpful in many ways, especially in pointing me to sources of pictures that I had not thought of and in identifying people long dead and locations that no longer exist. I am deeply grateful to Renate K. Milner, another first-rate historian, for the incredible amount of essential work that she performed in scanning every image included in the book. Quite literally, the book would not have been possible without her. I am obliged also to Maggie T. Bullwinkel, acquisitions editor at Arcadia Publishing, who kept me on course. Above all, I thank Norma, Lucy, Joe, and Tina for their love, support, and patience.

INTRODUCTION

Lowndes County is situated in the Wiregrass area of South Georgia, just north of Florida. The region had human inhabitants from ancient times, but until relatively recently in history, none of them stayed long. Few concrete traces of their existence remained to the modern era, and no Europeans were physically present before the founding of the neighboring Spanish missions of Santa Maria de los Angeles de Arapaja and Santa Cruz de Cachipile around 1623. Recent excavations have shown that Santa Cruz de Cachipile was within the bounds of what is now Lowndes County, but the mission did not endure.

The first American settlers in the vicinity arrived in 1821, four years before the creation of Lowndes County from the lower half of Irwin County. The Georgia General Assembly established Lowndes by carving it from Irwin in December 1825 and named it in honor of South Carolinian Williams Jones Lowndes, a planter, lawyer, Congressman, and candidate for vice president. Lowndes's first town, settled in 1827 and designated as the county seat in 1828, was Franklinville. Five years later, in 1833, Lowndesville, at the confluence of the Little and Withlacoochee Rivers, replaced Franklinville as county seat. Lowndesville became Troupville in 1837 to honor the popular Georgia senator and former governor, George Troup.

In 1859–1860, Lowndes County changed its seat again, this time owing to the building of the Atlantic and Gulf Railroad along a path four miles south of Troupville. The Atlantic and Gulf ultimately ran from Screven in the east to Thomasville in the west and provided a connection to Savannah via the Savannah, Albany, and Gulf Railroad at Screven. Wishing to enjoy the benefits of immediate access to the railroad and thereby to Savannah, many inhabitants of Troupville and of the county demanded the creation of a new town and county seat located directly on the Atlantic and Gulf. Consequently, the General Assembly in 1859 selected four commissioners to pinpoint a site for the new town. They bought 140 acres of land from William Wisenbaker, and the town placed there became Valdosta, for Val d'Aosta, a plantation belonging to George Troup, previously honored as the namesake of the old county seat. The Atlantic and Gulf's first train to Lowndes County, powered by a locomotive known as Satilla No. 3, arrived in Valdosta on July 4, 1860. These seemingly favorable developments occurred almost on the eve of the Civil War.

Lowndes County was not a scene of any military action whatever, but the war that raged from 1861 to 1865 had a substantial impact on the region. While local men served in the Confederate armies elsewhere, Lowndes became a refuge for civilians who had fled the fighting. From early in the war, an increasingly effective Union naval blockade of the Confederacy made consumer goods, including most necessities, nearly impossible to obtain. When needed items were available, they were unbearably expensive. Moreover, beginning in November 1864, Lowndes County lost its most important link to the outside world, the Atlantic and Gulf Railroad's tie with Savannah. Union major general William T. Sherman's "bummers" tore up miles of the tracks while carrying out their "march to the sea." Only in March 1866 did the Atlantic and Gulf have its tracks repaired and resumed sending trains through Lowndes County.

The impact of war upon the county was enduring, particularly in the sense that the local economy was sickly well into the 1880s, and some effects continued to linger far beyond that decade. When Sea Island, or long-staple, cotton began to be grown in the county in the 1880s, the economy showed signs of reviving, and Valdosta became a major inland market for Sea Island cotton. Also in 1889, the Georgia Southern and Florida Railroad extended its tracks through Lowndes and Valdosta, providing the county with a long-desired north-south rail line. The development that appeared to many residents to be a concrete indication of the county's economic recovery was the holding of a state fair in Valdosta in 1900. Indeed substantial changes were occurring. In 1904–1905, the county's two-story red brick courthouse, built in 1875, was razed, and a beautiful, new courthouse designed in the neoclassical Revival style by Frank P. Milburn was erected. In 1906, the general assembly chartered the South Georgia Normal College, for women, in Valdosta, and classes convened for the first time in 1913. In the same period, three additional railroads came to Lowndes County, giving the county significant rail connections in almost every direction.

On the negative side, the highly destructive boll weevil invaded Georgia in 1915 and had a devastating effect on the still shaky farm economy by ravaging cotton crops across the state. Southern agriculture, still feeling some of the consequences of the Civil War, fell into persistent depression that simply worsened when the Great Depression struck in the 1930s. In the meantime, after the First World War, which involved the United States most directly in 1917–1918, local leaders, in the hope of easing dependence on the unsound farm economy, tried to attract non-agricultural industry and also began to campaign for tourism, then in its formative stages. The new National Road or Dixie Highway, eventually designated as U.S. Highway 41, ran through the county, including Hahira in northern Lowndes, Valdosta, and Lake Park in southern Lowndes. Tourism was a major local business by the mid-1920s and continued as an important segment of the economy, especially after the construction of Interstate Highway 75 through the county in the 1960s.

The hard times that accompanied the Great Depression and continued throughout the 1930s finally ended when the United States entered World War II in 1941. As tragic as the conflict was, it generated a boom that restored full employment and benefited almost every element of the economy, including agriculture. Lowndes County shared in the return of prosperity. Particularly important was the establishment of Moody Field, later Moody Air Force Base, on rural land on the east side of Georgia Highway 125 ten miles north of Valdosta. Moody operated until 1946, when it was deactivated. The Korean War of 1950–1953 led to the base's reopening in 1951, and it has remained active since then. Moody became Lowndes County's largest employer and probably is the single most important factor in the local economy to the present.

Through time, Lowndes County experienced substantial population growth. The first census after its creation, that of 1830, showed 2,453 persons living in the county. Over the next decade, the population grew to 5,574 and by 1850 had reached 7,714. The trend continued to be similar in the last decades of the 20th century. By 1970, the county's population had reached 55,112; in the next decade, it grew to 67,972. In 1990, 75,981 persons were residents of the county, and the figure was up to 92,115 by 2000. The increase between 1970 and 2000 was 67.1 percent. Moreover, the Bureau of the Census estimated the population of the county in 2005 to be 96,705, meaning that Lowndes had surpassed Dougherty County and had become the most populous county in southern Georgia.

One

Schools, Students, and Education

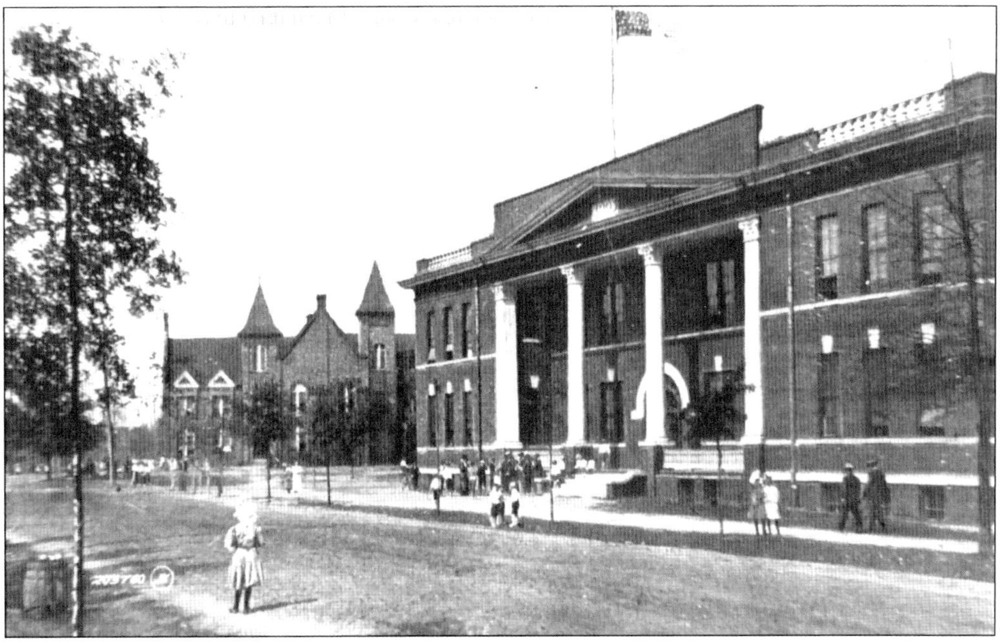

In a photograph from prior to 1921, the essential parts of the independent Valdosta City Schools are shown. The street is West Central Avenue, and on the left is the former Valdosta Institute, then serving as a grammar school and later to be the Valdosta Junior High School until 1950. To the right is Valdosta High School, which was replaced by a new building on Williams Street in 1921 and subsequently became an elementary school, a junior high school, and again an elementary school.

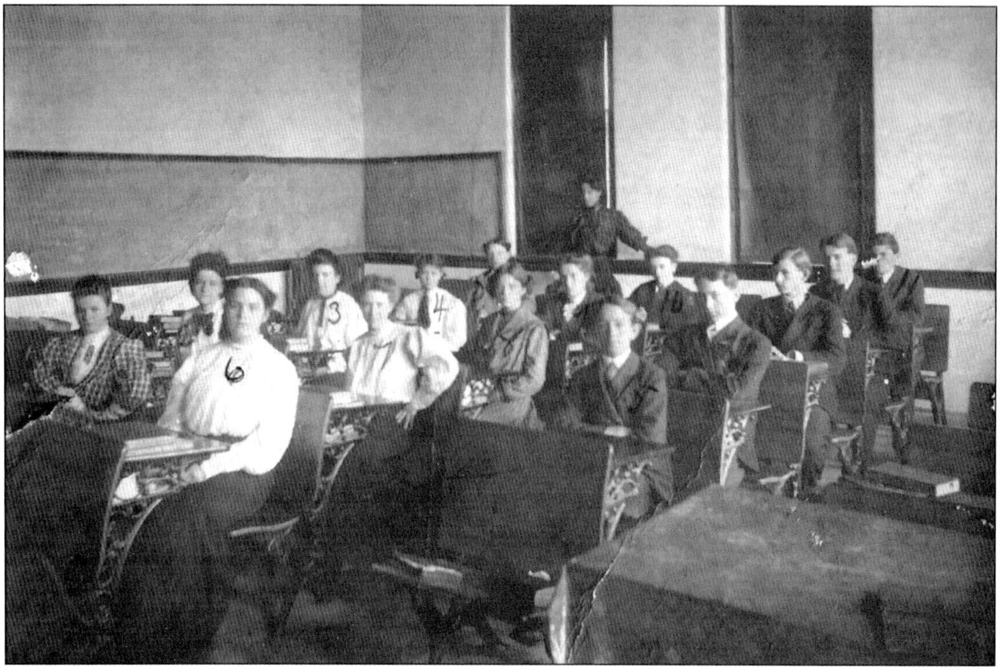

This is an undated classroom scene in the Valdosta Institute prior to its becoming a public school belonging to the City of Valdosta. The notable aspect of the image is the well-dressed appearance of all the students, which indicates the affluence of their families.

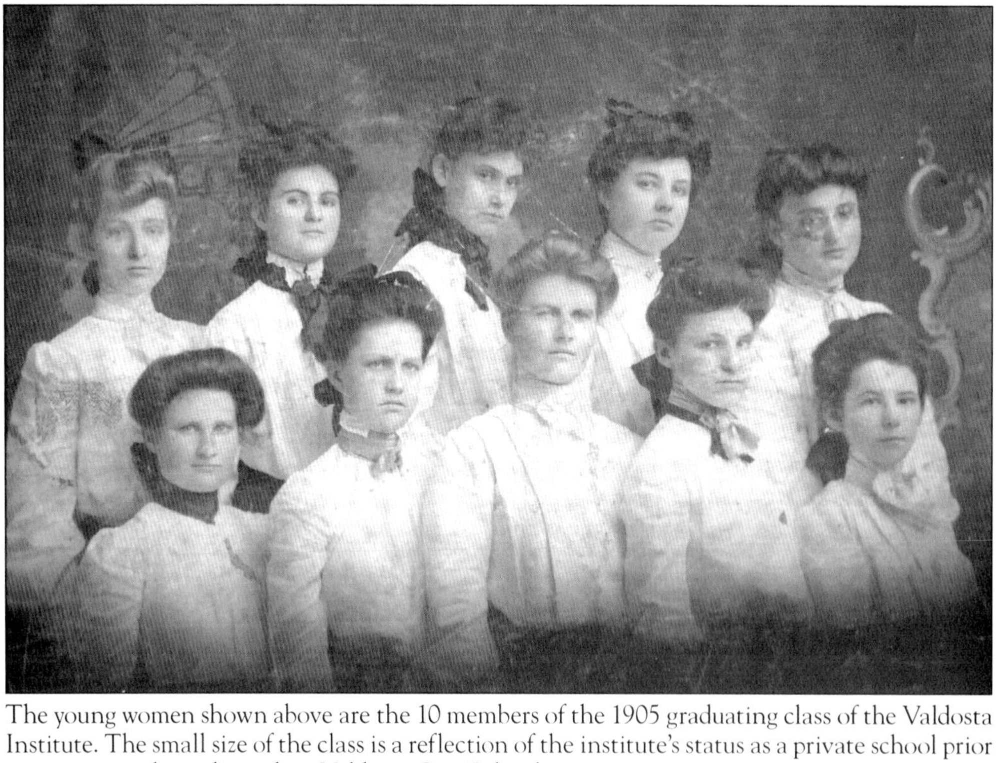

The young women shown above are the 10 members of the 1905 graduating class of the Valdosta Institute. The small size of the class is a reflection of the institute's status as a private school prior to its joining the independent Valdosta City Schools.

This small but apparently well-kept building was a school in the Lowndes County System. It was situated in the county, south of Valdosta and in the direction of Statenville. The date of the picture is uncertain, but it appears to be from the 1890s or perhaps early in the 20th century.

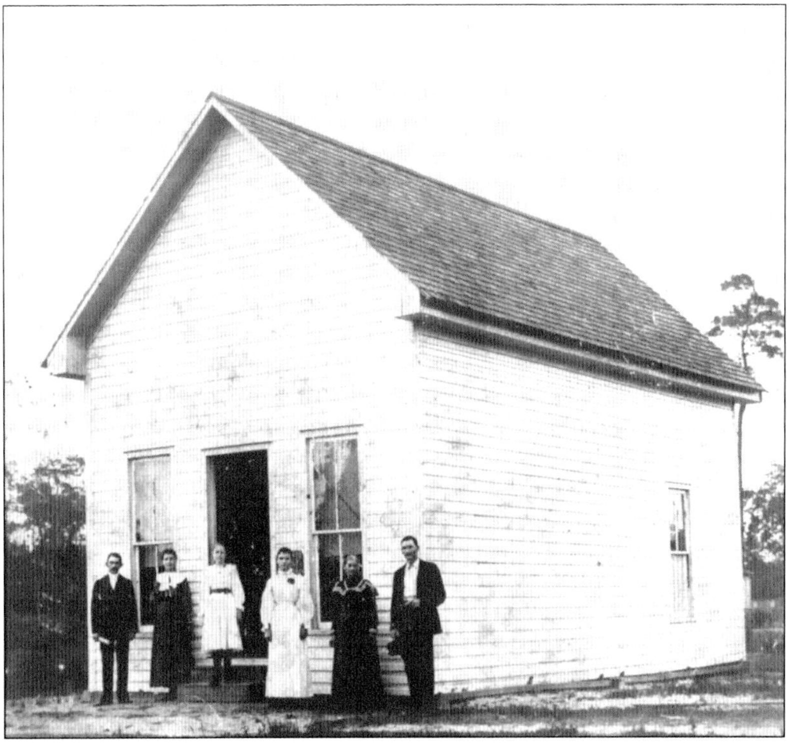

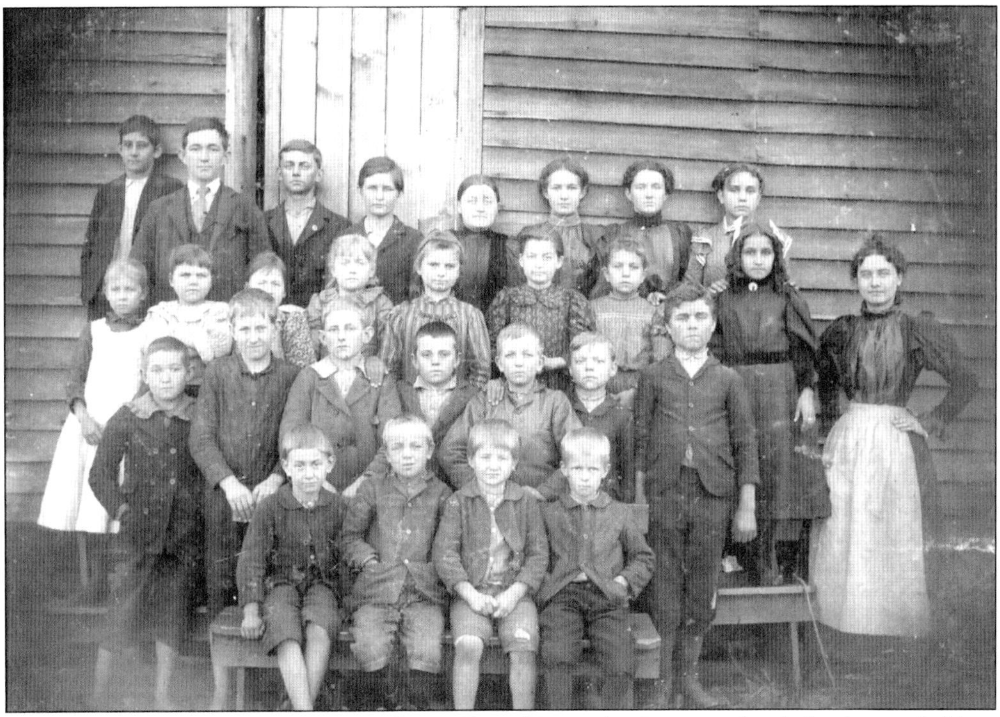

These are the students and teachers of a small rural Lowndes County school; the date probably is late in the 19th century, but the precise location in the county is unknown. The school structure is unpainted and appears to be quite primitive and basic.

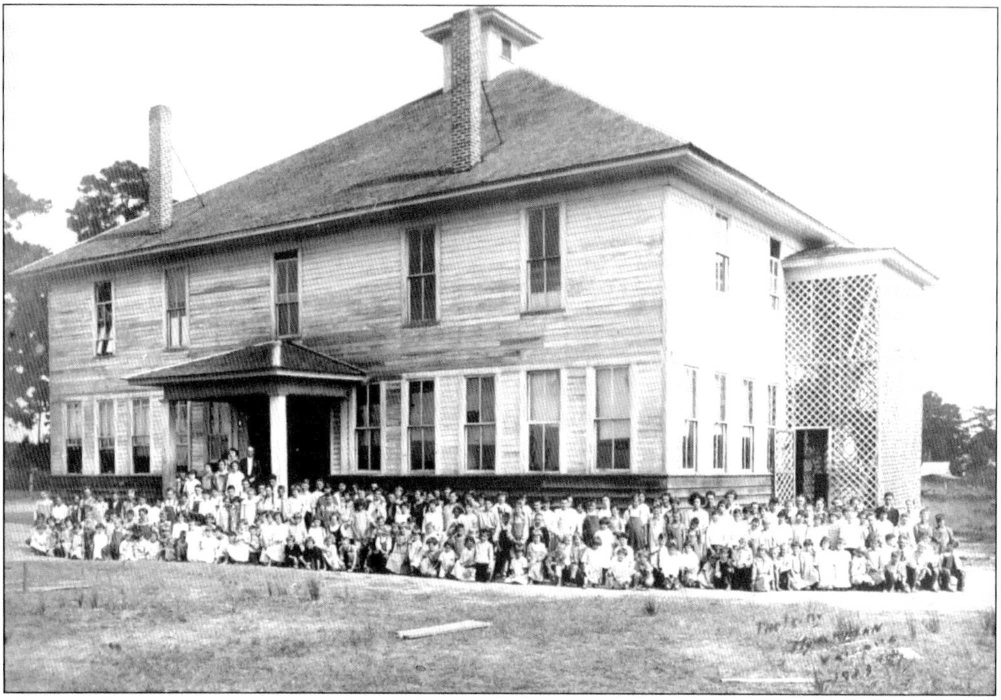

The wooden structure pictured above with its students was the Clyattville School in southern Lowndes County. The image bears a message about how strapped for cash many school systems in the South were in the 1920s. The building is badly in need of paint and seems generally to be in a state of deterioration.

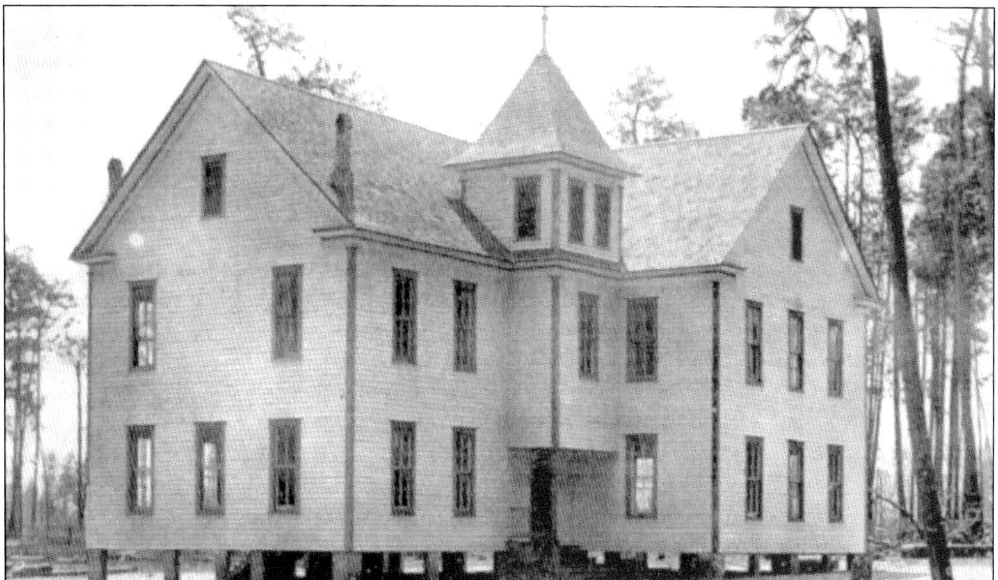

Shiloh School was situated in northern Lowndes County near the town of Hahira. The neat, seemingly well-kept building once was considered to be the largest wooden school edifice in the state of Georgia.

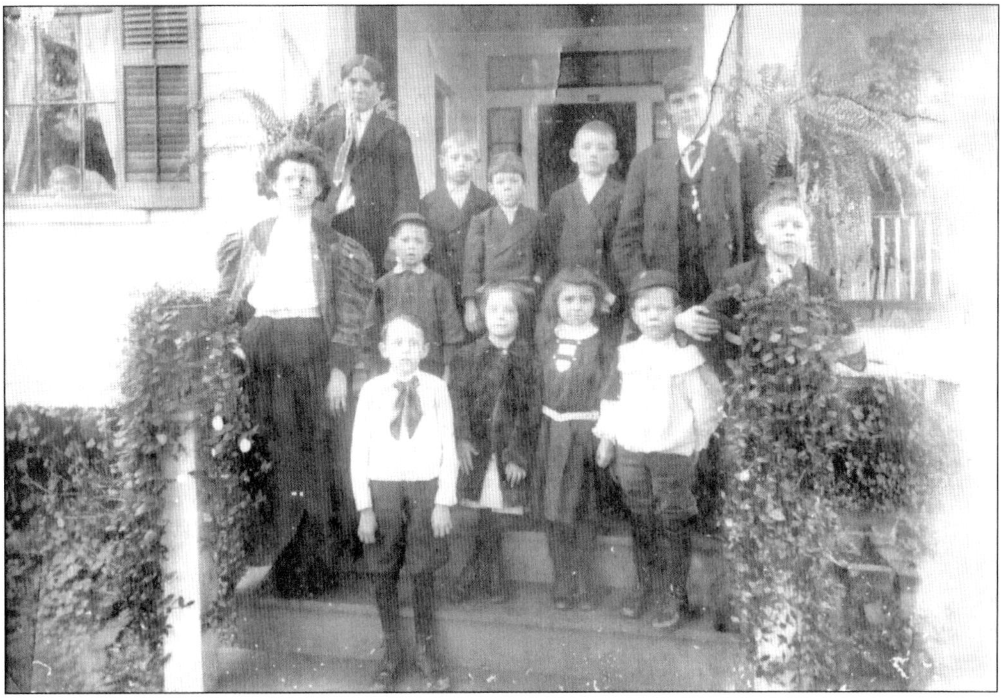

Seen here are the students of the small home school of Annabelle Myddleton at 409 North Troup Street in Valdosta. Annabelle Myddleton is the woman at the left of the picture.

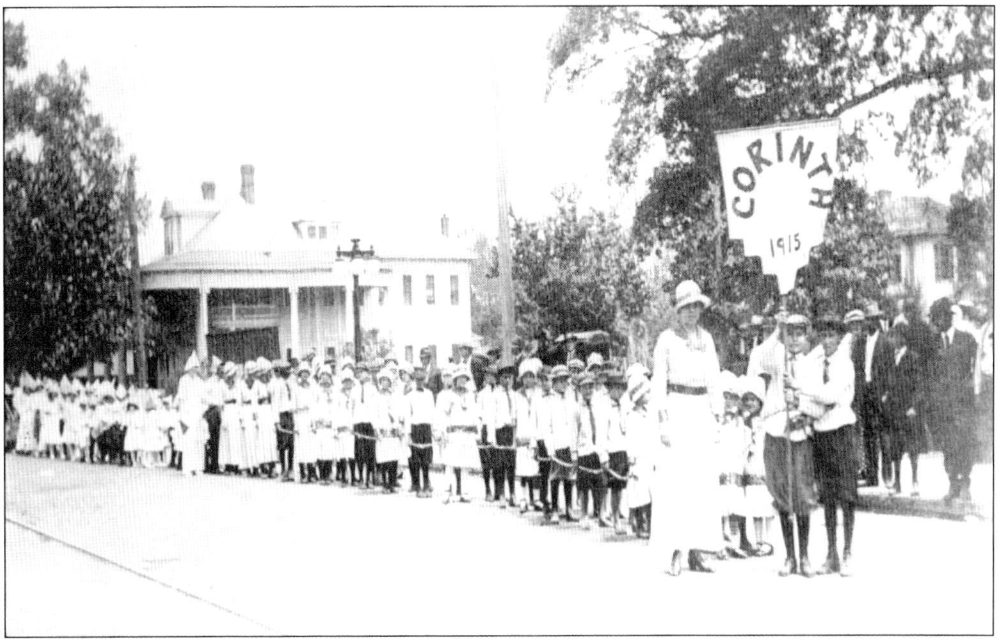

In 1915, students from Corinth School in the northern section of Lowndes County prepare to participate in a parade in Valdosta. Standing on the east side of North Patterson Street, they are holding a rope so as to stay in line. Given the date, the occasion may have been a "preparedness parade" in support of Pres. Woodrow Wilson's program of military preparedness because of the Great War then raging in Europe.

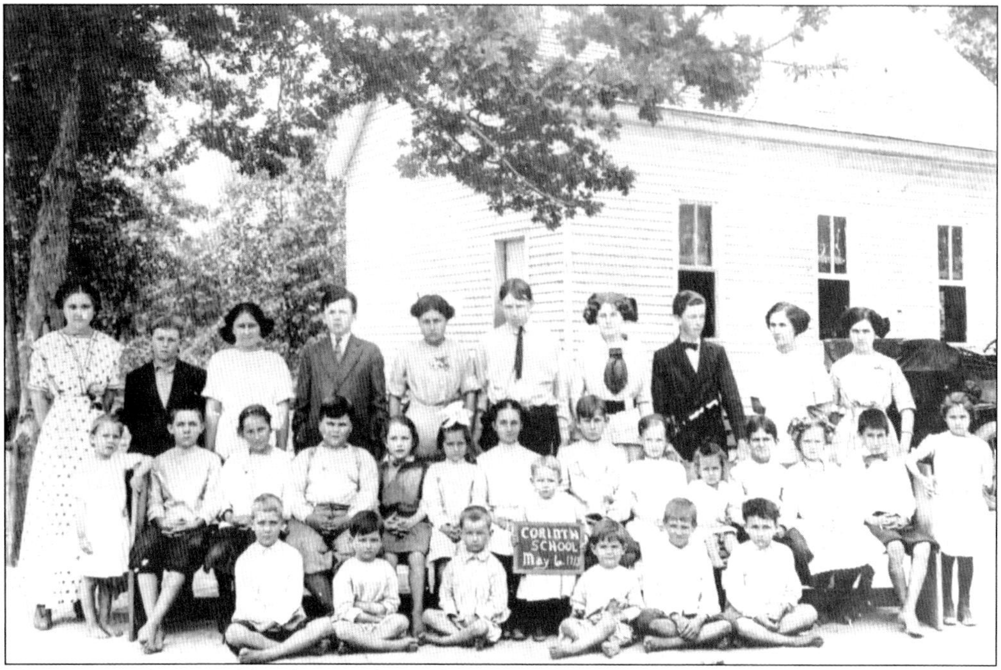

These are students and faculty members of Corinth School in north Lowndes County. The date of the photograph is May 6, 1913. From the evidence presented by the picture, Corinth was a small school, but it seems to have been tidy, well maintained, and nicely shaded by trees.

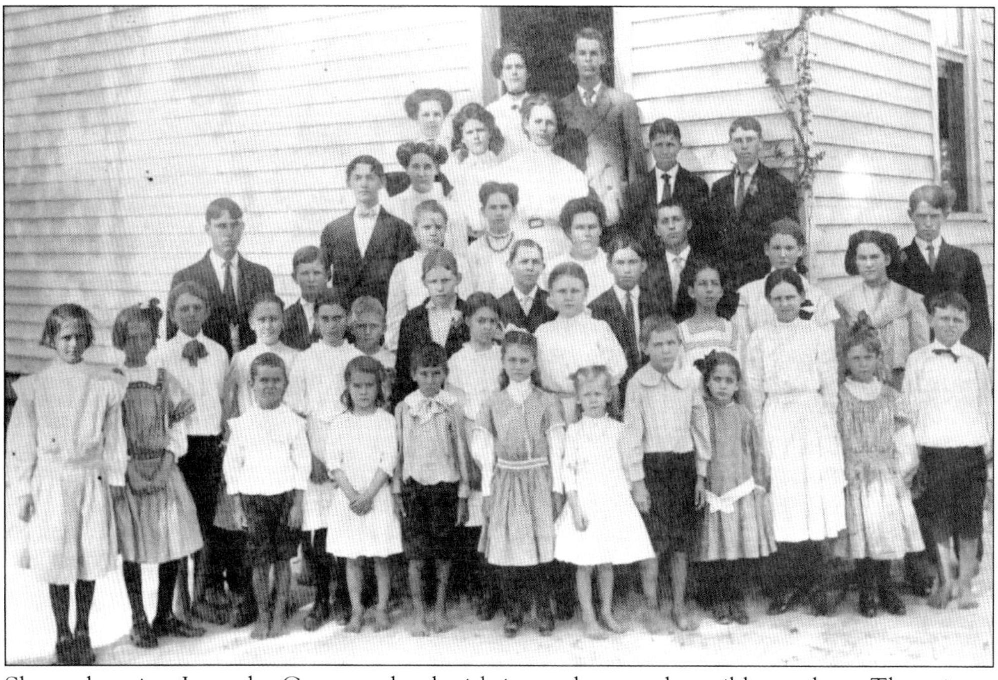

Shown here is a Lowndes County school with its students and possibly teachers. There is no specific information about the school's location or the time of the picture. However, careful examination of the building's configuration indicates that it is Corinth, the same school that appears in the image above.

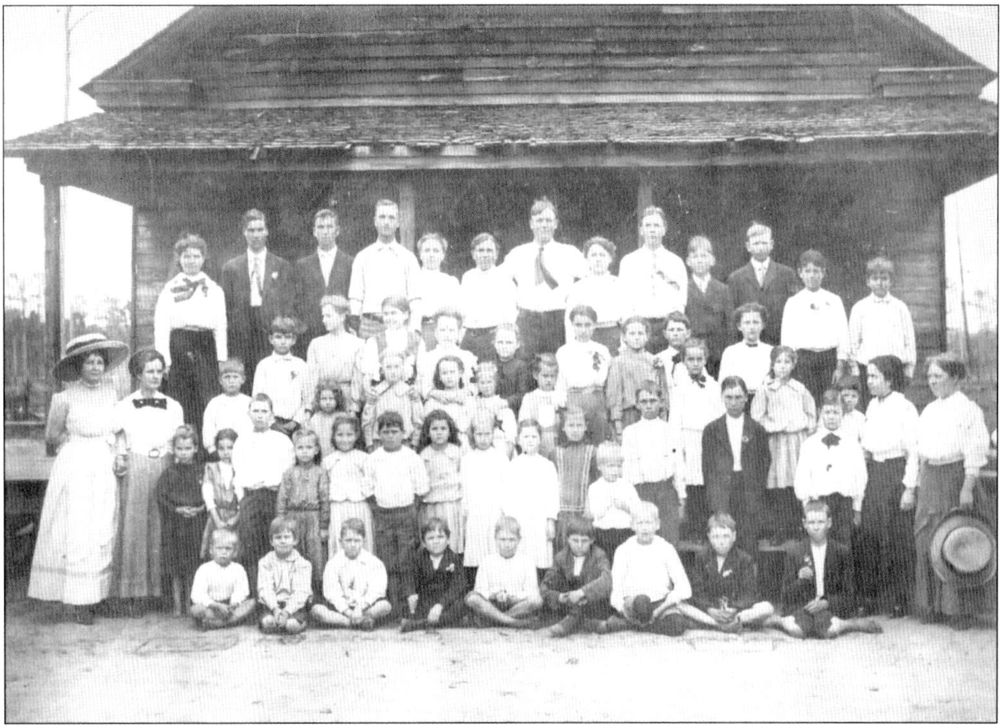

The school pictured here is probably Blanton in the Lowndes County system in the 1890s or possibly the very early 20th century. This is another building that suffered from lack of maintenance, as the building is unpainted and the roof is deteriorating.

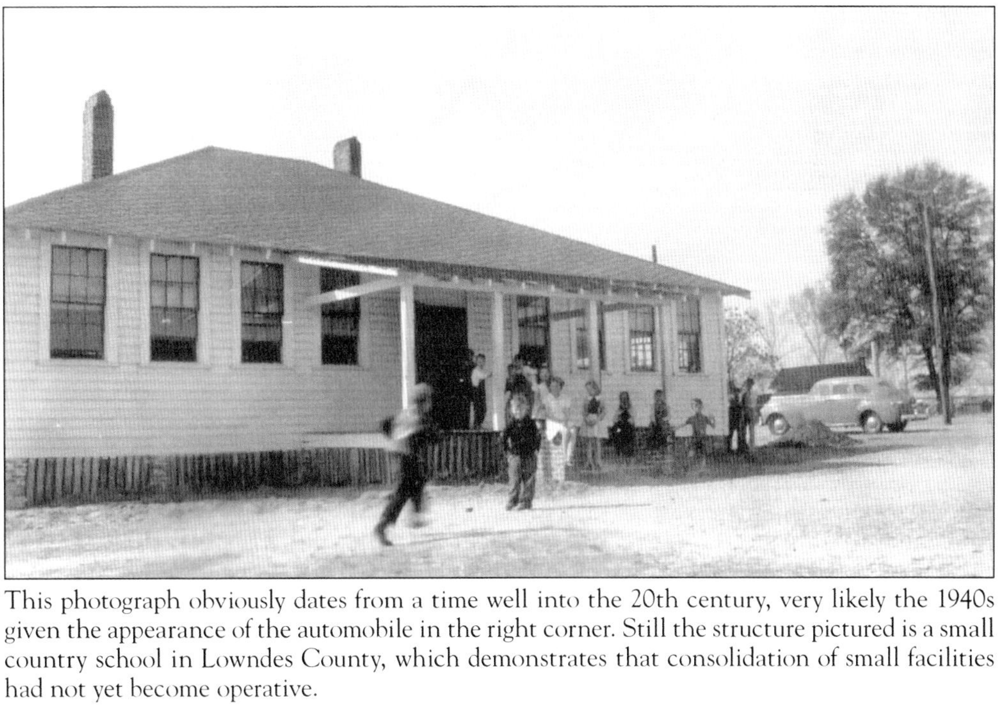

This photograph obviously dates from a time well into the 20th century, very likely the 1940s given the appearance of the automobile in the right corner. Still the structure pictured is a small country school in Lowndes County, which demonstrates that consolidation of small facilities had not yet become operative.

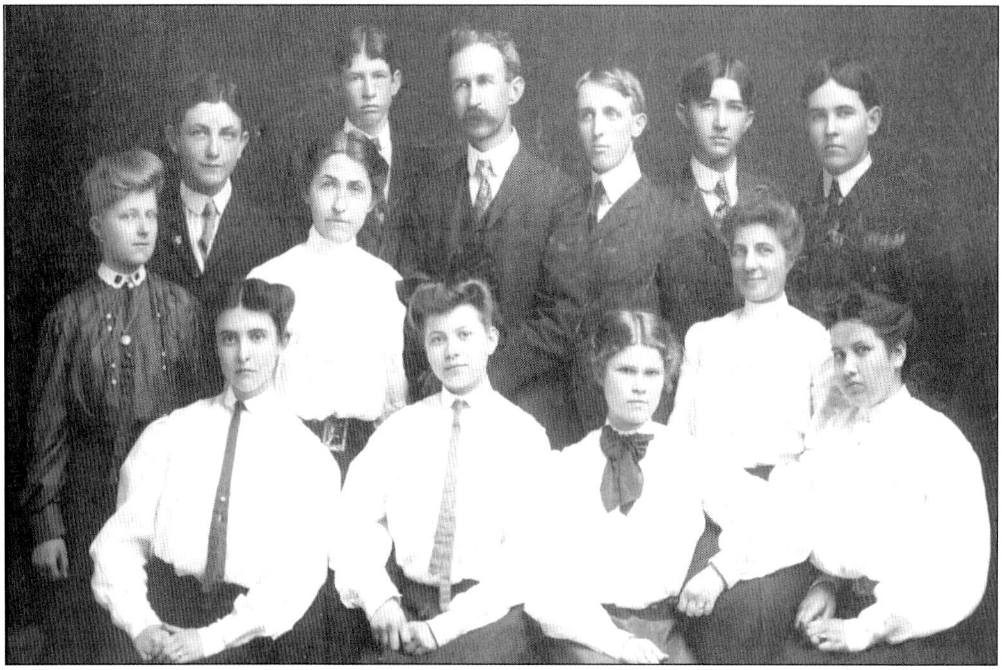

These young men and women were members of the Valdosta High School graduating class of 1905. The size of the group makes obvious that the city's high school was still small at the time, partially because it was still in competition with the Valdosta Institute for students.

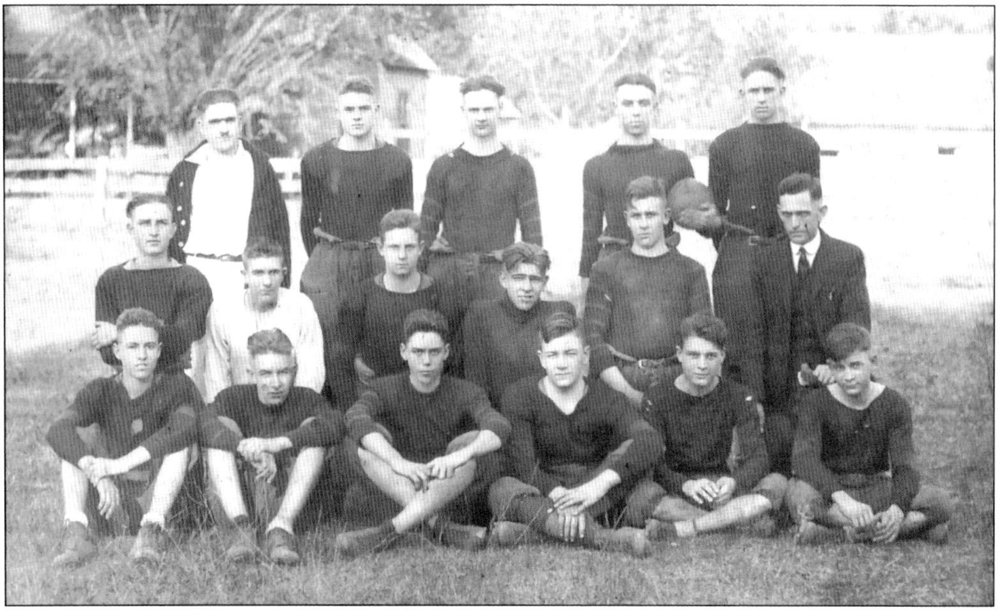

Above is one of the earliest photographs of a high school football team in Lowndes County, the Valdosta High School team of 1919. In the picture are, from left to right, (first row) Joe Legg, Billy Brooks, Maxwell Oliver, Reid Hill, Everall Dash, and Howard Pollard; (second row) Decar Sims, John Ritch, Emmett Pope, Carl Jones, Terry Almand, and J. L. Newbern Sr. (coach); (third row) Leon Paine (assistant coach), Gordon "Tuny" Converse, Norman Felder, James Johnson (team captain), and Thomas Tillman.

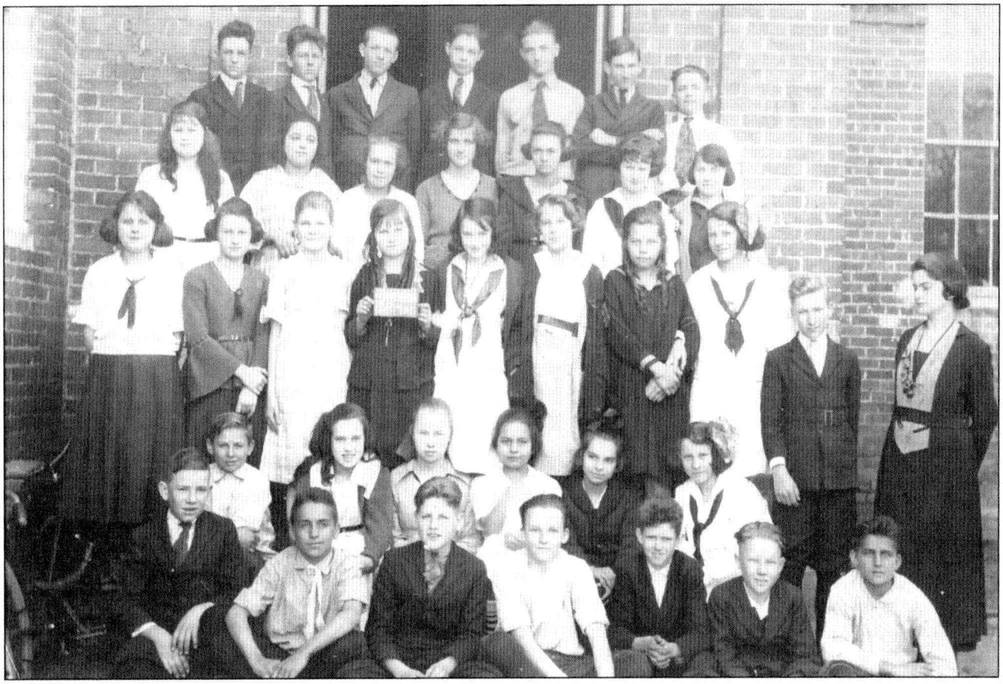

In 1921, a Valdosta Junior High class poses on the steps of the school building, which was the former Valdosta Institute. Standing at the right is the teacher, Margaret Roberts, who served in the Valdosta City Schools until well into the 1950s.

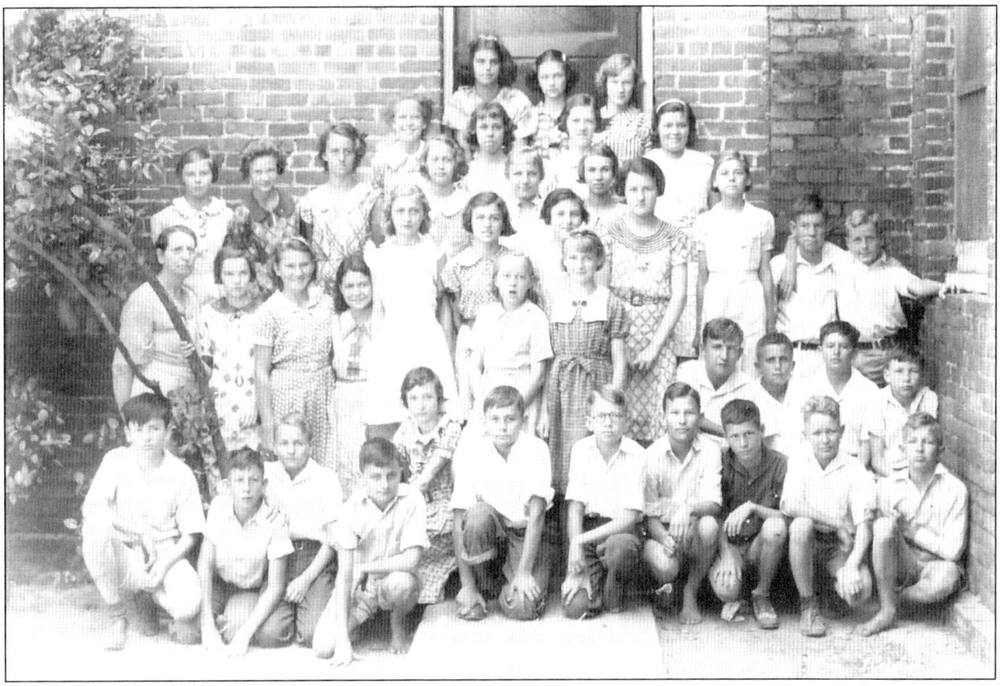

A much more casually dressed class of Valdosta Junior School students than the group above appears in this photograph from 15 years later. The date is May 7, 1936, and the teacher is Miss Cora Mahone, one of the two women for whom Sallas-Mahone Elementary School later was named.

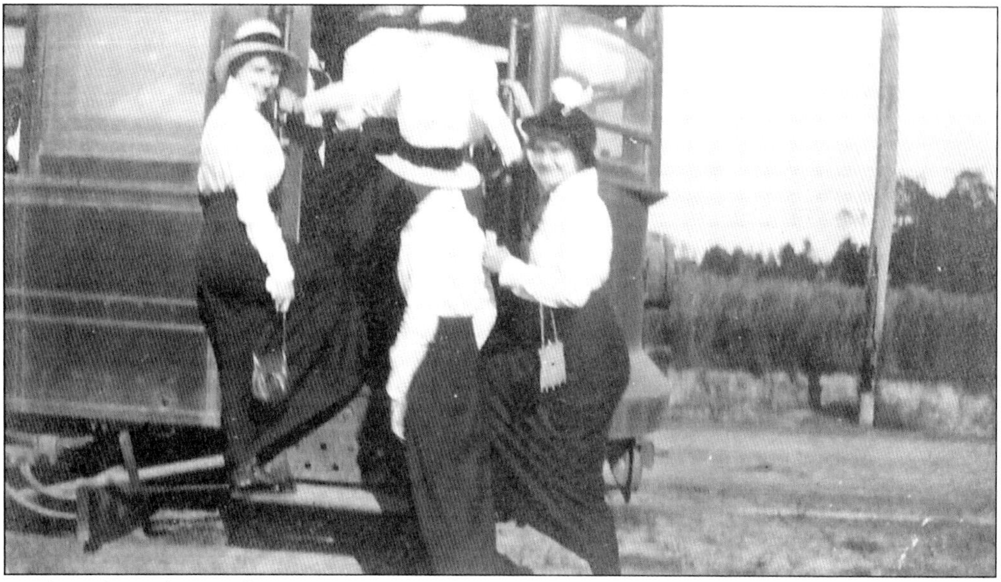

Students from the South Georgia Normal College board a car of the Valdosta Street Railway on North Patterson Street sometime between the college's opening in 1913 and the demise of the street railway system in 1924.

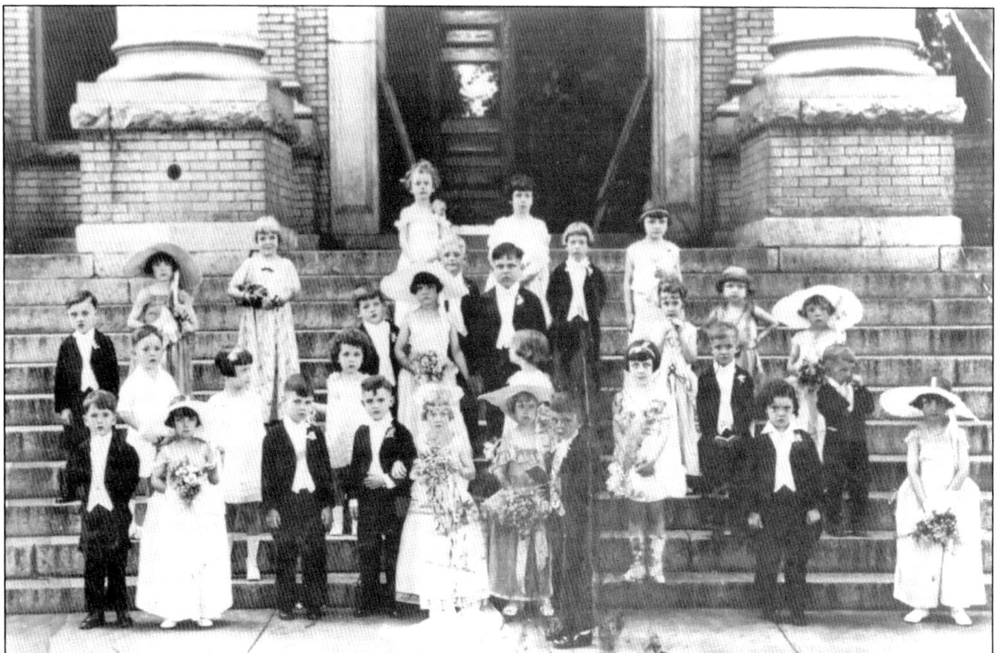

This picture is of young Valdosta students who participated in a so-called "Tom Thumb Wedding" in the mid-1920s. The scene of the photograph is the steps of the Lowndes County Courthouse, and the date is approximately 1925.

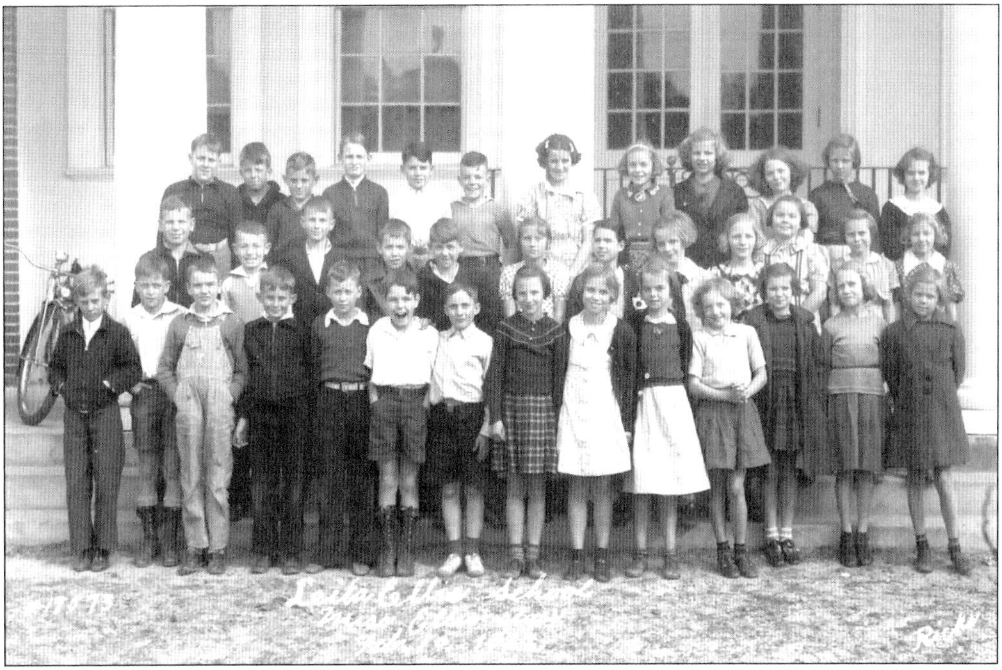

Pictured above is an elementary class at Leila Ellis School on North Lee Street in Valdosta in 1937. The photograph identifies the teacher as Leila Ellis, the school's namesake.

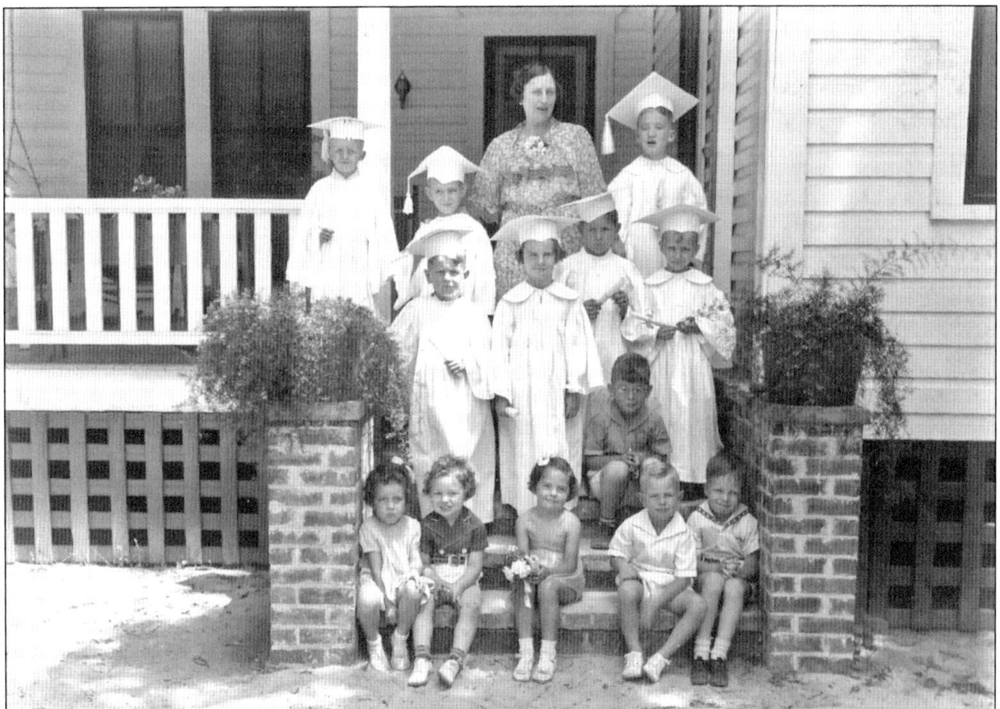

The date of this image, 1937, is certain, but little additional information is available. It is clearly a small, privately owned school held in a neat, well-maintained home, but the location and the identity of the teacher both remain unknown.

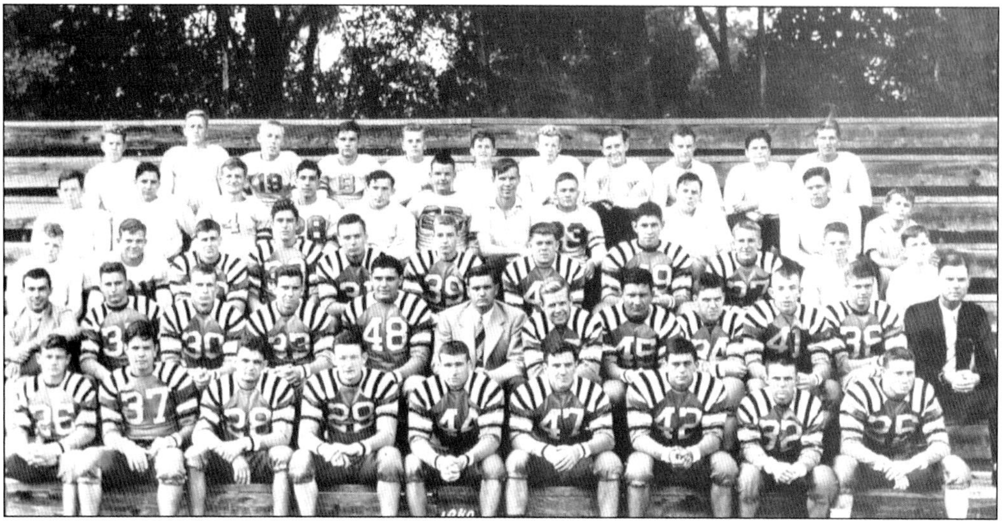

The Valdosta High School Wildcat football team of 1940 poses in the wooden stands of Cleveland Field, adjacent to the school on Williams Street. This was the first Valdosta High team to win a state championship. Since 1940, the team has won an additional 22 such championships and has the most victories of any high school team in the country.

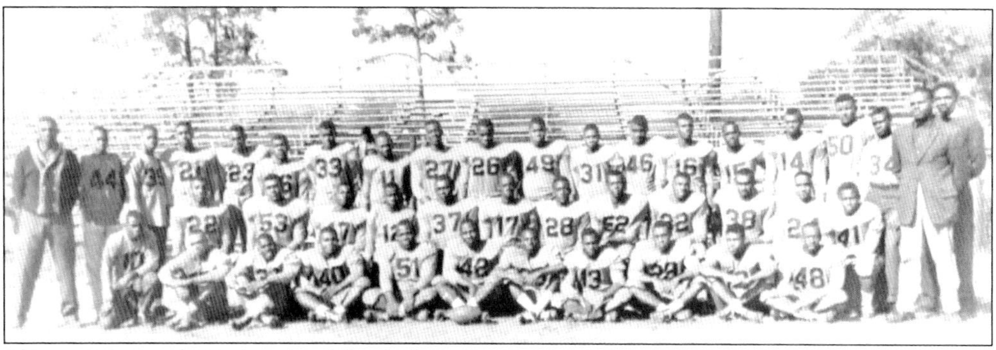

The 1963 Pinevale High School football team won the Georgia Class A championship for that season. This photograph emphasizes the point that, nearly 10 years after the U.S. Supreme Court's decision of 1954 that invalidated racial segregation in public education, the Valdosta City School System remained segregated.

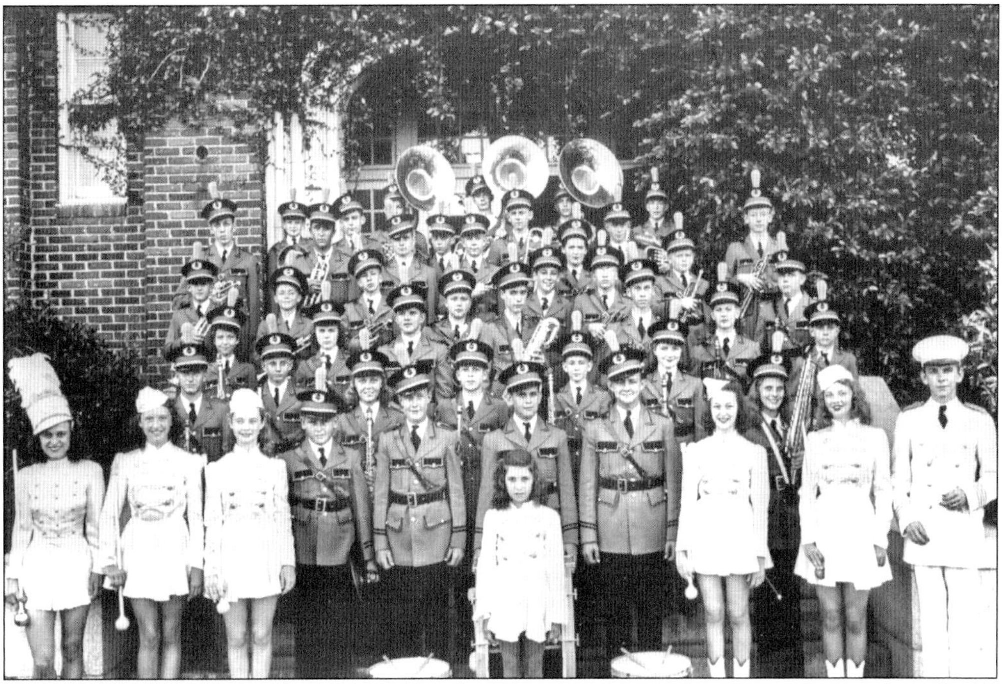

Posed in uniform on the front steps of Valdosta High School is the 1941–1942 marching band. Among its various purposes, the band became and remained a significant adjunct to the school's football program in the 1940s and on to the present.

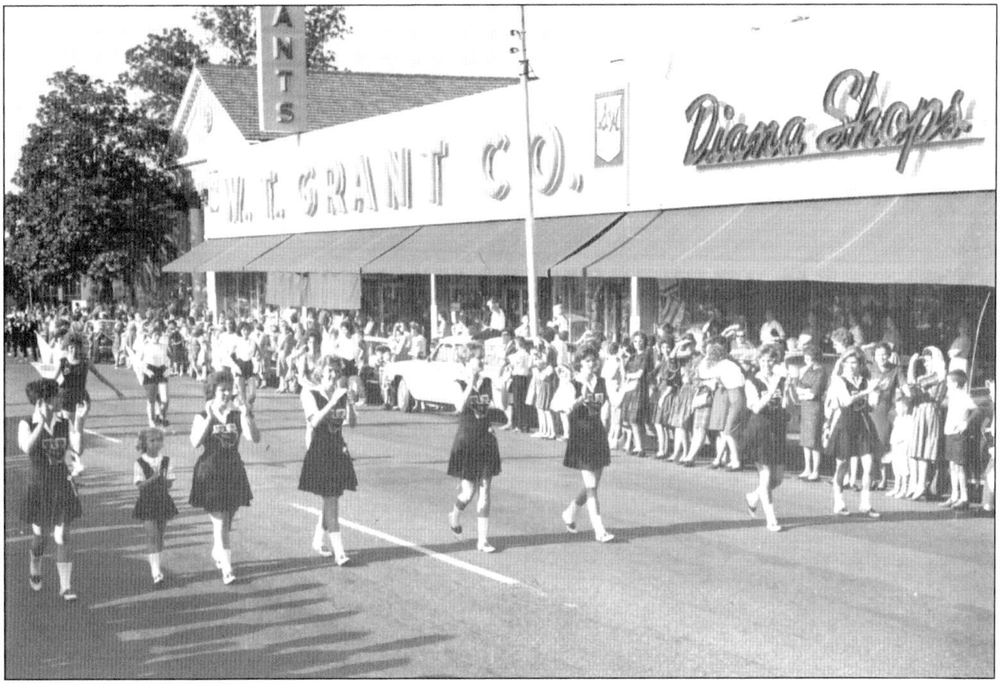

A quarter of a century later, in the 1960s, Valdosta High School cheerleaders and band members participate in a parade. They are marching southward on North Patterson Street, just south of the First Presbyterian Church, which is partially visible in the background.

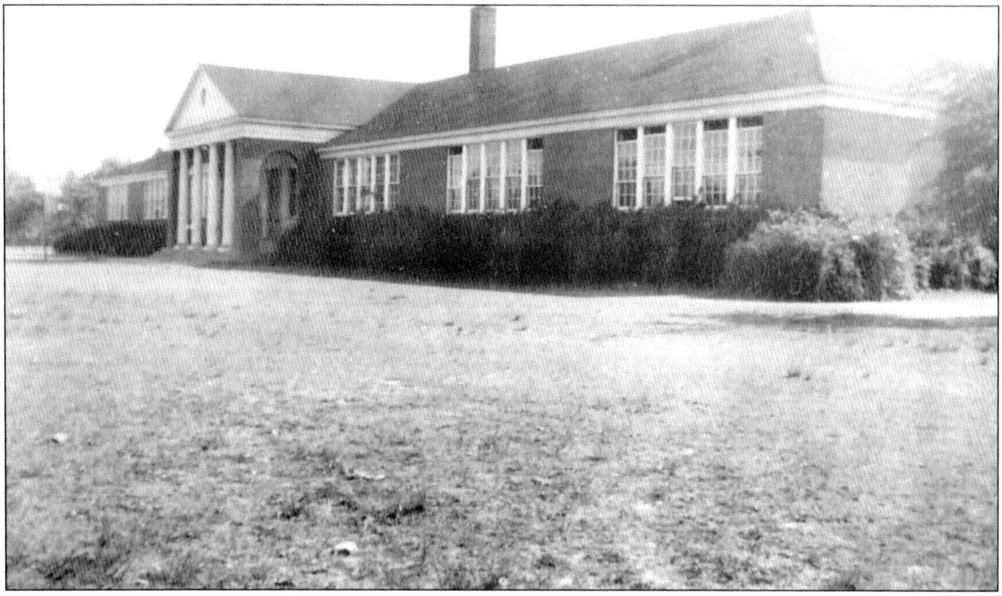

This is Leila Ellis Elementary School on North Lee Street in Valdosta. Having long since served out its useful life in public education, the structure still stands and in recent years has been renovated and put to use as the headquarters of the Lowndes Associated Ministries to People, usually known simply as LAMP. Leila Ellis is the only school of considerable age in Valdosta that has survived to the present.

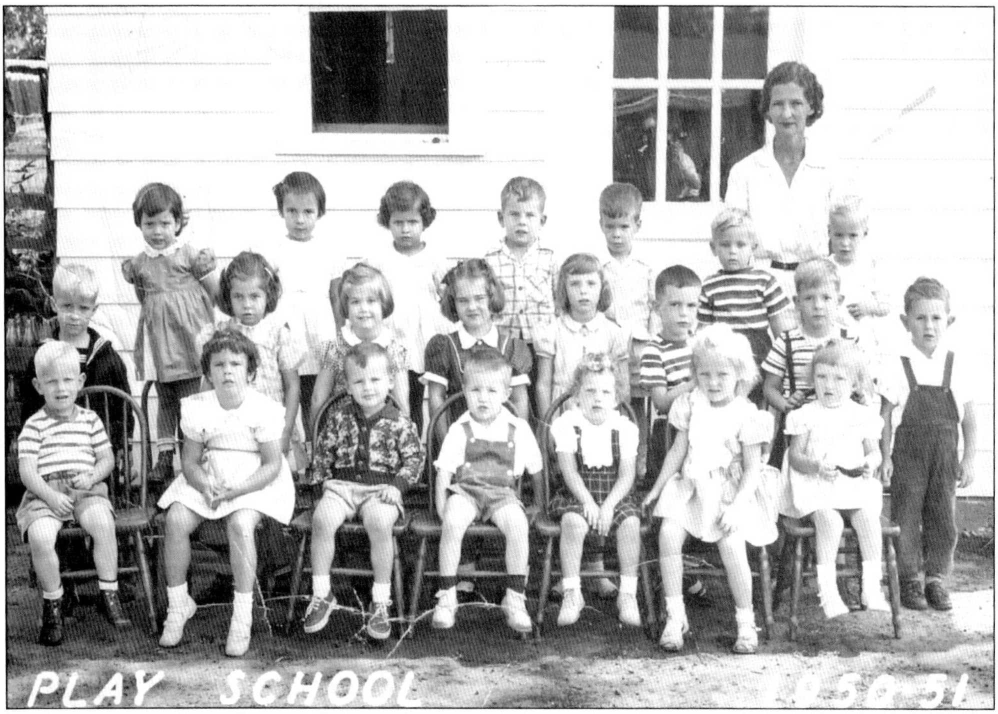

The image above is of a private Valdosta preschool class in 1951–1952, taught by Meta Shaw Coleman. Coleman was an extremely popular preschool teacher, as is demonstrated by the size of the class.

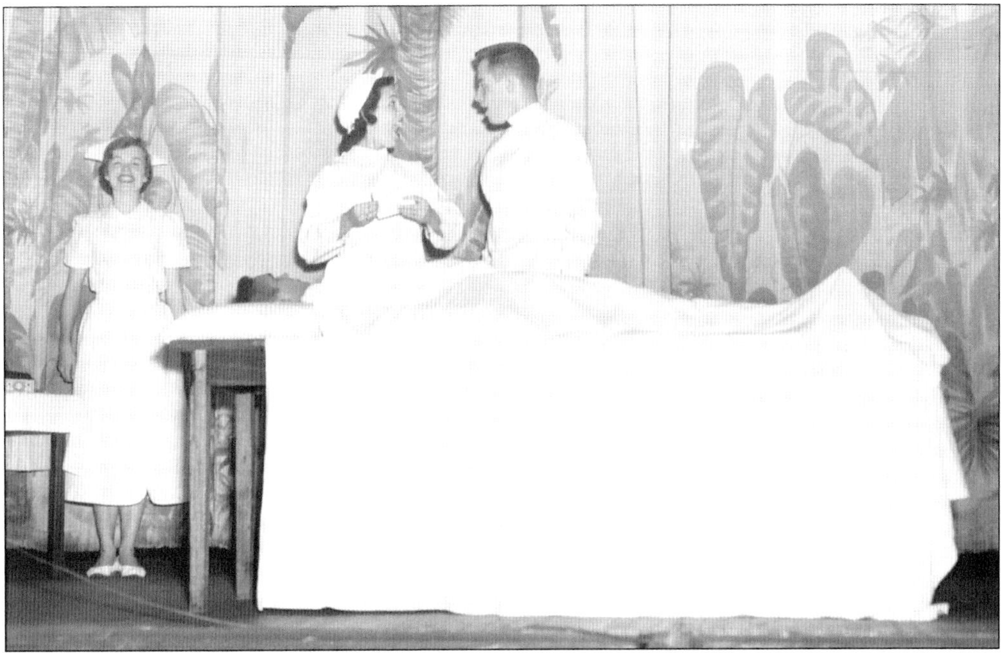

On the stage of the Ritz Theater in 1954, a skit is performed by students from Valdosta High School. The participants standing are, from left to right, Cay Cranford, Lucille Helms, and Charles Bryan. On the "bed" is Charles O. Templeton. The occasion was the distribution of awards to members of the 1953 state championship Valdosta High School football team.

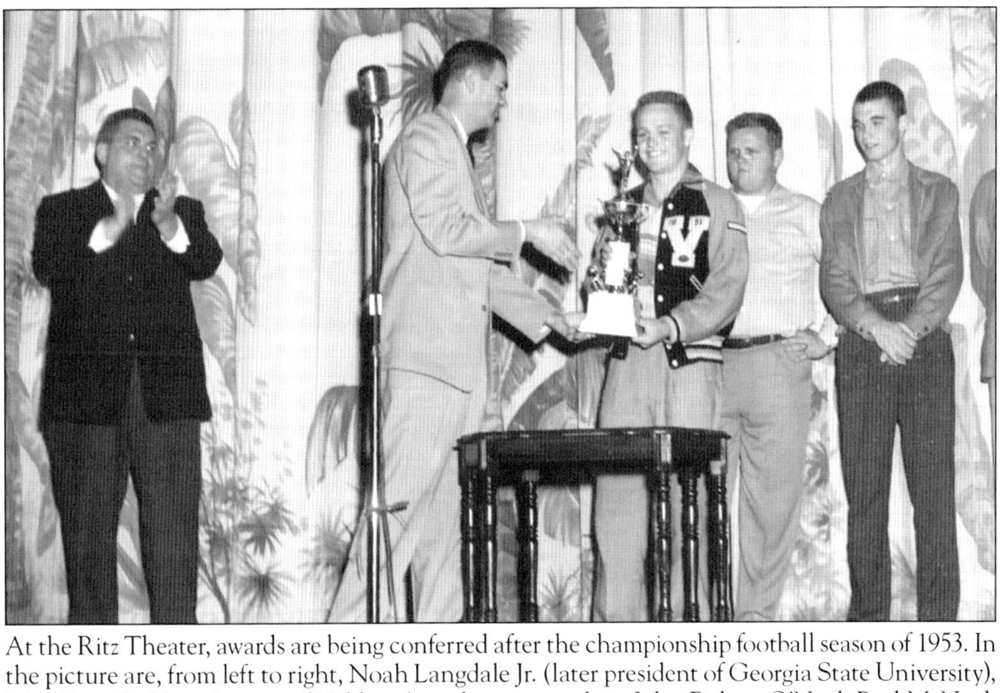

At the Ritz Theater, awards are being conferred after the championship football season of 1953. In the picture are, from left to right, Noah Langdale Jr. (later president of Georgia State University), John Bray Giddens (mayor of Valdosta), and team members John Robert O'Neal, Paul McNeal, and Willie Webb. This image highlights the importance of football in the city of Valdosta and in Lowndes County.

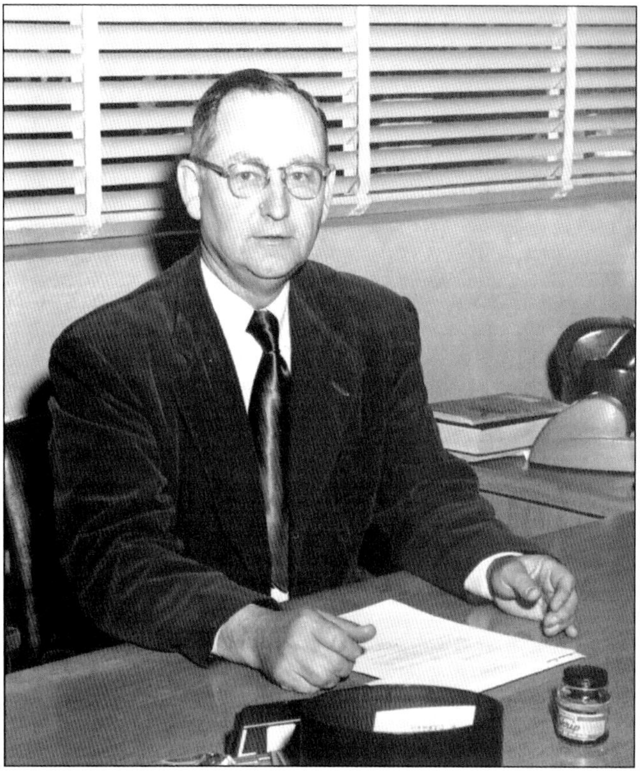

W. G. Nunn was superintendent of the Valdosta City Schools from 1948 until his retirement in 1968. During his tenure, he was responsible for much of the growth of the system and the construction of new school facilities.

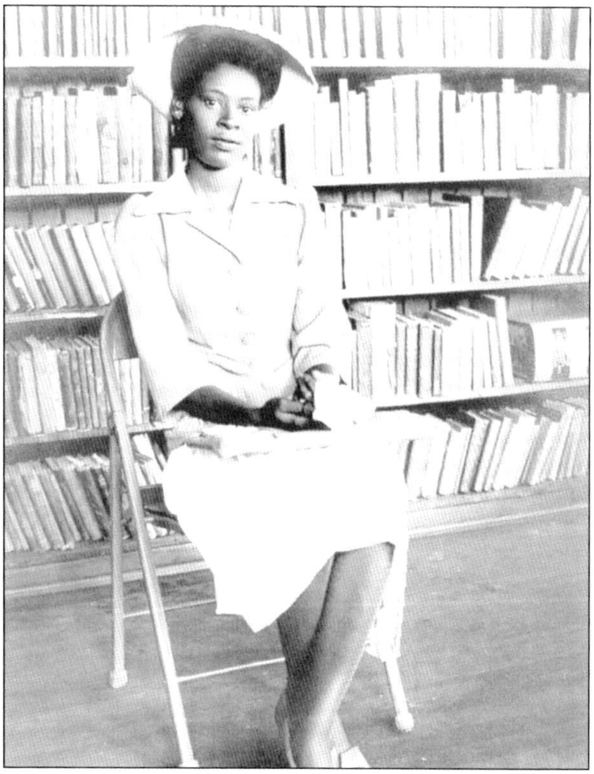

A senior at Westside High School in the Lowndes County Schools poses for her class photograph in 1964 at a time when racial segregation continued to be the norm in the county. The tattered condition of the library books behind her stresses the handicaps with which segregated black schools had to contend.

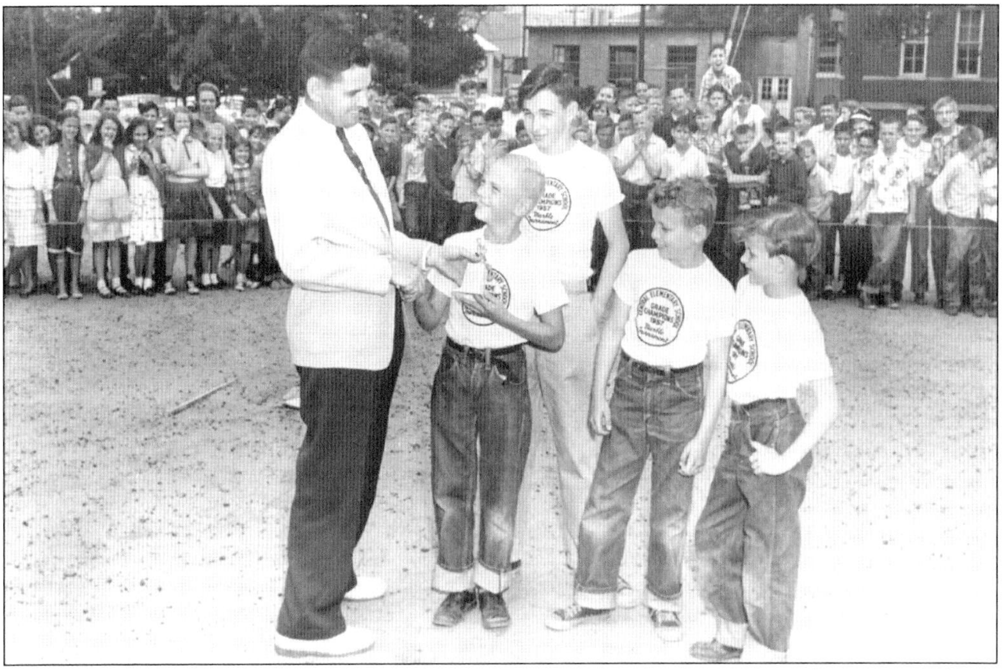

These two images illustrate an activity that was common in many Southern elementary schools until the 1960s: the marble tournament. In the picture below, two students participate in such an event at Central Elementary School in Valdosta in the late 1950s, with an interested crowd of onlookers behind them. Above, Principal Hadley McDuffie of Central Elementary awards prizes to winners of a marble competition. From left to right, the recipients are Dawson Vickery, Donnie Tinsley, John Barrett, and Lewis McGill.

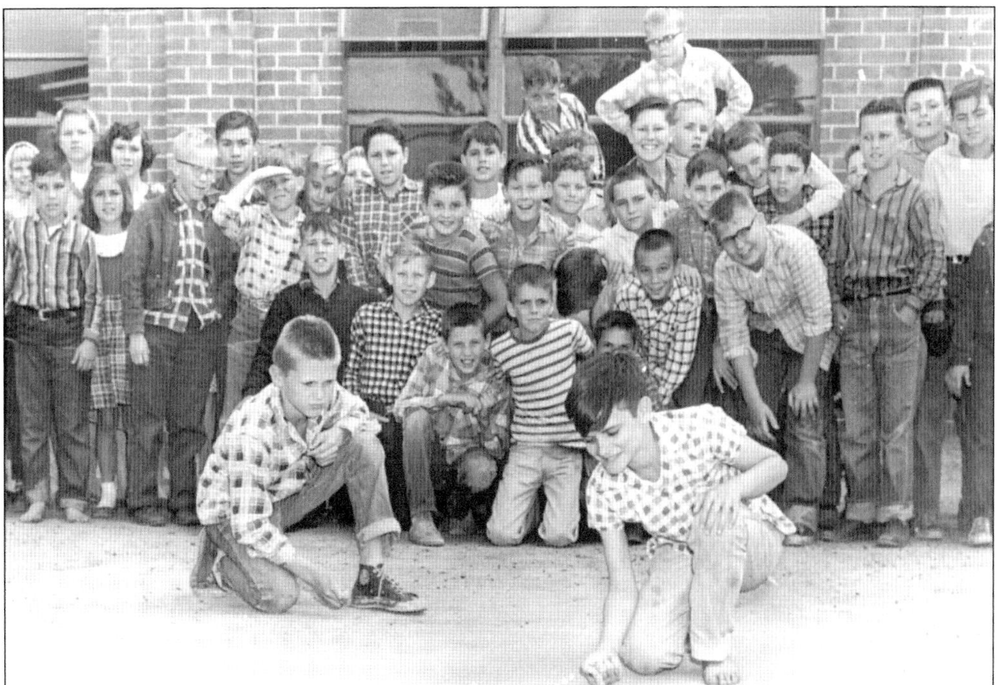

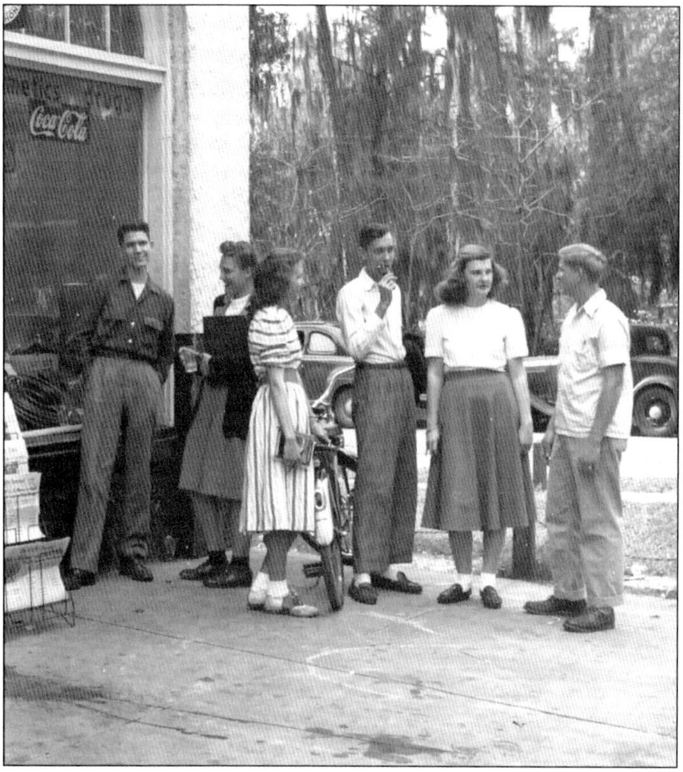

These Valdosta High School students, c. 1948, are "hanging out" at the Brookwood Pharmacy on North Patterson Street, which was near the school and was a favored gathering place. From left to right are James Puckett, Helen Scott, Betty Jo Garrison, Edward "Sonny" Barnum, Marguerite DeLoach, and Billy Mayes.

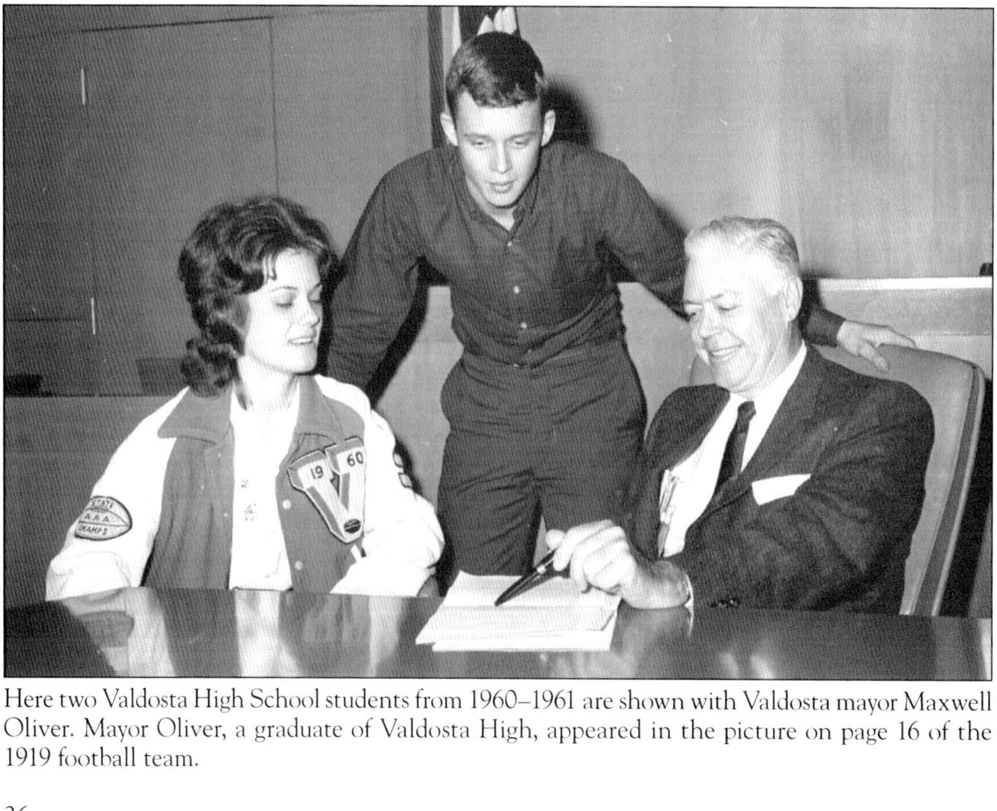

Here two Valdosta High School students from 1960–1961 are shown with Valdosta mayor Maxwell Oliver. Mayor Oliver, a graduate of Valdosta High, appeared in the picture on page 16 of the 1919 football team.

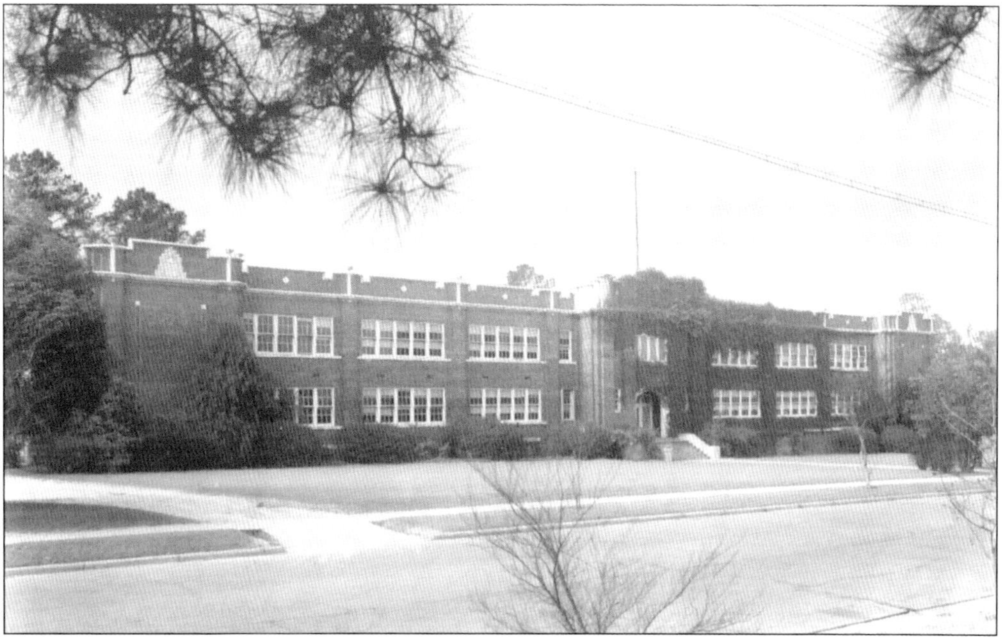

This page features two views of Valdosta High School on Williams Street. At the top is the school as it appeared in the 1940s and 1950s when ivy covered the wall above the front entrance. The building, along with an auditorium, gymnasium, home economics facility, and lunchroom, was in use from 1921 until 1971, when a new Valdosta High School opened on North Forrest Street. The picture below shows the ultimate fate of the old structure, which burned in 1977.

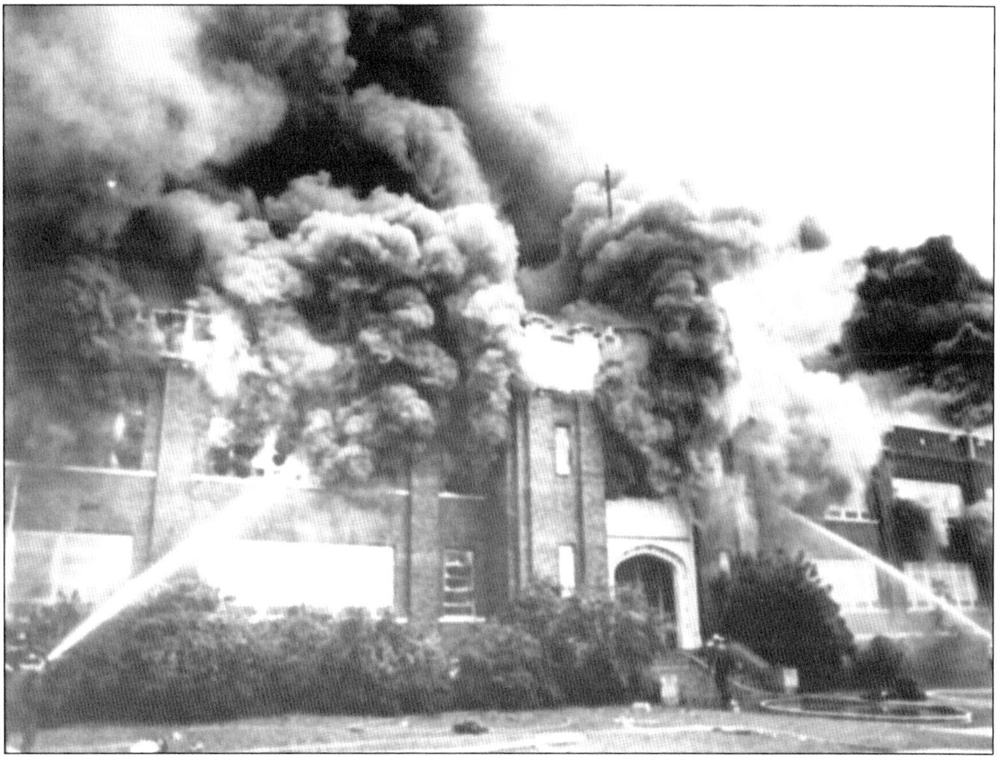

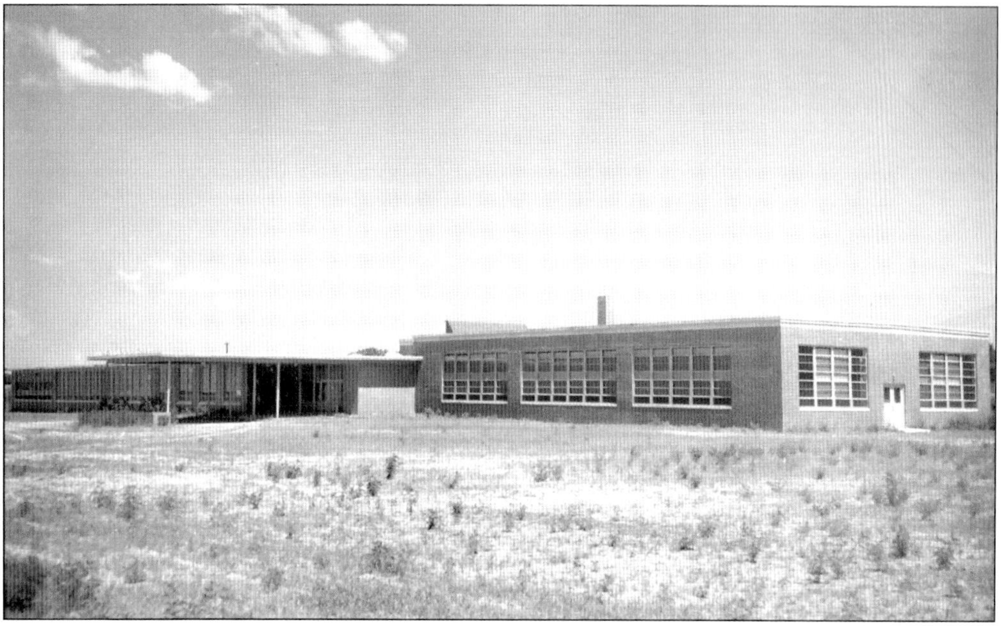

The Valdosta City Schools launched a program of constructing new facilities in the 1950s. One of the first schools to emerge from the program was the Valdosta Junior High School at 110 Burton Avenue, between North Patterson Street and North Oak Street. This image shows the building as it appeared when just completed and before any landscaping had been done. In the early 21st century, a new middle school replaced this facility, which was then torn down.

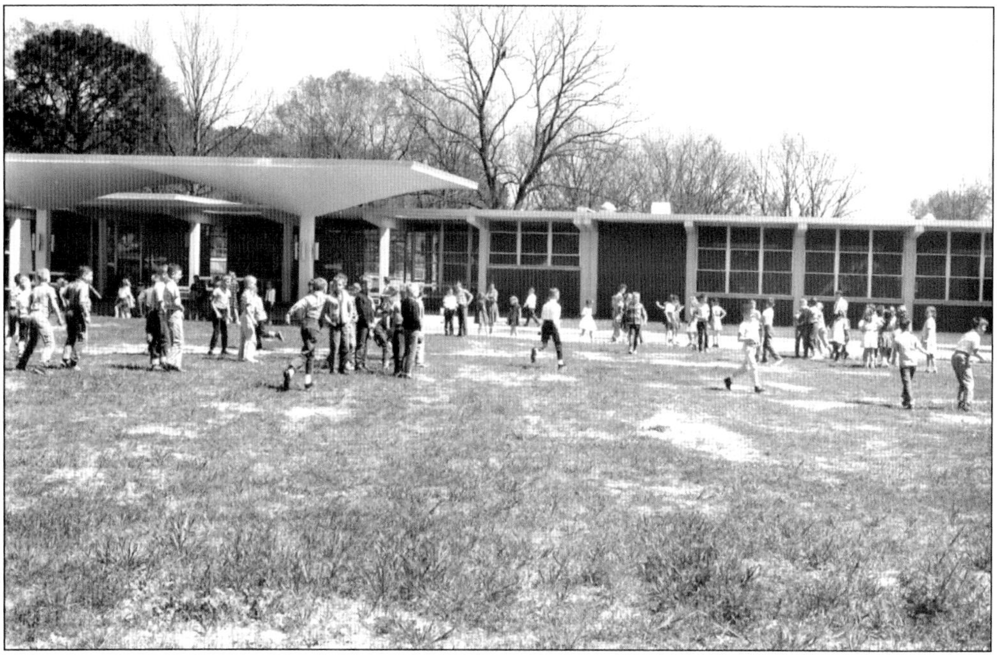

S. L. Mason Elementary School, named for Stuart L. Mason, a former member of the Valdosta Board of Education, was another product of the expansion and construction program that began in the 1950s and continued into the 1960s and beyond. The school, located on Azalea Drive, is shown with the front campus swarming with students at recess.

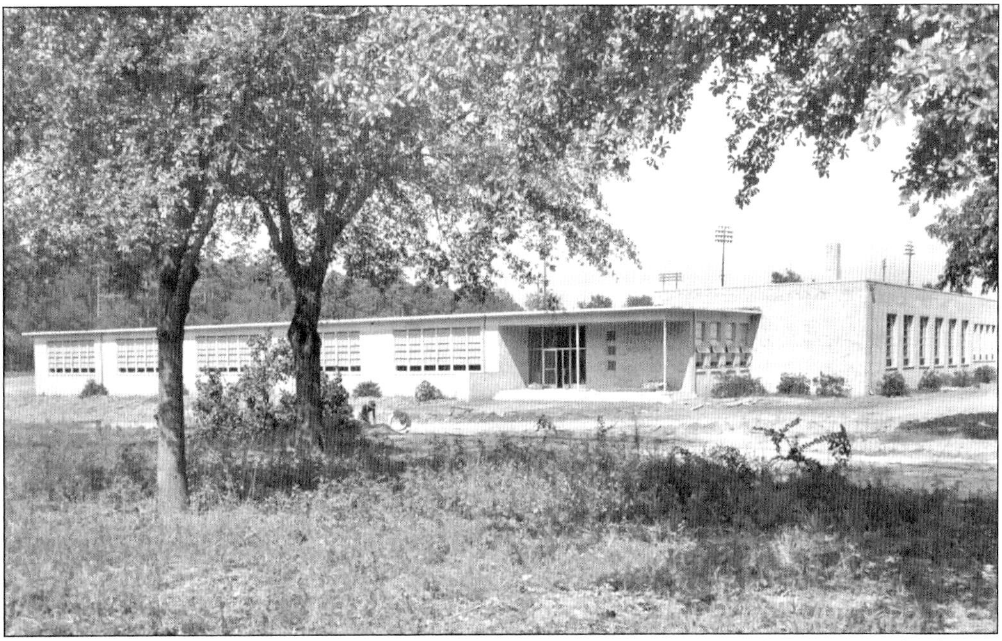

This is Sallas-Mahone Elementary School on North Patterson Street, the first new facility to be built in Valdosta in the 1950s. After serving students for several decades, this structure was closed when a new Sallas-Mahone was constructed at a different place. The building was razed, and the land is now the property of South Georgia Medical Center.

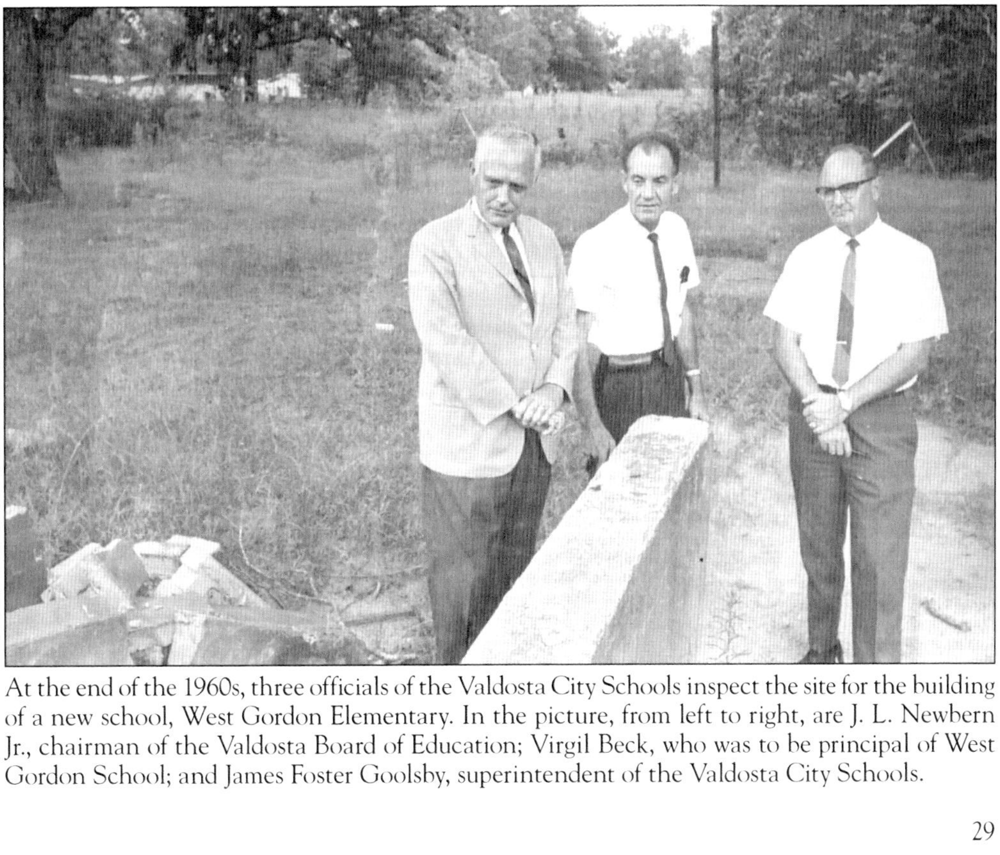

At the end of the 1960s, three officials of the Valdosta City Schools inspect the site for the building of a new school, West Gordon Elementary. In the picture, from left to right, are J. L. Newbern Jr., chairman of the Valdosta Board of Education; Virgil Beck, who was to be principal of West Gordon School; and James Foster Goolsby, superintendent of the Valdosta City Schools.

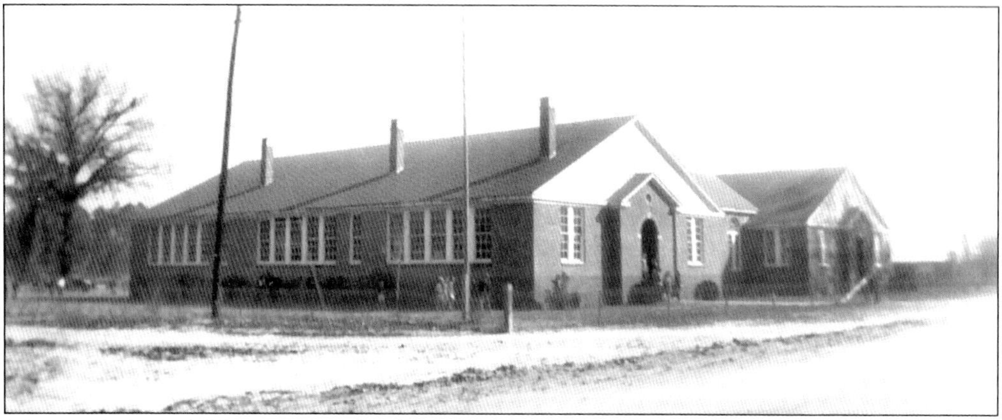

Above is Lake Park Elementary School in Lake Park in southern Lowndes County. This building is fairly typical of the brick structures that during the waves of consolidation in the 1940s and 1950s replaced the wooden rural schools displayed earlier in this chapter. Since this picture in the 1950s, the school complex at Lake Park has significantly expanded.

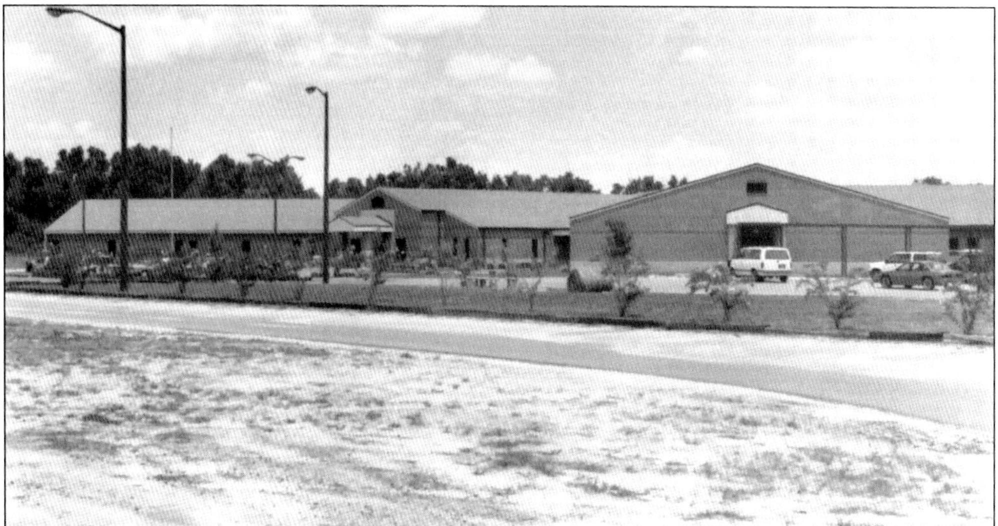

In a photograph of fairly recent vintage, the new Hahira Elementary School, in the Lowndes County School System, is shown. This set of structures in 1994 replaced the previous Hahira Elementary that was situated elsewhere and is representative of the continuing program of expansion and construction carried on in the Lowndes County School System.

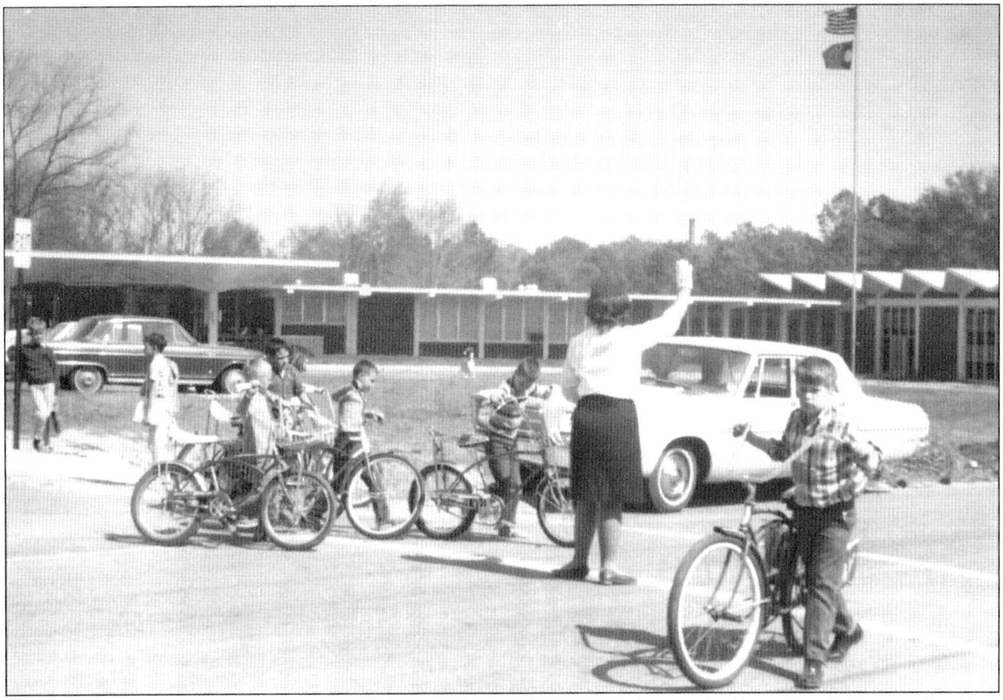

Students from S. L. Mason School in Valdosta depart at the end of a school day in the late 1960s. They are crossing Azalea Drive in front of the school under the watchful eye of a civilian crossing guard.

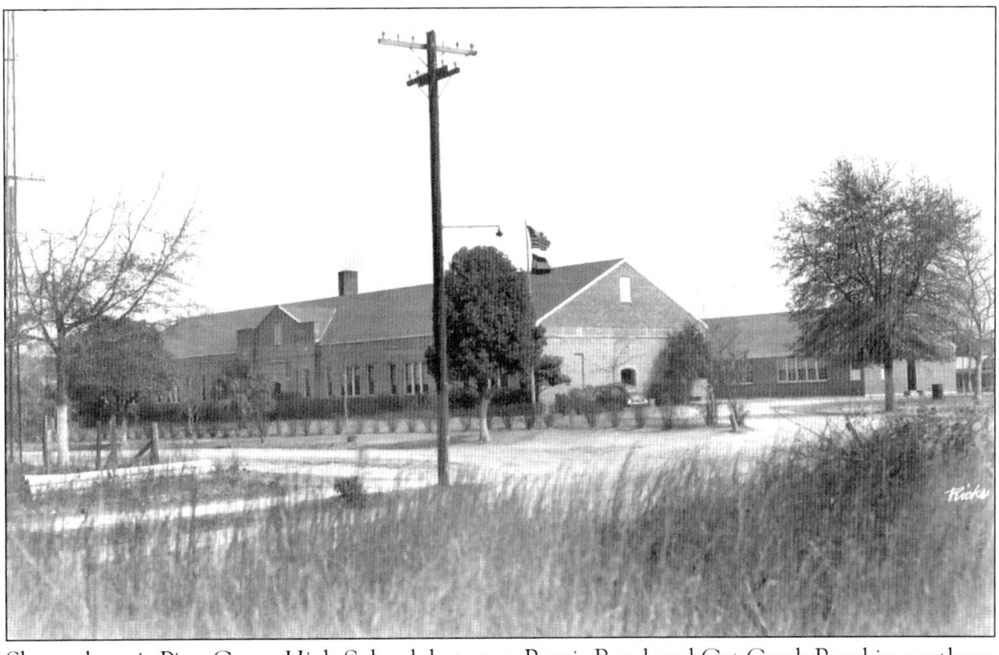

Shown here is Pine Grove High School, between Bemis Road and Cat Creek Road in northern Lowndes County. This relatively modern brick structure continued as a high school until consolidation of rural and small town high schools in the county in the 1960s. Since then, all county students have attended a single county high school, Lowndes High.

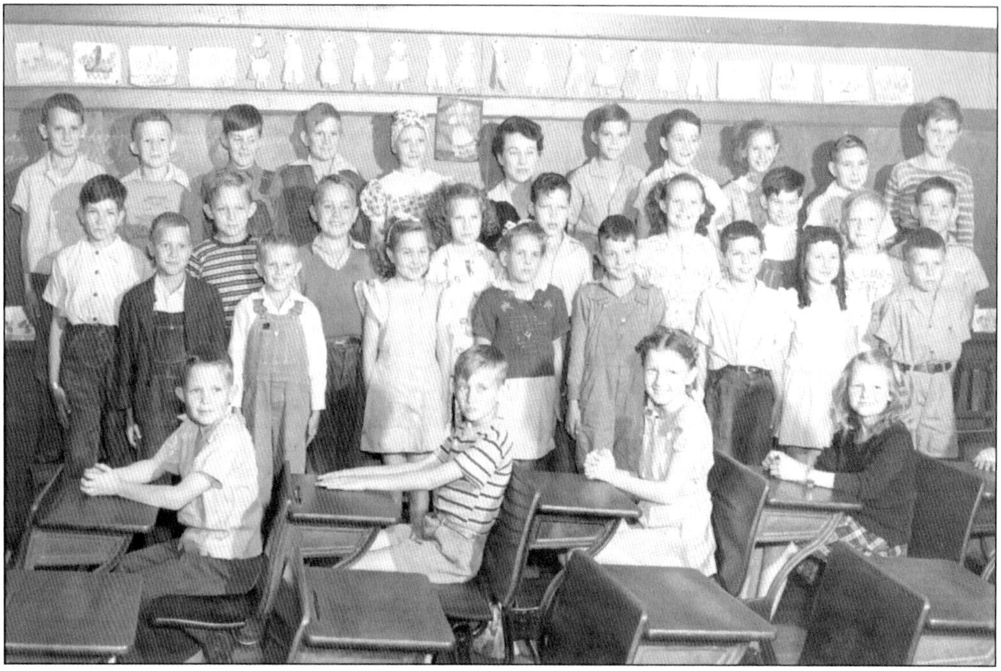

Pictured above is a third-grade class at Central Elementary School in Valdosta in 1946–1947. The teacher is Lena Jenkins Branch Mathis. These students, some of whom came from rural areas of Lowndes County to attend the city schools, were members of the Valdosta High School class of 1956.

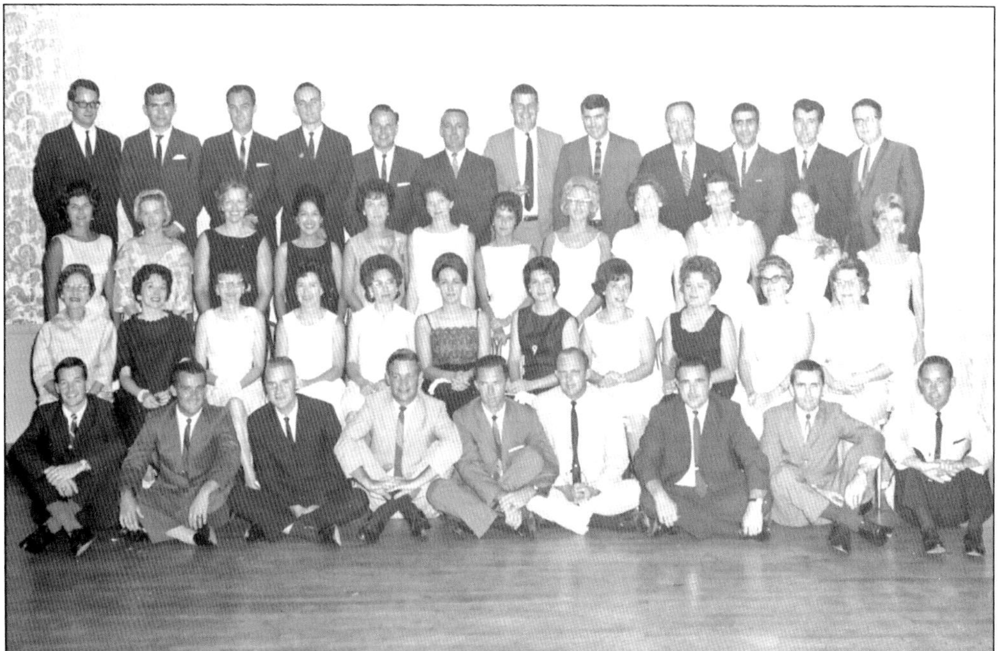

Forty-two members of the Valdosta High School class of 1955 assembled with two of their teachers for a 10-year class reunion at the Valdosta County Club in the summer of 1965. This class graduated from Valdosta High School on May 30, 1955.

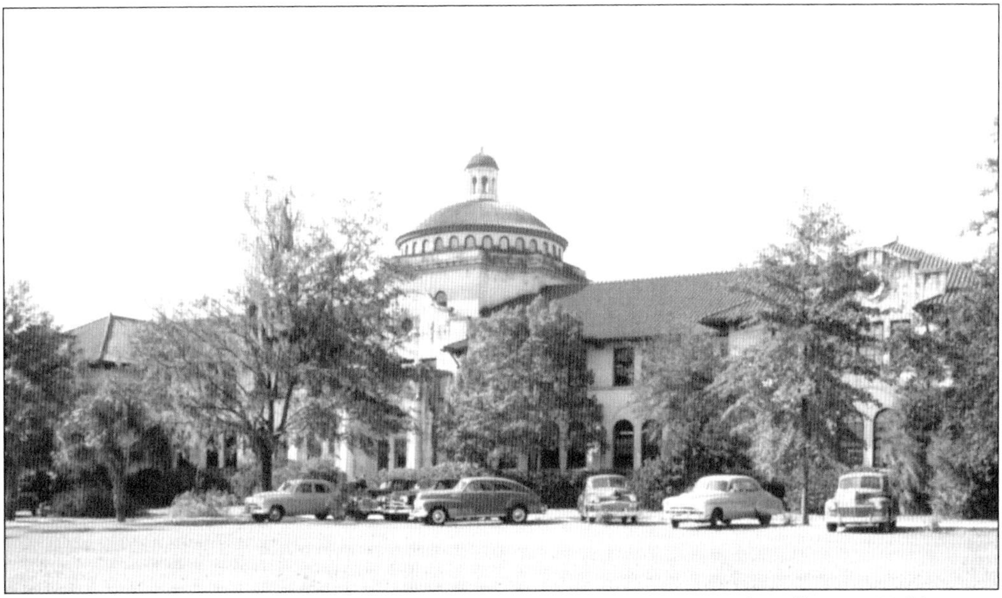

The Georgia General Assembly chartered the South Georgia Normal College in Valdosta in 1906, and the college began its operations in 1913. Eventually the institution became Georgia State Woman's College (GSWC), Valdosta State College, and, in 1993, Valdosta State University. This view is of GSWC's administration building, West Hall, at the end of the 1940s. Note the automobiles that are parked on the front lawn.

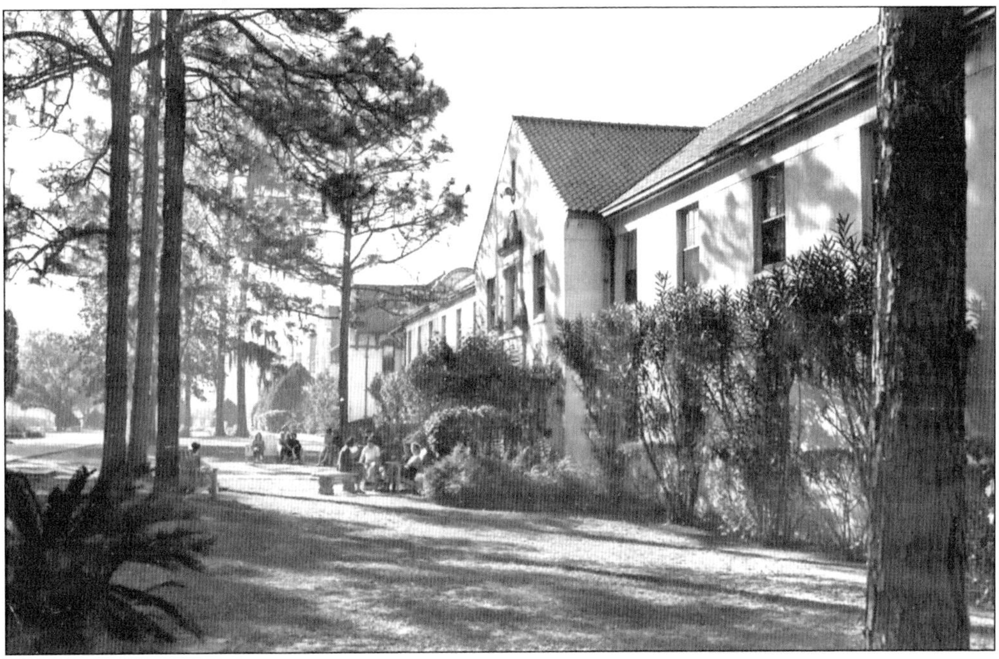

This picture features the three dormitories that housed women on the GSWC campus until the arrival of coeducation in the 1950s. The dormitory in the foreground was then Senior Hall but has for many years been known as Reade Hall. Behind it, in the center, is Ashley Hall, and at the rear is Converse Hall. The original Converse Hall burned in the 1970s and has since been replaced by a new structure.

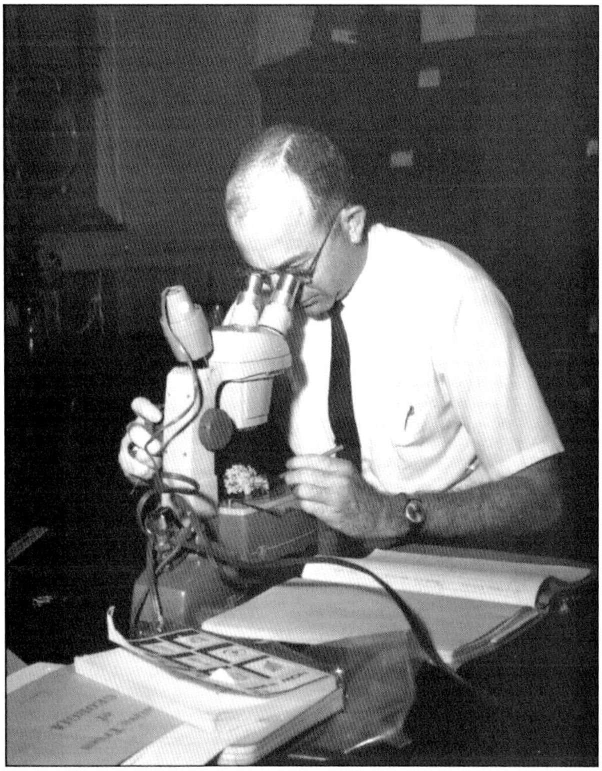

Dr. Wayne Faircloth, Valdosta State University professor of biology, who arrived on campus at the beginning of the 1960s and served well into the 1990s, uses a microscope to examine a plant specimen for a botany class.

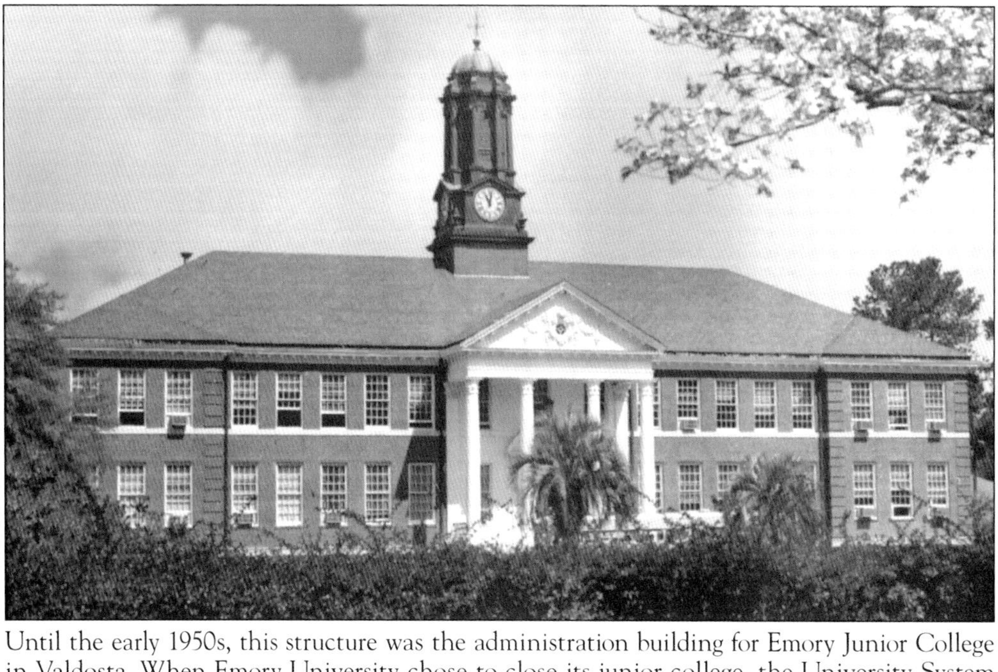

Until the early 1950s, this structure was the administration building for Emory Junior College in Valdosta. When Emory University chose to close its junior college, the University System of Georgia acquired the facilities for Valdosta State College (VSC). The former Emory Junior College became the North Campus of Valdosta State, and the administration building was named Pound Hall.

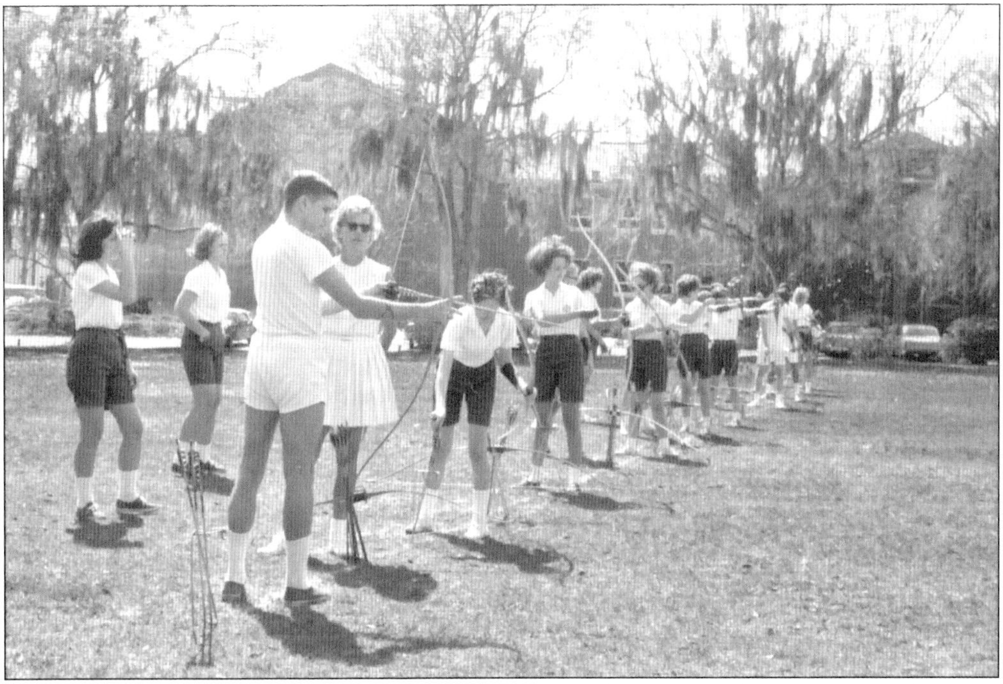

For many years, physical education courses were required of most students as a normal part of their academic programs at GSWC and VSC. Shown above is a VSC archery class being taught by Prof. Gertrude Veatch in the early 1960s.

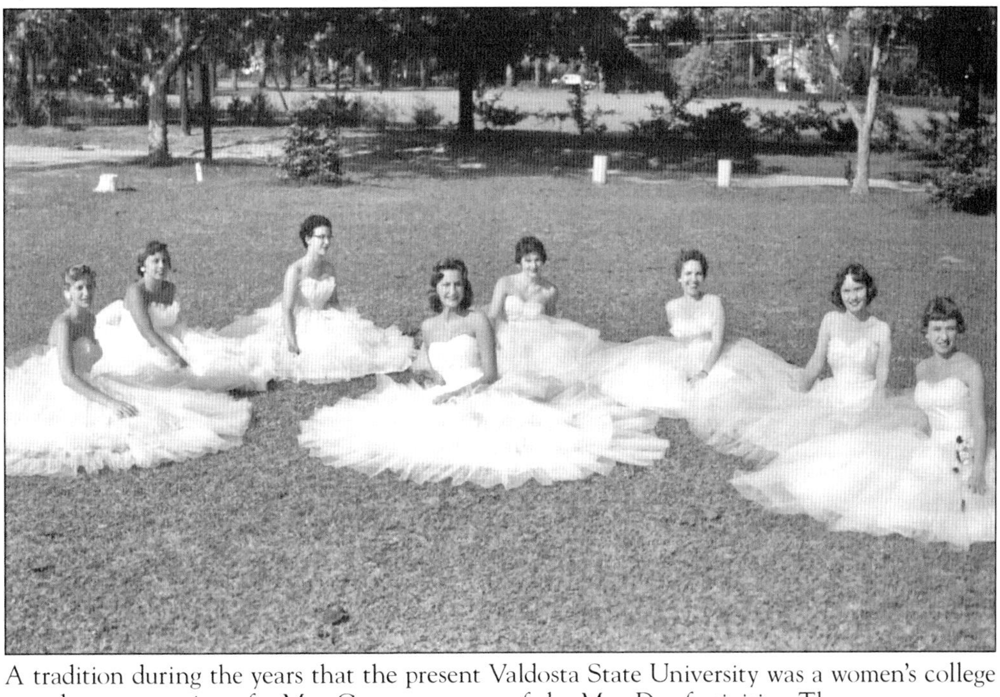

A tradition during the years that the present Valdosta State University was a women's college was the presentation of a May Court as a part of the May Day festivities. The young women pictured above in their gowns were the members of the 1956 May Court, when May Day was still being observed.

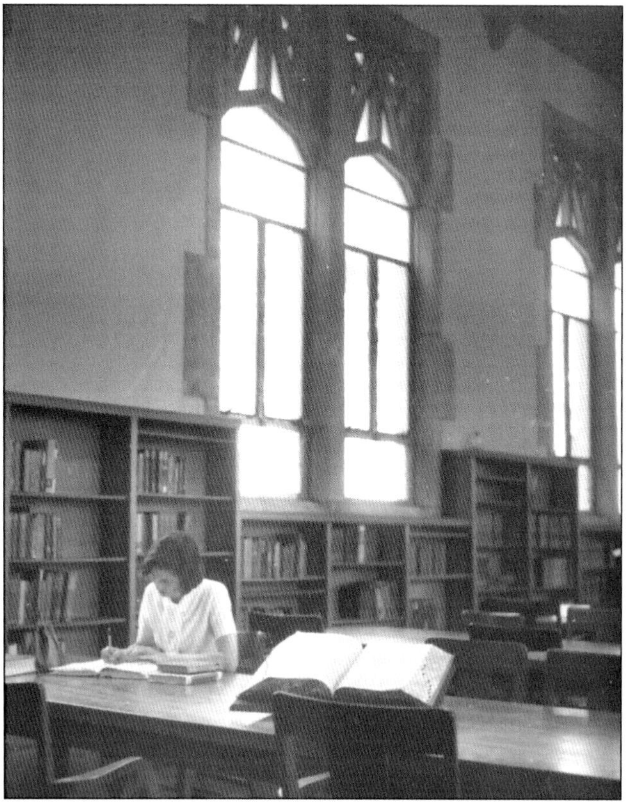

The picture to the left is of a female student of the 1950s or 1960s at work in the reading-reference room of the Richard Holmes Powell Library at Valdosta State College. Built by the New Deal Works Progress Administration and dedicated by Eleanor Roosevelt in 1941, the Powell Library was succeeded by a much larger facility, the Odum Library, in the 1970s.

On March 19, 1971, at Valdosta State College, John W. Langdale, left, of Valdosta, a longtime member of the University System of Georgia Board of Regents, is presented a citation to honor him for his service by Dr. George Simpson, chancellor of the University System.

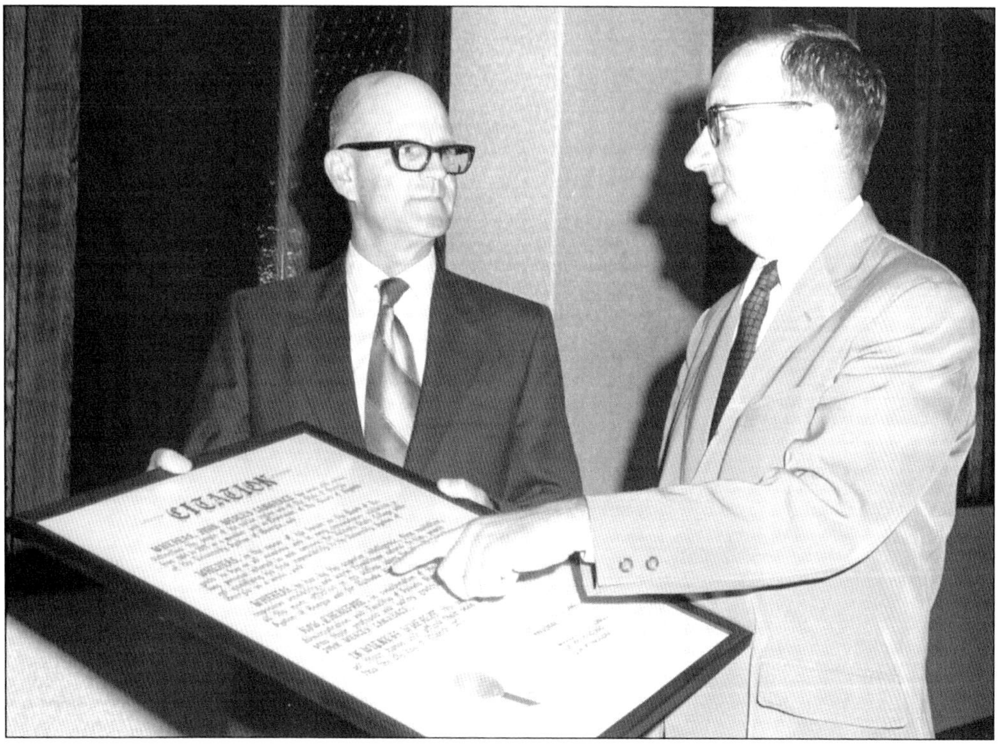

Two

TRANSPORTATION

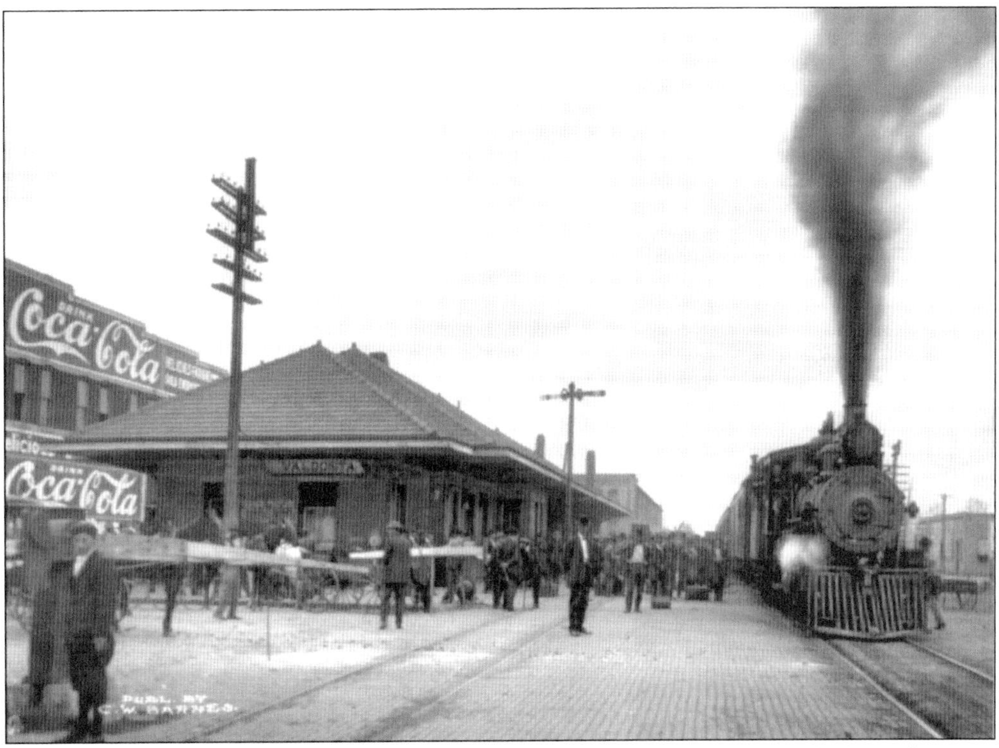

Pictured around 1900 is the Atlantic Coast Line Railroad's Valdosta depot, which was between South Ashley Street on the east and South Patterson Street on the west. The crowd between the station and the passenger train exemplifies the importance of the railroad as the king of overland transportation at the turn of the 20th century. The Atlantic Coast Line was only one of five different railroads that served Lowndes County and Valdosta at the time.

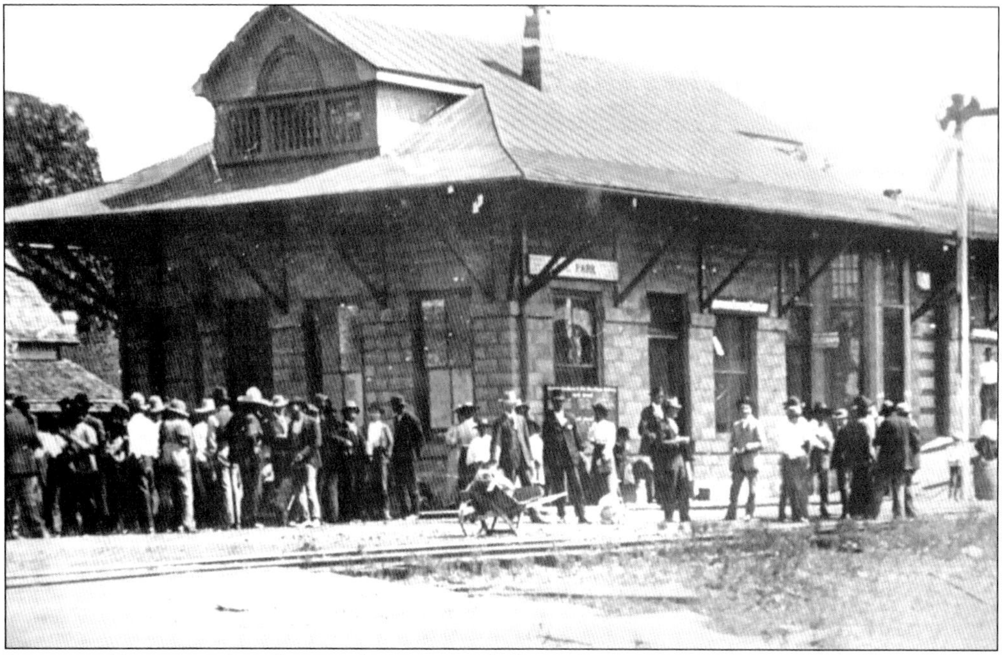

Just as Valdosta travelers frequently patronized the railroads in the late 19th century and well into the 20th century, so also did travelers elsewhere in the county. Shown here is a large group of people at the Lake Park railroad station in southern Lowndes County around 1900.

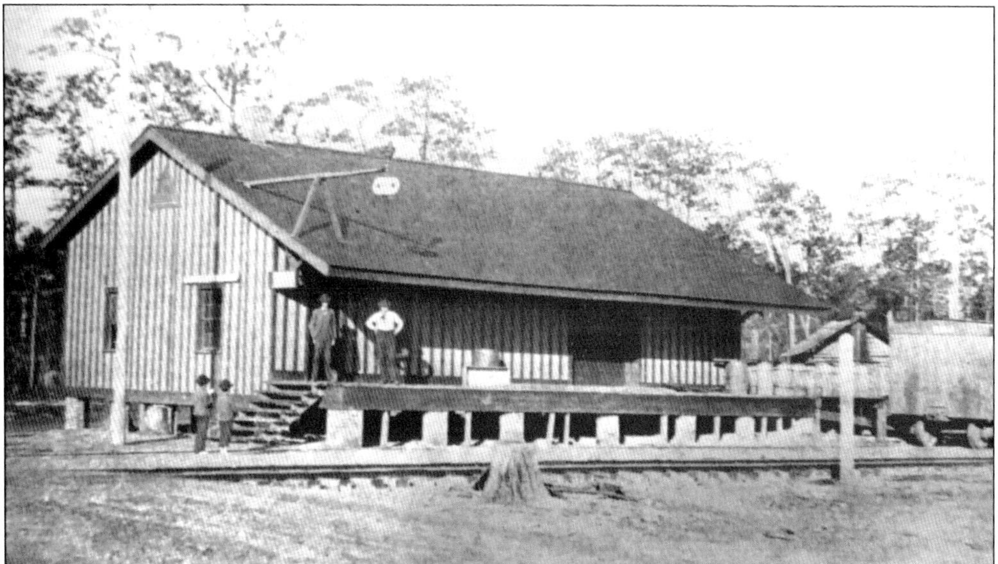

Though the above *c.* 1900 picture of the Hahira railroad station in northern Lowndes County does not show large numbers of passengers, it does emphasize another of the railroads' functions, the hauling of freight, such as the barrels at the right side of the photograph.

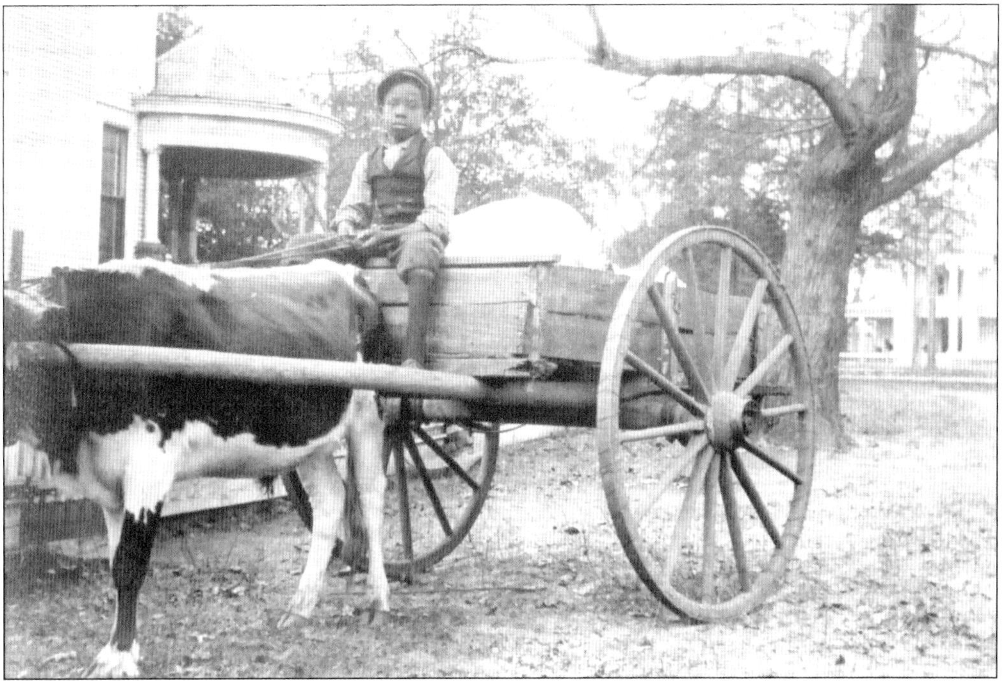

An alternative means of travel in the 19th century and even into the 20th century was the oxcart. Here a youngster is shown driving an oxcart in Valdosta probably in the 1890s, though the exact date is unknown.

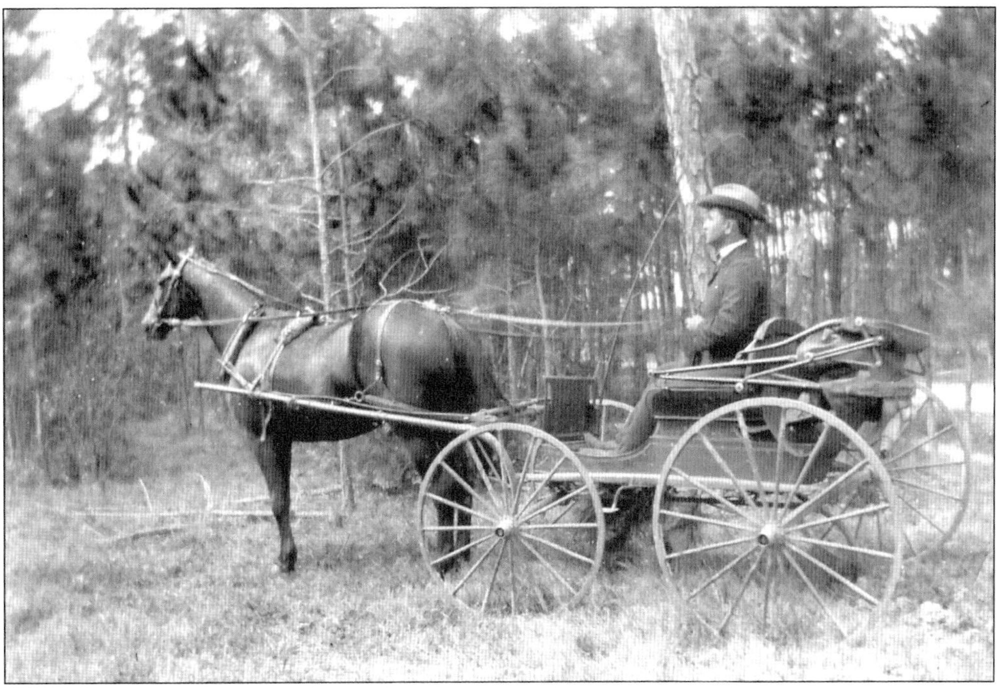

A common form of transportation in Lowndes County in the 19th century was the horse-powered wagon, buggy, or other vehicle. This obviously affluent Lowndes resident is driving his buggy, pulled by a well-groomed horse, on the edge of a pine grove in the 1890s.

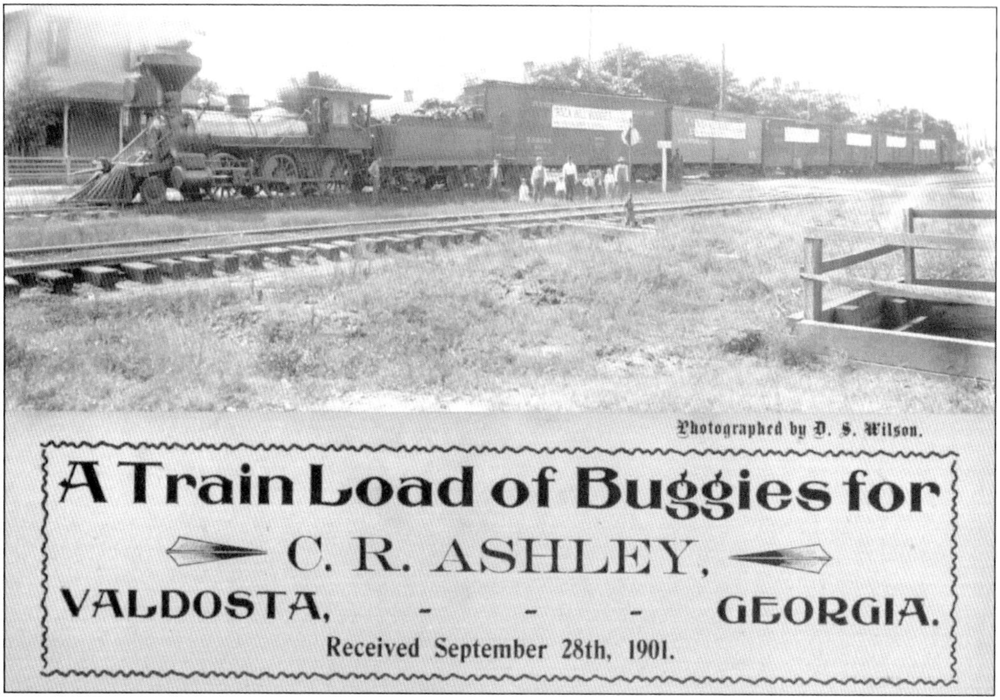

This image, advertising "A Train Load of Buggies for C. R. Ashley" and dating from 1901, displays an interesting contrast in transportation. The railroad, then the ultimate form of overland travel, is being used to carry buggies, another common means of transportation. At the same time, automobiles were already being manufactured, and the first airplane flew about two years later. In a relatively short period, the automobile and the airplane far surpassed both the buggy and the railroad; the buggy virtually disappeared, and the railroads almost stopped carrying passengers.

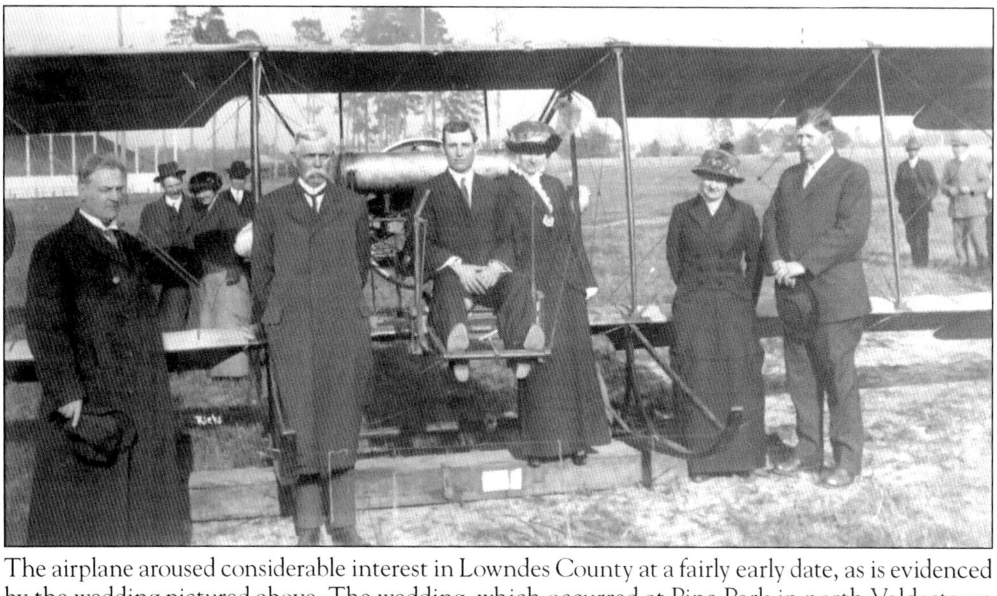

The airplane aroused considerable interest in Lowndes County at a fairly early date, as is evidenced by the wedding pictured above. The wedding, which occurred at Pine Park in north Valdosta on December 10, 1913, was set around a "flying machine." The bride and groom are in the center, and the minister, Aubrey L. Johnston, is second from the left at the front.

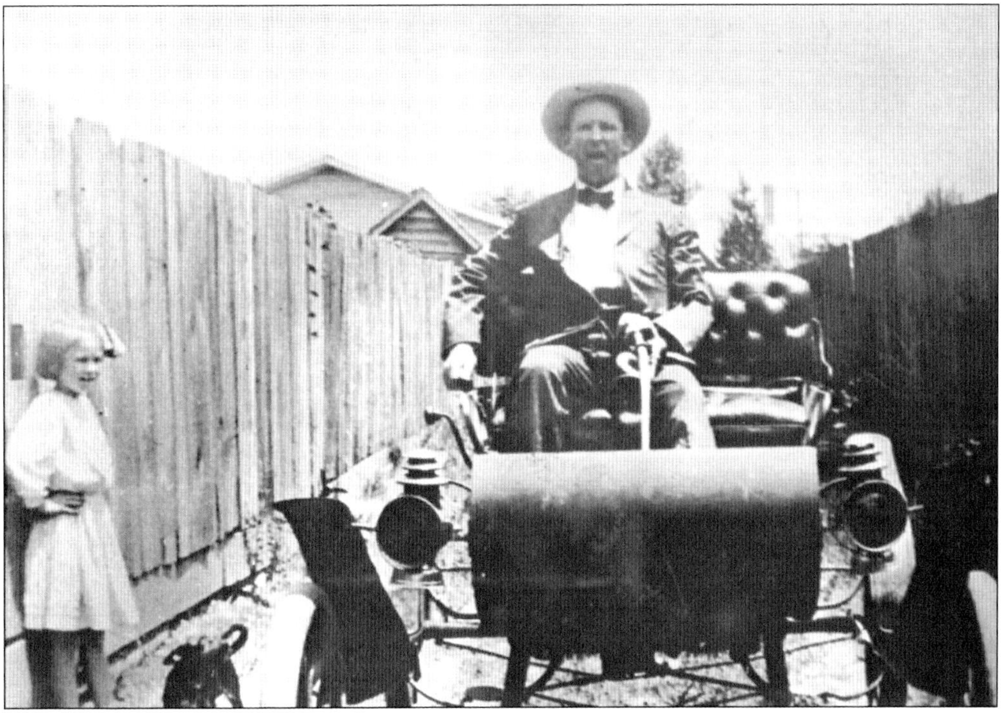

At the very beginning of the automobile age, E. R. Barber, a prominent Valdosta businessman, is shown sitting in or perhaps driving an early model of the "horseless carriage."

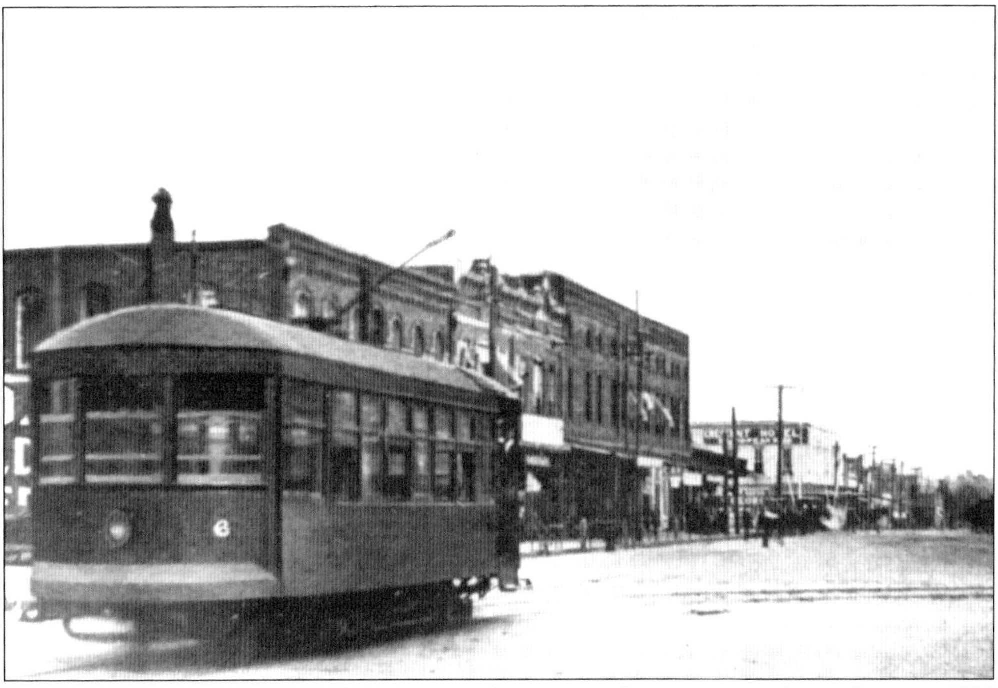

For residents of Valdosta, the county seat, an efficient way of moving around town between 1899 and 1924 was the Valdosta Street Railway. The street railway car pictured was in the downtown area at the time.

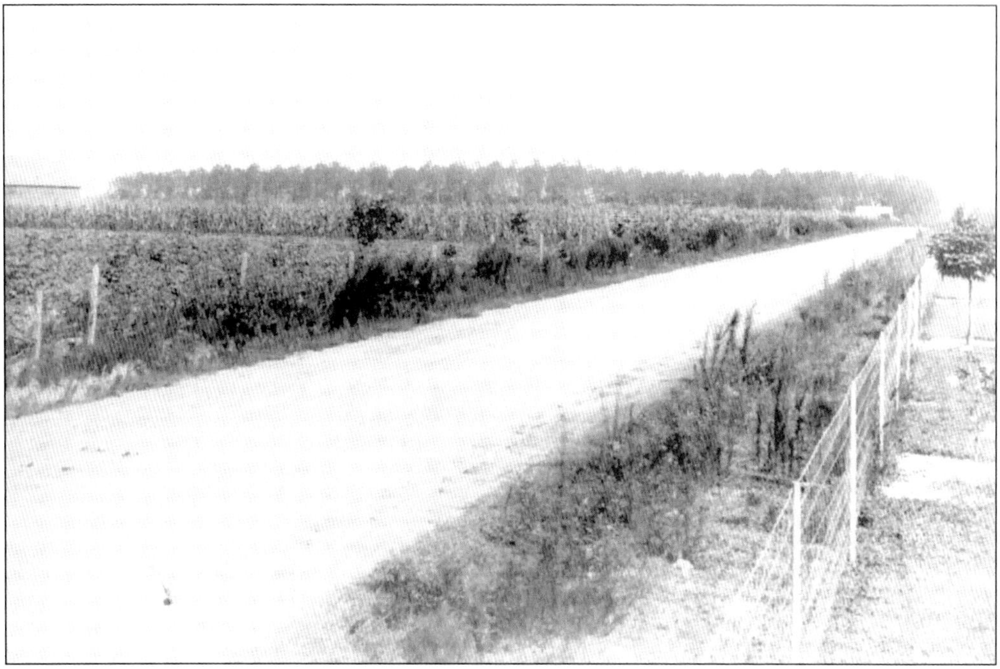

Rural residents of the county did not enjoy the same transportation advantages as those living in Valdosta. This image, from well before 1950, shows a typical county farm road with a sand and clay surface that would have been extremely dusty in dry times and deeply muddy when wet.

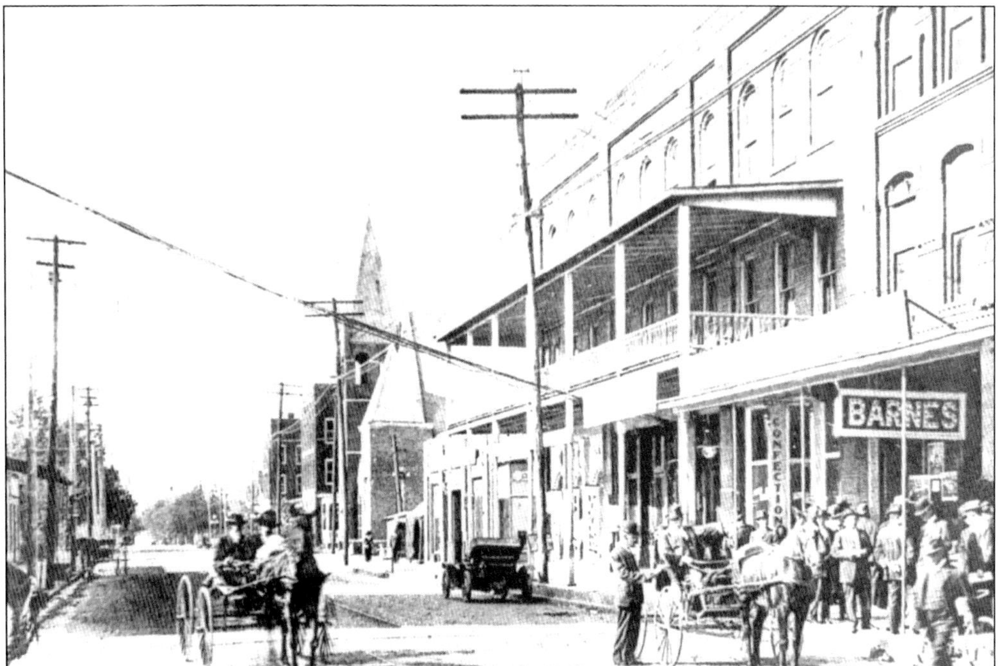

This interesting view of West Hill Avenue in Valdosta, from around 1905–1910, displays a mixture of horse-drawn vehicles and one automobile. Running down the middle of the street are the tracks for the Valdosta Street Railway.

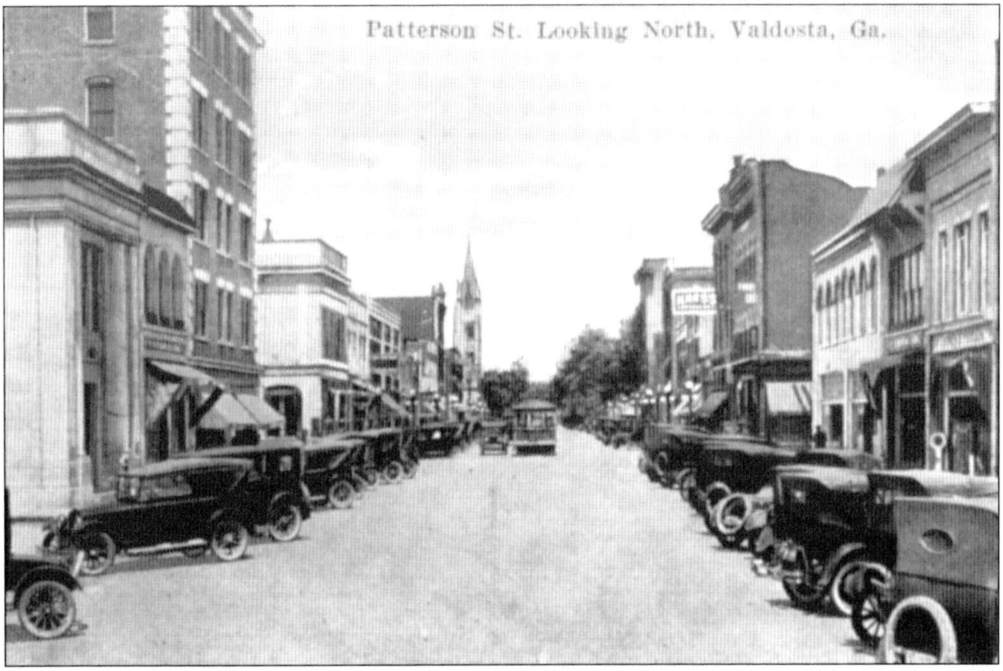

This image of North Patterson Street looking toward the north is from the early 1920s, certainly prior to 1924, when the Valdosta Street Railway ceased business. The striking aspect of the picture is the large number of automobiles parked on either side of the street, which demonstrates just how popular they had become. At the same time, the street railway continues to drive down the middle of the street.

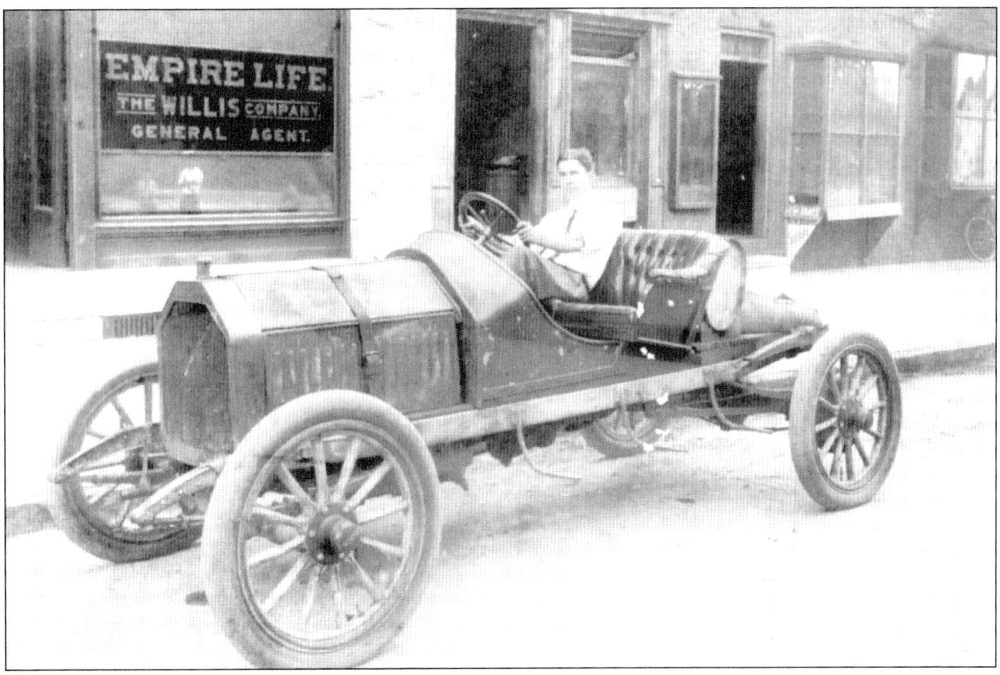

Willard Parrish of Valdosta sits in his open automobile in the 1920s. The car gives the appearance of being very basic, offering few amenities other than a means of moving around the county.

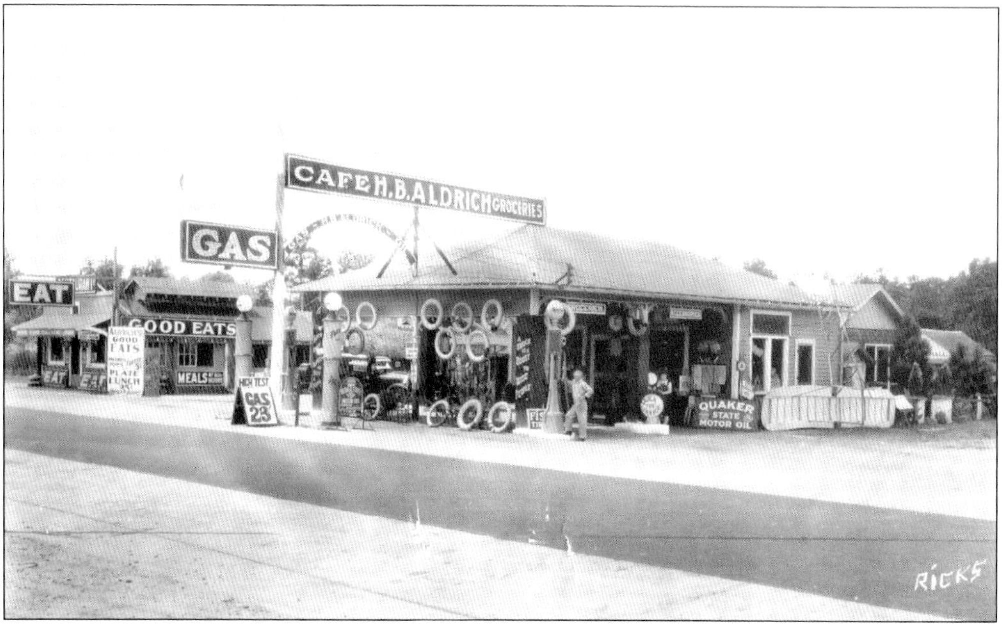

The growing popularity of the automobile spawned a great variety of related businesses, such as gasoline stations to provide fueling facilities. H. B. Aldrich put together three businesses in one—a gasoline station, restaurant, and grocery store—on North Ashley Street in Valdosta in the early 1920s. Later in the 1920s, Aldrich's location became the site of Pines Camp, the first "tourist court" in Lowndes County.

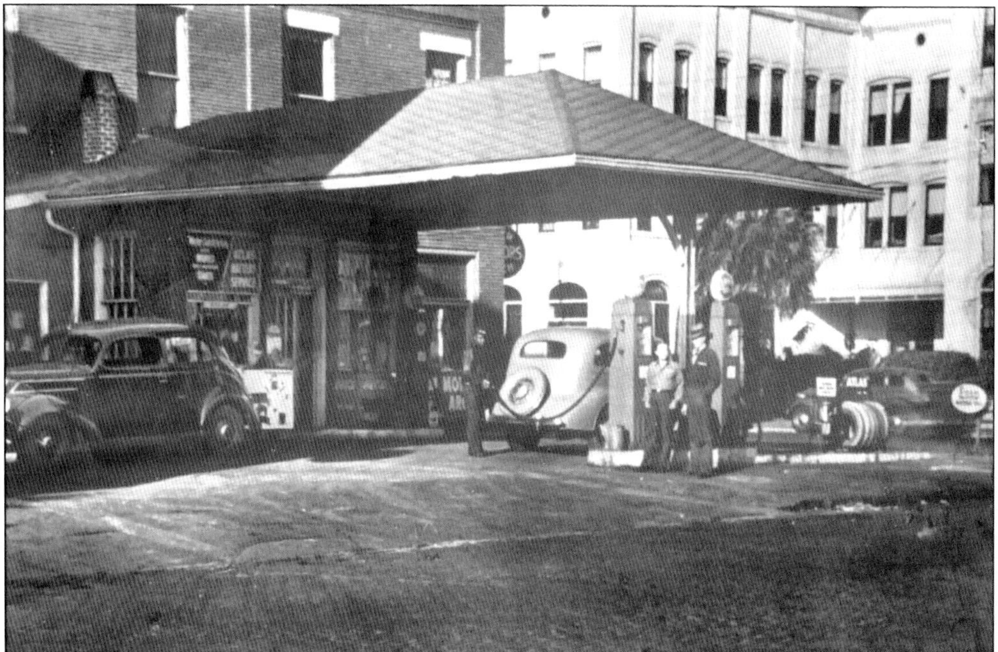

Another popular source for repairing and fueling automobiles in Valdosta was Bobby Daugharty's service station, adjacent to the Valdes Hotel at the corner of West Hill Avenue and North Toombs Street. This picture of the station dates from the 1930s.

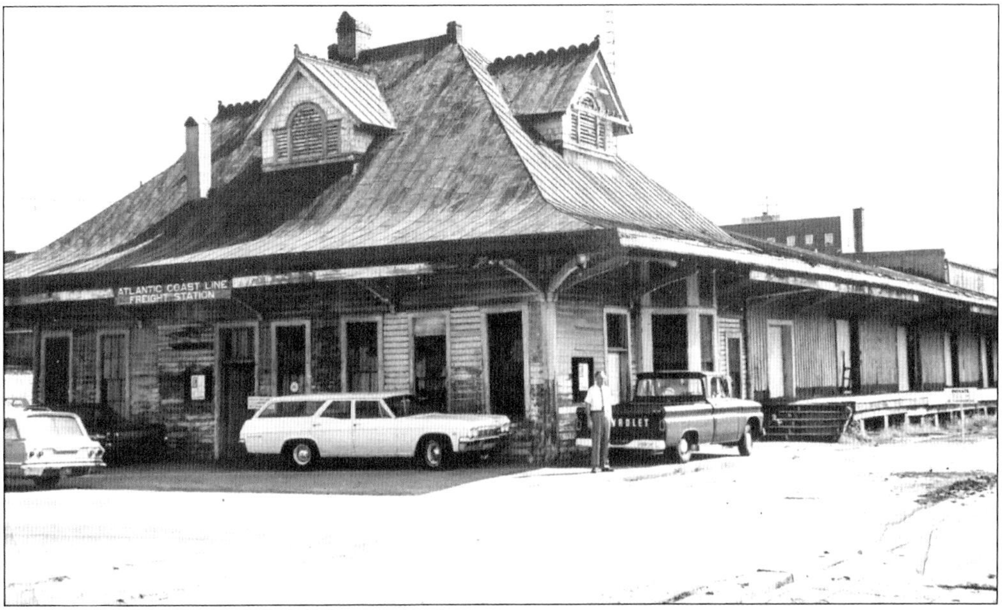

Shown here in its last days of business in the 1960s is the Atlantic Coast Line Railroad's old freight station in Valdosta.

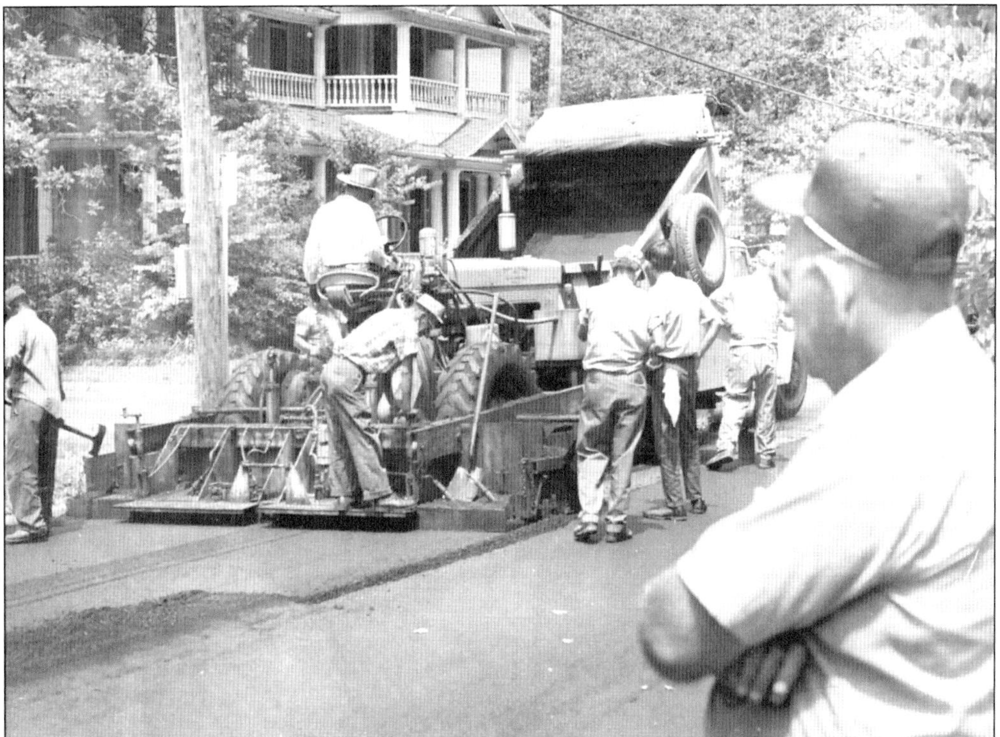

In the 20th century and beyond, the almost limitless use of the automobile as a means of transportation demanded good paved roads and streets and frequent repairs or repaving when needed. Here a paving crew resurfaces West Hill Avenue in Valdosta in the 1950s or 1960s.

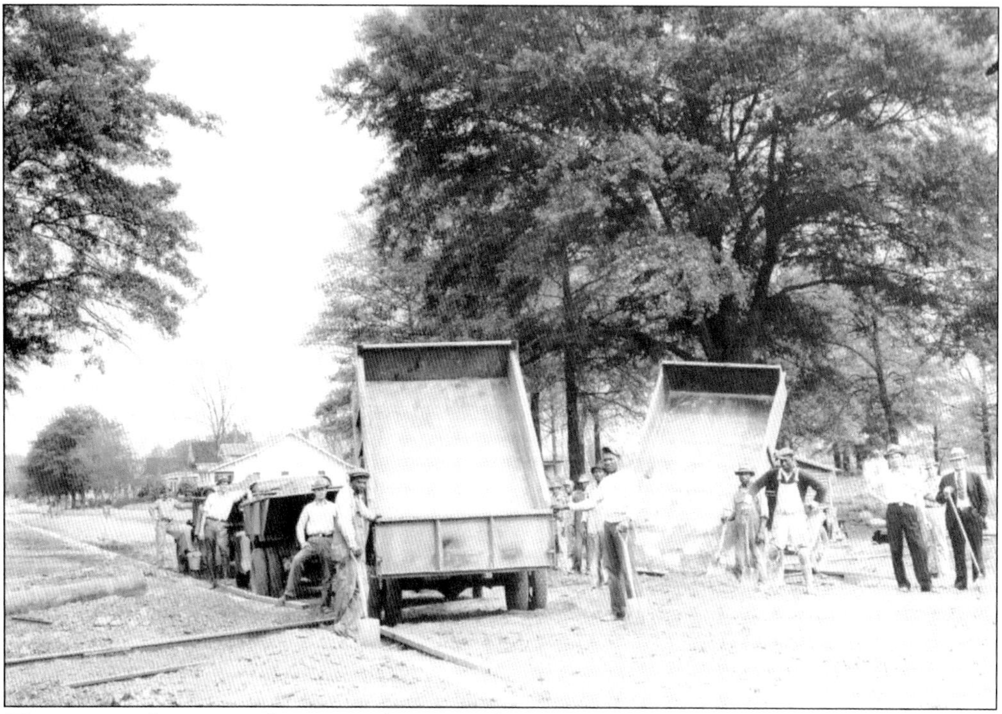

This picture shows a work crew grading a road and a crossing at a set of railroad tracks at an unidentified location in Lowndes County in the 1930s or 1940s.

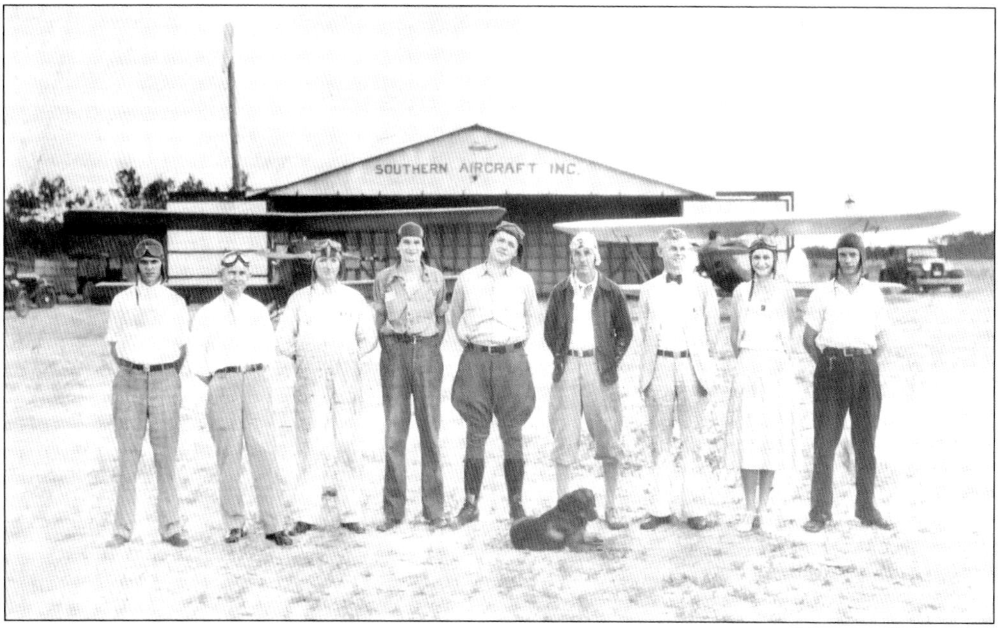

Aviation was unusually popular in Lowndes County, especially in the 1930s after Charles Lindbergh's 1927 solo crossing of the Atlantic Ocean to Paris. The local aviators shown in this image include, from left to right, Ray Kinsey, Pete Robinson, Tom Steadman, L. E. Futch, ? Jolly, Ray Bridges, Fred Pultar, Louise Clifford, and Tom Clifford. According to a note on the original picture, Louise Clifford was the first licensed female pilot in Georgia.

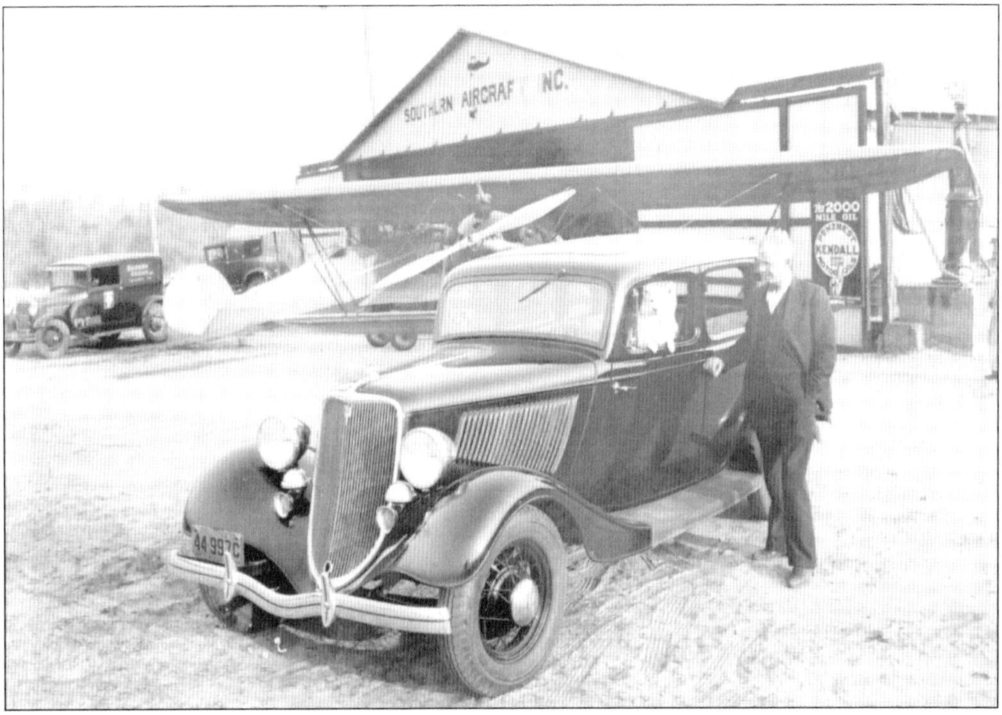

Fred W. Pultar, one of Lowndes County's leading advocates of aviation, is shown at the county's first airport adjacent to the Madison Highway south of Valdosta in 1934.

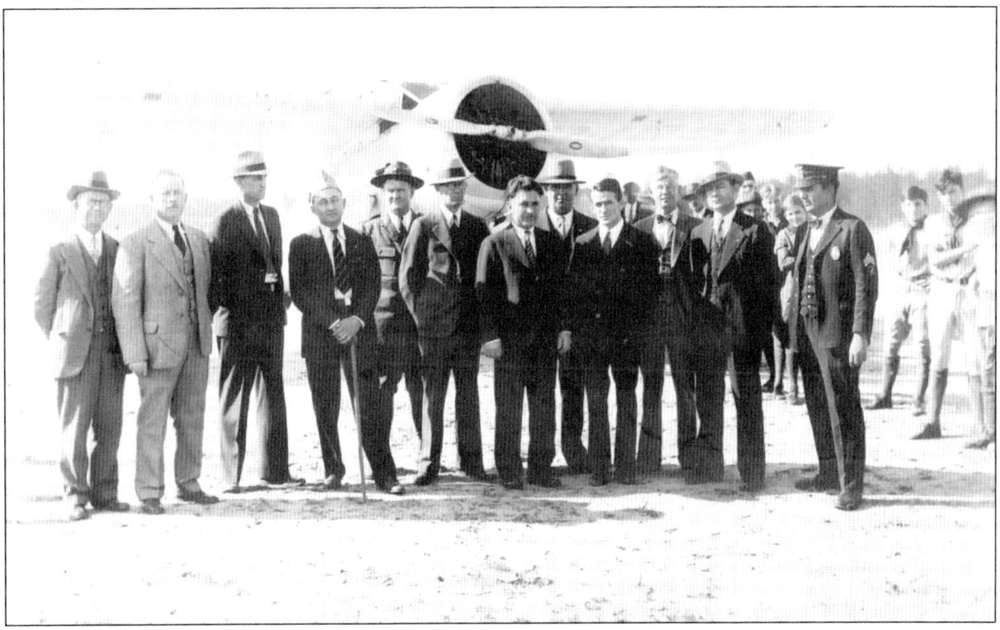

An event that probably helped to popularize aviation in Lowndes County was the visit by the famous pilot Wiley Post, flying the *Winnie May*, in 1931. Shown with Post (bareheaded in the center, directly under the propeller of the *Winnie May*) are, from left to right, P. W. Robertson, Emory P. Bass, R. E. Miller, L. F. Howell, unidentified, Winston C. McKey, unidentified, Harold Gaddy, Fred Pultar, J. P. "Pat" Kelly, and Valdosta police chief William P. Kendall.

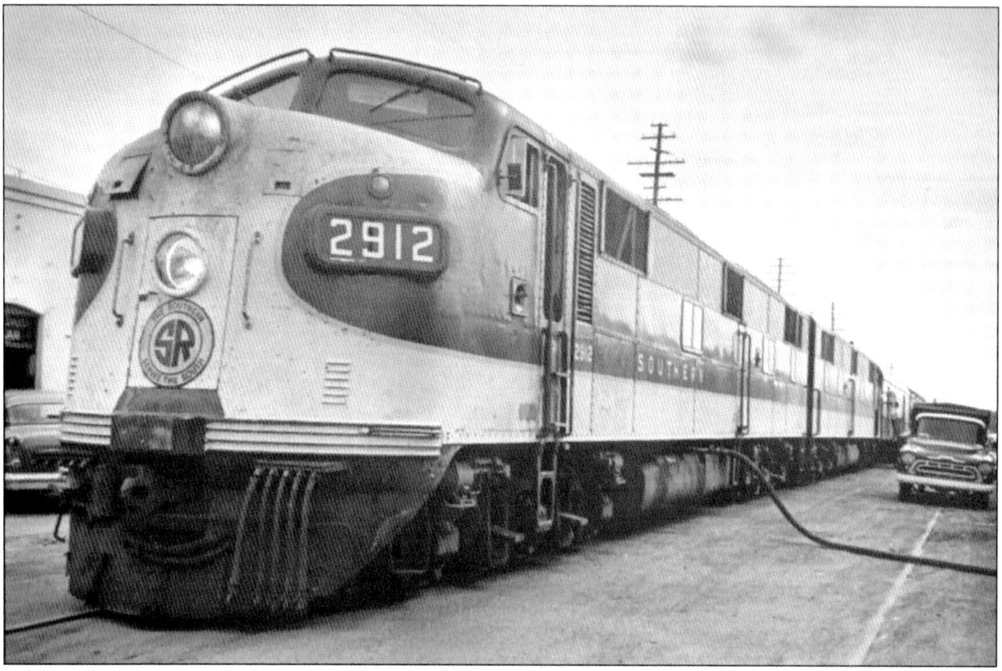

Although the railroads doing business in Lowndes County have not carried passengers for many years, they have continued their significance as freight carriers down to the present. Here, from the 1950s, is a Southern Railway train during a stop in Valdosta. Note the contrast between the modern diesel engine and the coal-powered locomotive shown on page 37.

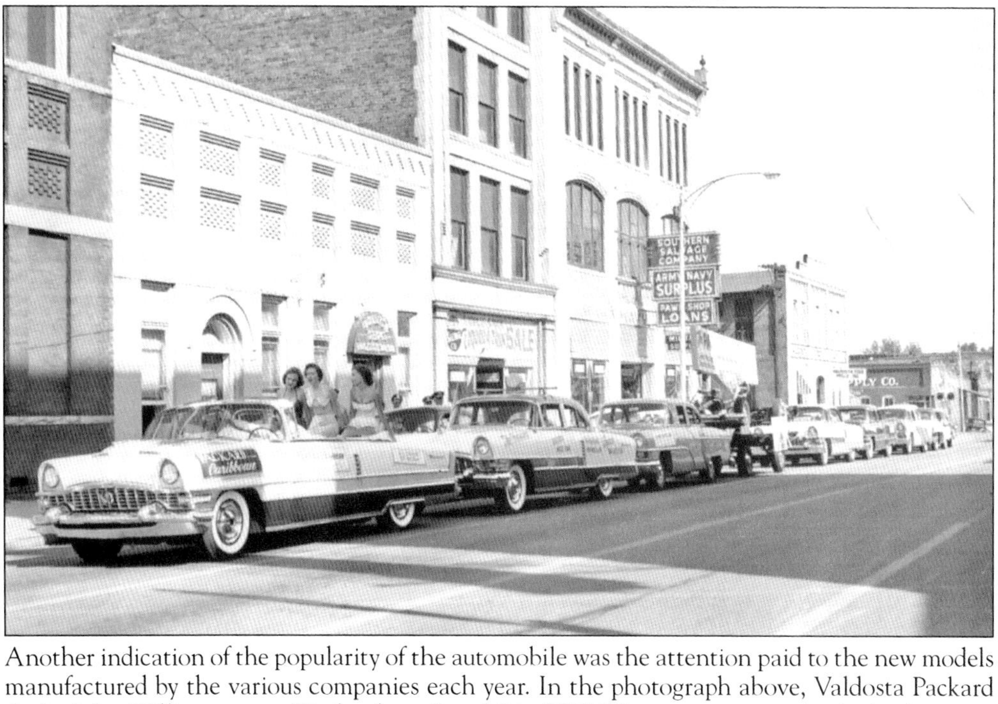

Another indication of the popularity of the automobile was the attention paid to the new models manufactured by the various companies each year. In the photograph above, Valdosta Packard dealer John Williams stages "Packards on Parade" in 1955. The young women in the lead car are, from left to right, Josephine Bogle, Annette Howell, and Sandra Shaw.

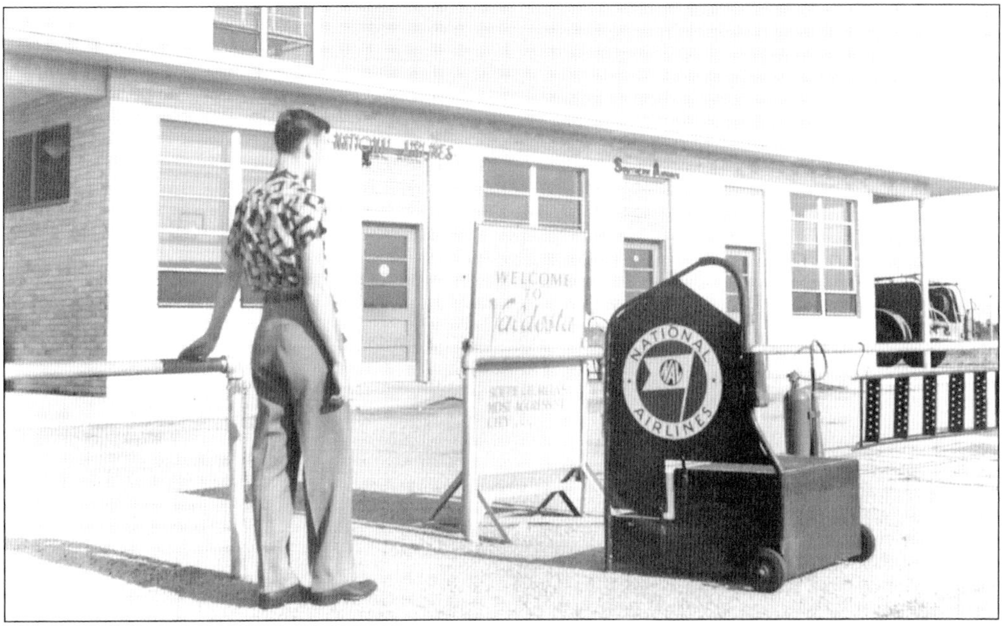

In the late 1940s, a passenger terminal was constructed at the Valdosta Municipal Airport on the south side of town next to the Madison Highway, and commercial passenger service became available for Lowndes County travelers. At the time of this picture, about 1957, both Southern Airways and National Airlines served the airport. The man in the image is Albert Pendleton.

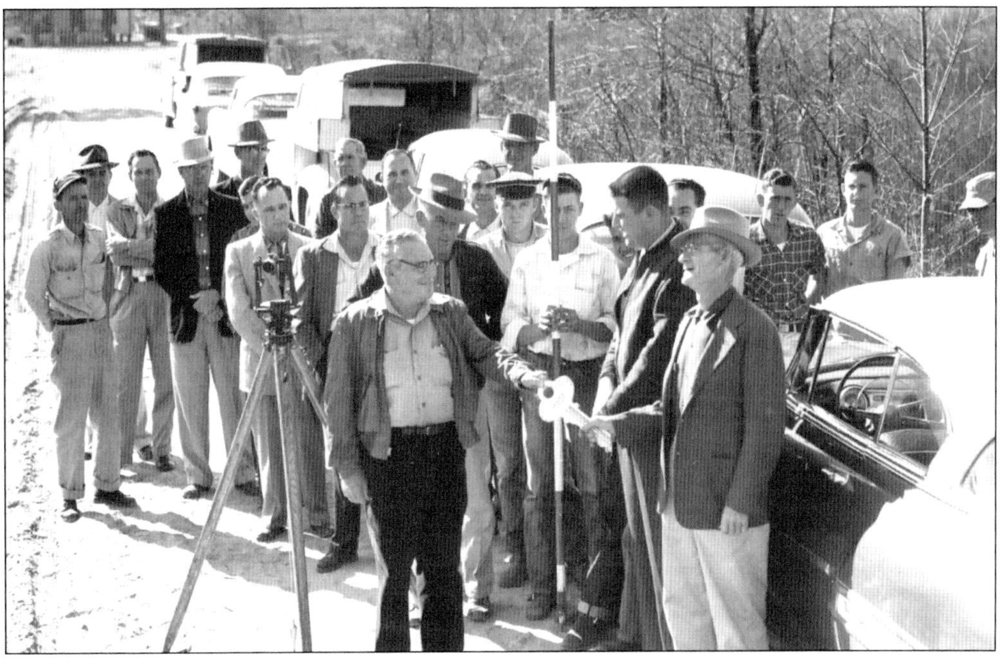

A highly important transportation development that originated in the Eisenhower administration between 1953 and 1961 was the launching of the interstate highway system. One of the main north-south interstate arteries is Interstate 75, which runs through Lowndes County and has been of major economic benefit. Shown here is an early step in the process, the survey of the route within Lowndes in 1957, years before actual construction could begin.

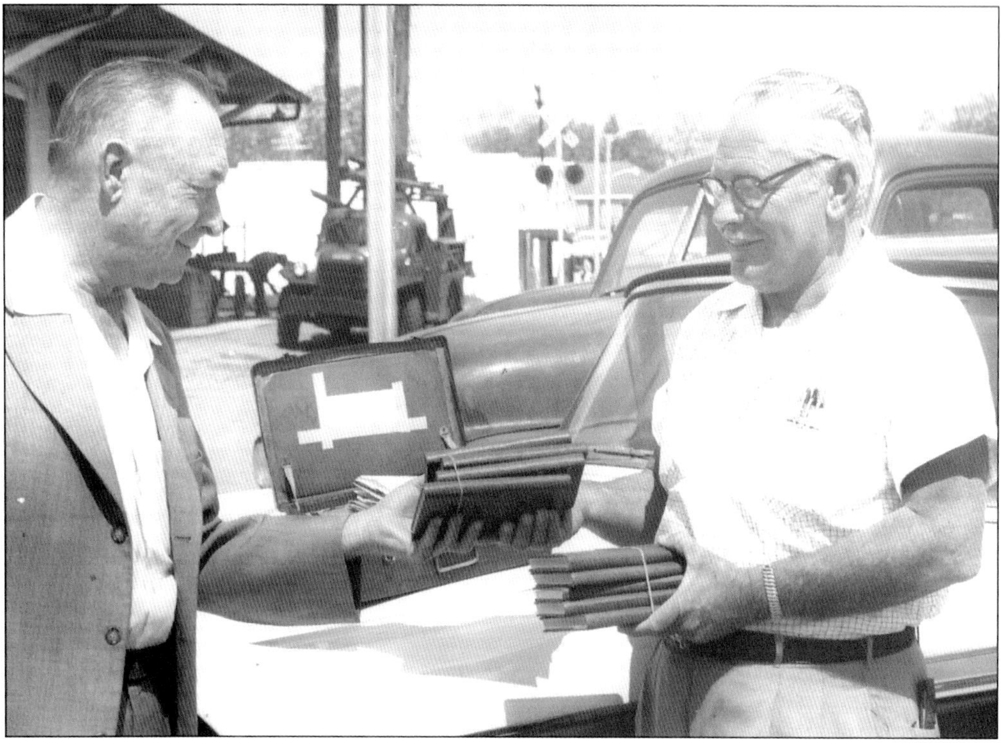

In this photograph, from 1957, the survey books for Interstate 75 in Lowndes County are delivered.

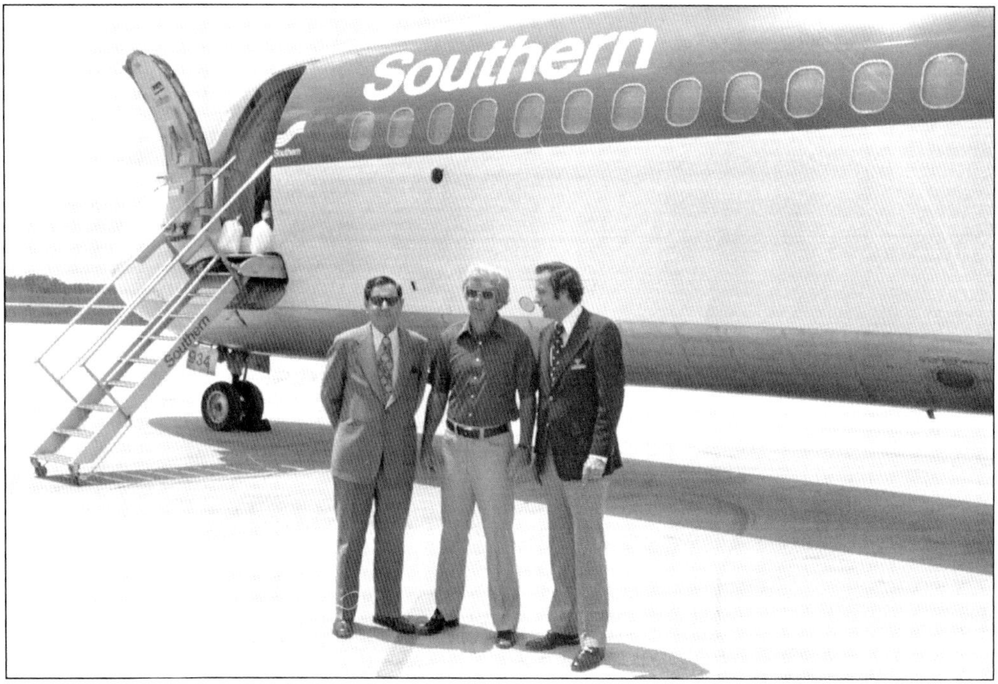

Pictured above is the arrival of the first Southern Airways jet airliner at the Valdosta Municipal Airport in 1974. Shown with the aircraft, from left to right, are James M. Beck, Ferrell Scruggs, and Gil Harbin, prominent Valdosta businessmen.

Three

Agriculture, Business, and Industry

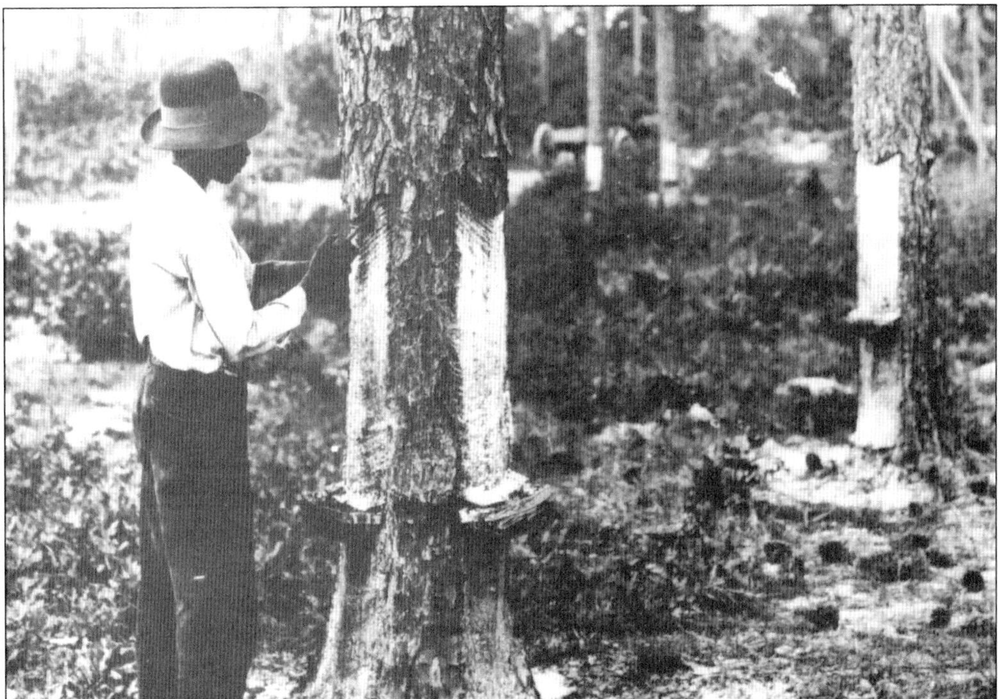

With the use of a special tool, a turpentine worker cuts a "cat face" on a pine tree so the resin will run from the wound into a cup at the bottom. The next part of the routine procedure was the gathering of the resin from the cups to be transported to a distillery for processing. The naval stores or turpentine industry was a major economic activity in Lowndes County, where Valdosta was the headquarters of the American Turpentine Farmers Association, until the 1970s. (Valdosta–Lowndes County Chamber of Commerce.)

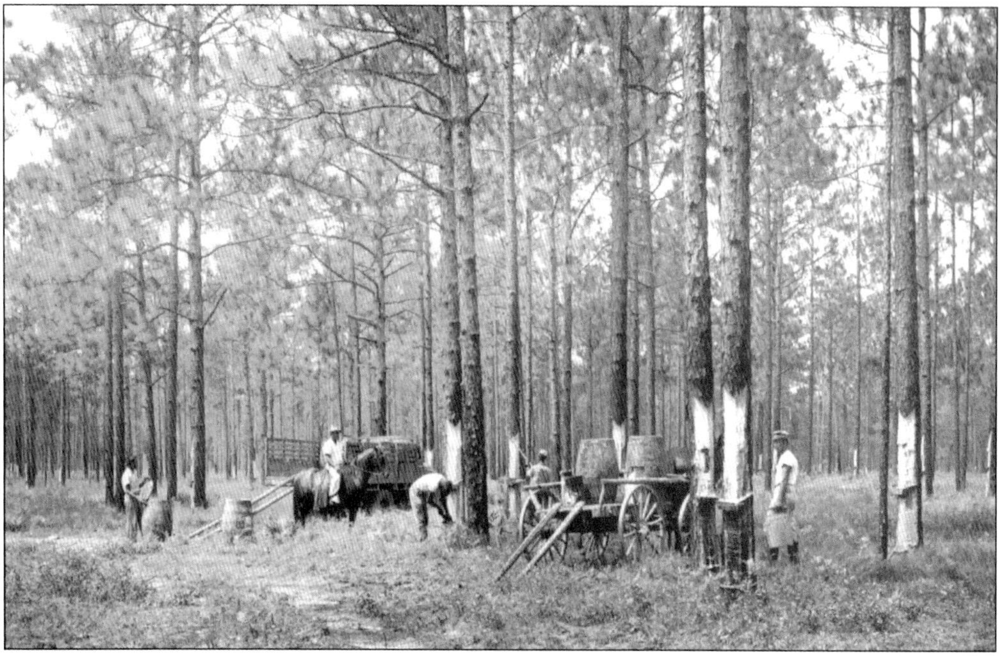

In sharp contrast with the photograph on the previous page of a single worker cutting a "cat face," this picture is of a crew of turpentine workers in a rather open pine forest collecting the resin from the cups attached to the trees. The image features a foreman on horse or mule, a wagon to be used to haul the barrels of resin in the woods, and a truck to transport the barrels to the still.

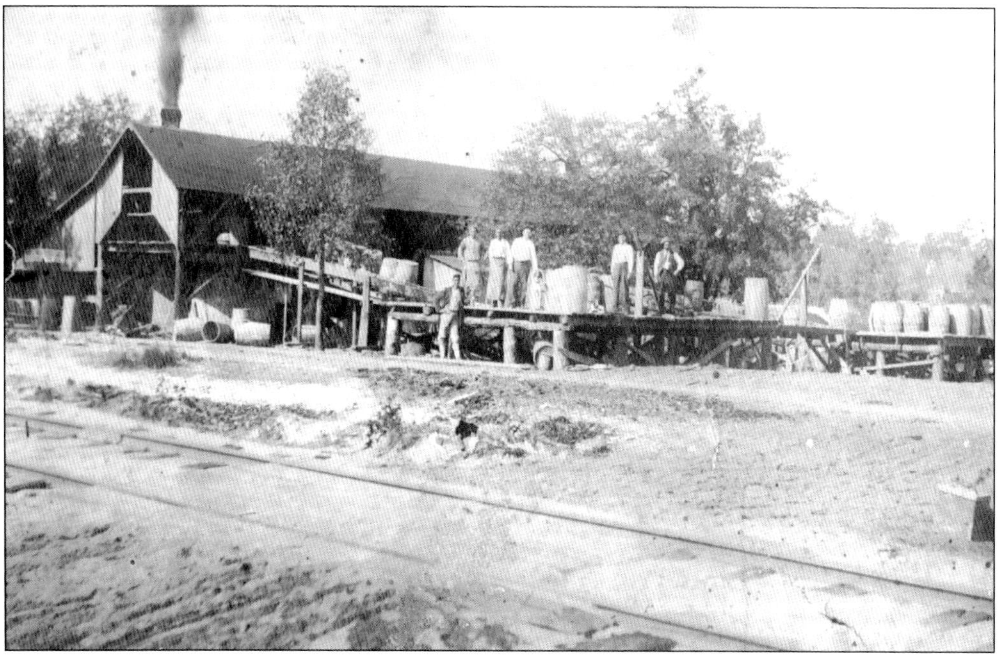

In the prime of the naval stores industry, turpentine distilleries dotted the landscape in Lowndes County. Shown above is one such still, where the smoke from the chimney indicates that the distilling process is underway. As the tracks in the foreground point out, this seems to be one of the larger distilleries that had a direct rail link.

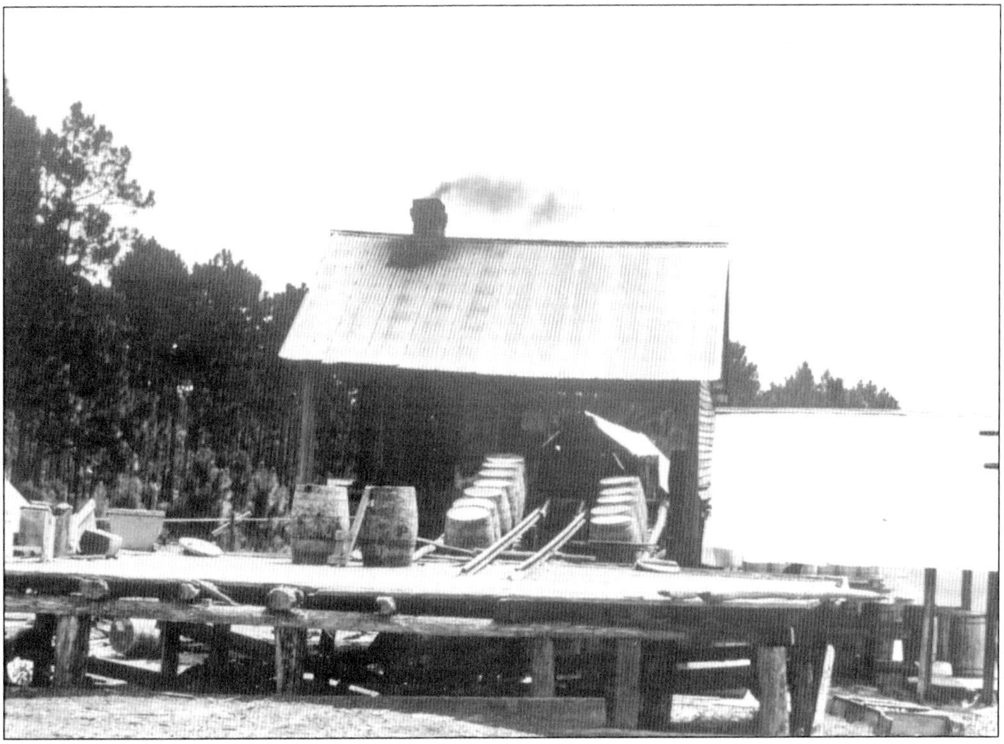

Compared to the distillery on page 52, this one appears to be a fairly small operation. Great variations in size were, in fact, typical of the turpentine industry. The smoke shows that the still was processing at the time of the picture, and the number of barrels on the loading/unloading platform at the front is evidence of plentiful business at the moment.

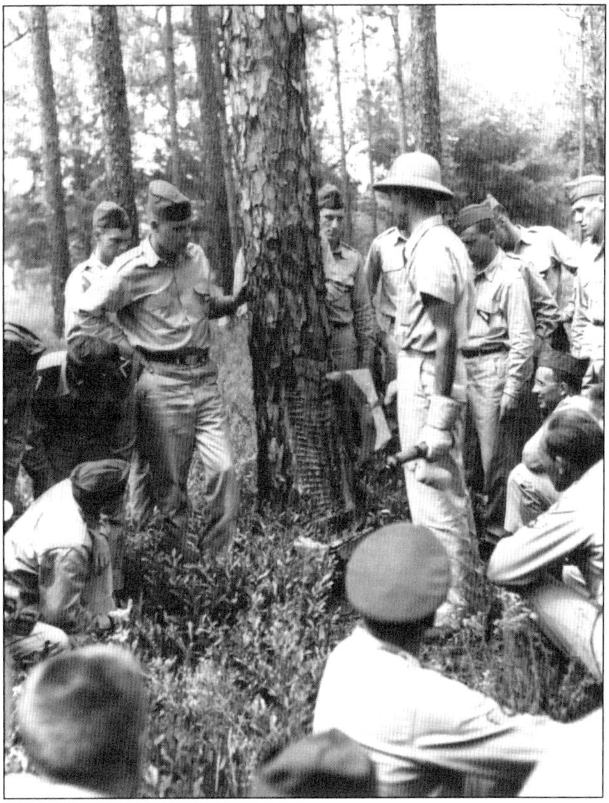

The picture is from the later 1950s, after the reopening of Moody Air Force Base during the Korean War of 1950–1953. This image depicts a demonstration of the method of cutting a "cat face" to Air Force enlisted–personnel. (Valdosta–Lowndes County Chamber of Commerce.)

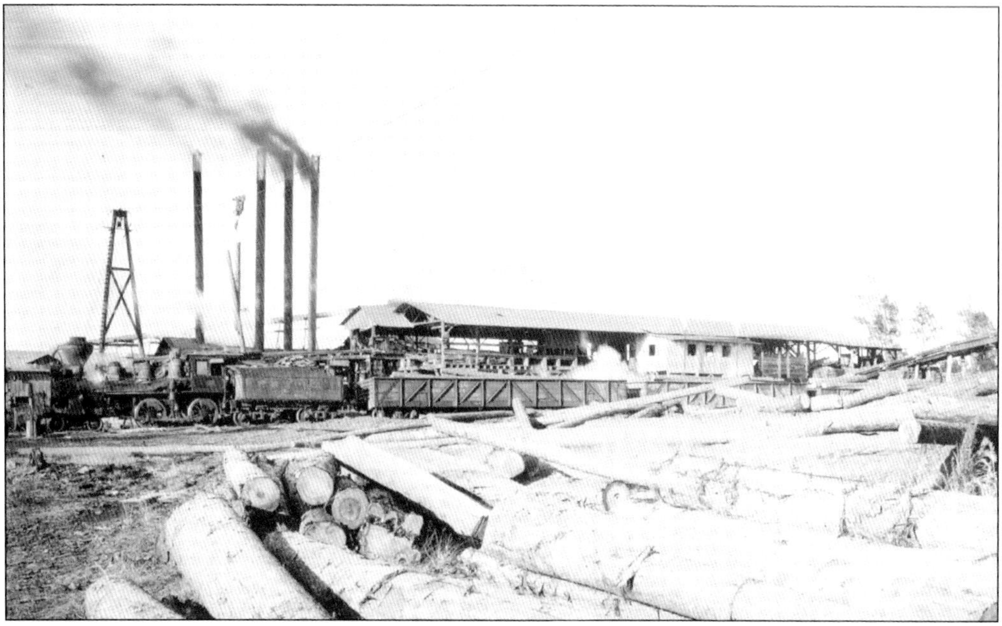

Above is an image of an old Lowndes County business, the J. N. Bray Lumber Company, apparently at the height of its operations. This was a major sawmill operation as evidenced by the four smoke stacks in the background, the presence of a company train in the middle of the picture, and a huge stack of logs in the foreground. J. N. Bray continues in business in Lowndes County to the present day. (Valdosta–Lowndes County Chamber of Commerce.)

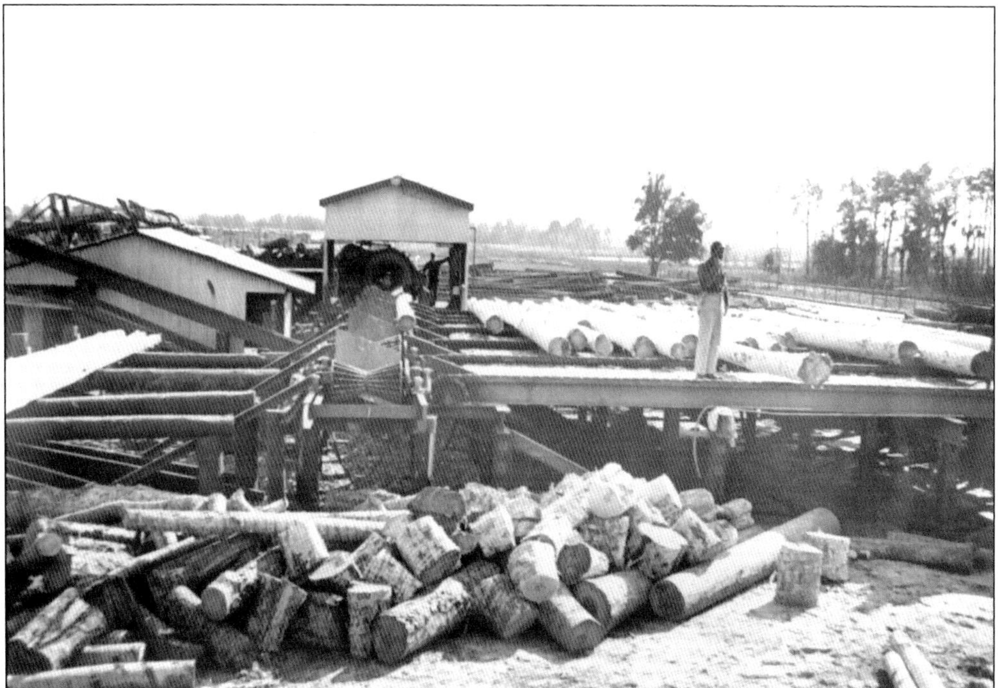

The identity of this sawmill is not shown on the photograph, but it is further evidence of the extent and importance of the lumber industry in Lowndes County in the 20th century.

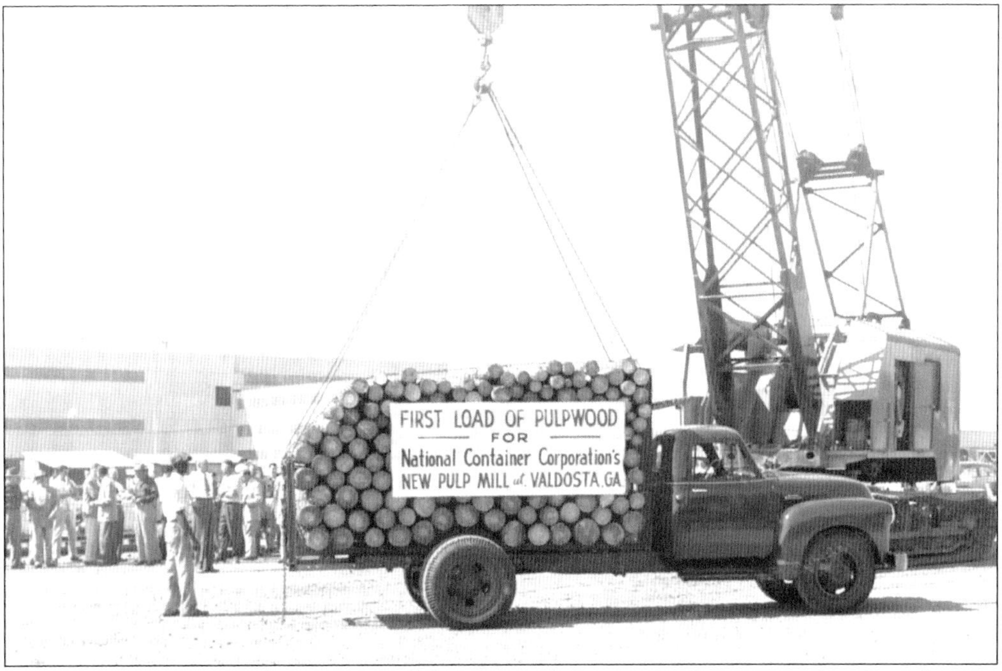

These images focus on the opening of the National Container Corporation's pulp and paper mill at Clyattville in southern Lowndes County in 1952. They make obvious another use of the pine tree that is not related directly to either naval stores or lumber. The top picture shows the ceremonial arrival at the mill of the first load of pulpwood to be processed for paper, with an audience in the background. The bottom photograph is of local dignitaries being interviewed for a radio broadcast marking the opening of the mill. The figures that can be identified are, third from the left, former governor Melvin E. Thompson, holding the microphone, and on the far right, Judge Harley Langdale. (Valdosta–Lowndes County Chamber of Commerce.)

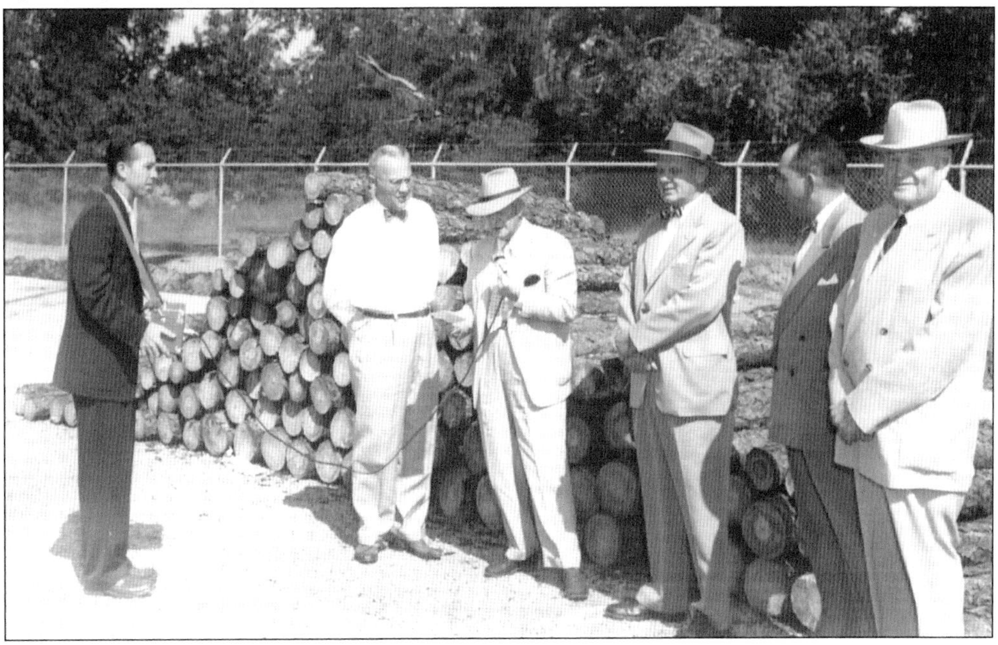

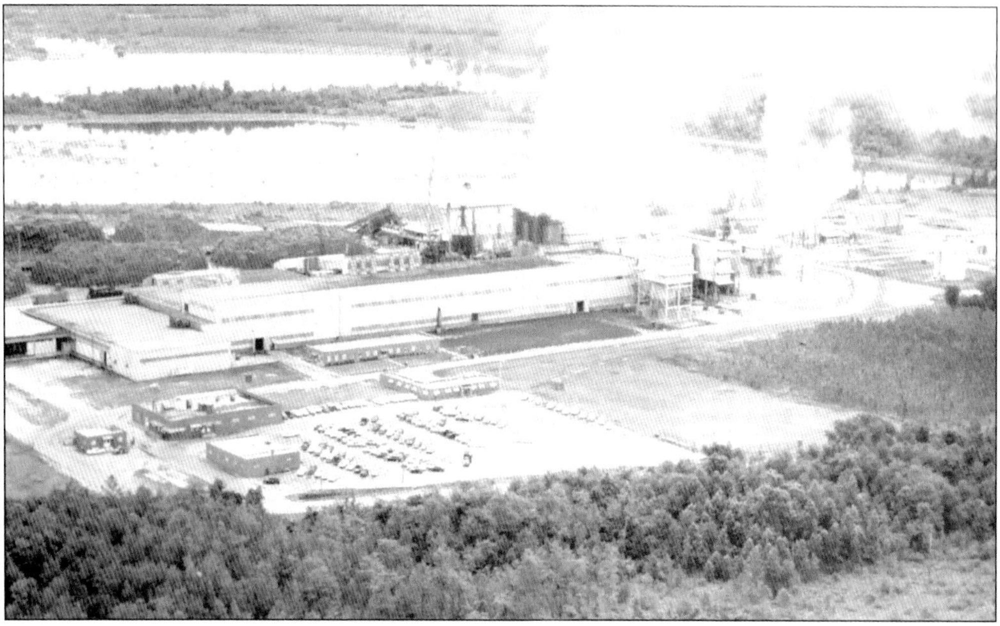

This is an aerial view of the pulp and paper mill at Clyattville. Having been initiated by the National Container Corporation in the early 1950s, the plant has gone through a variety of changes of ownership and of names in the years since. It has been Owens-Illinois, Tenneco, Georgia Pacific, and at the present, it is Packaging Corporation of America. (Valdosta–Lowndes County Chamber of Commerce.)

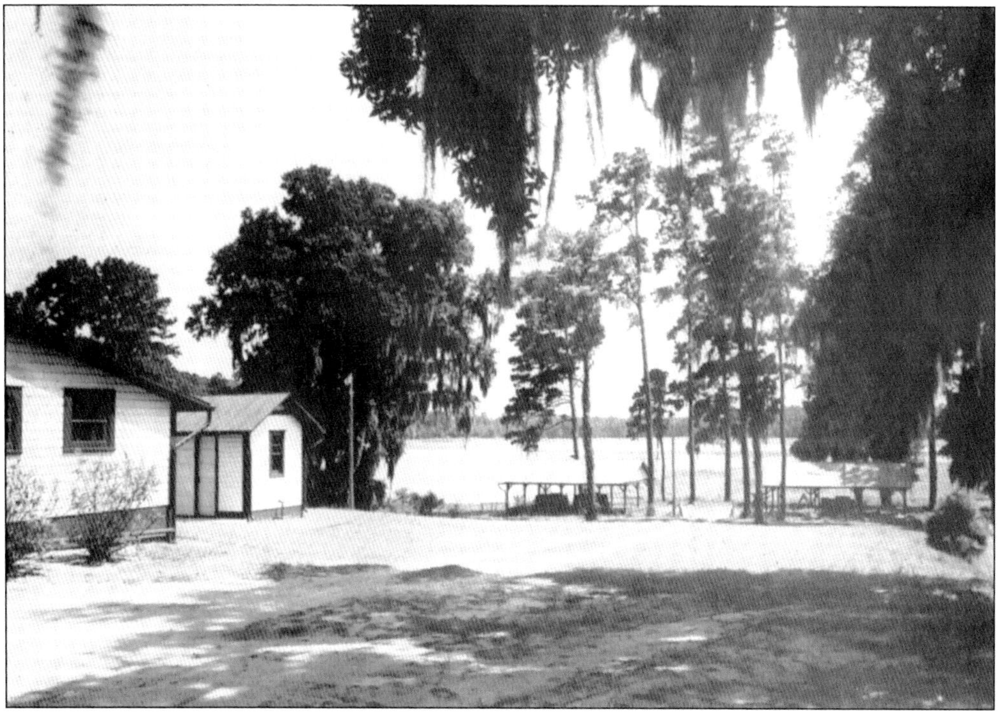

This U.S. Fish Hatchery on a Lowndes County lake south of Valdosta represented an unusual form of farming. The date of the photograph is unclear, but it is perhaps from the 1930s or 1940s.

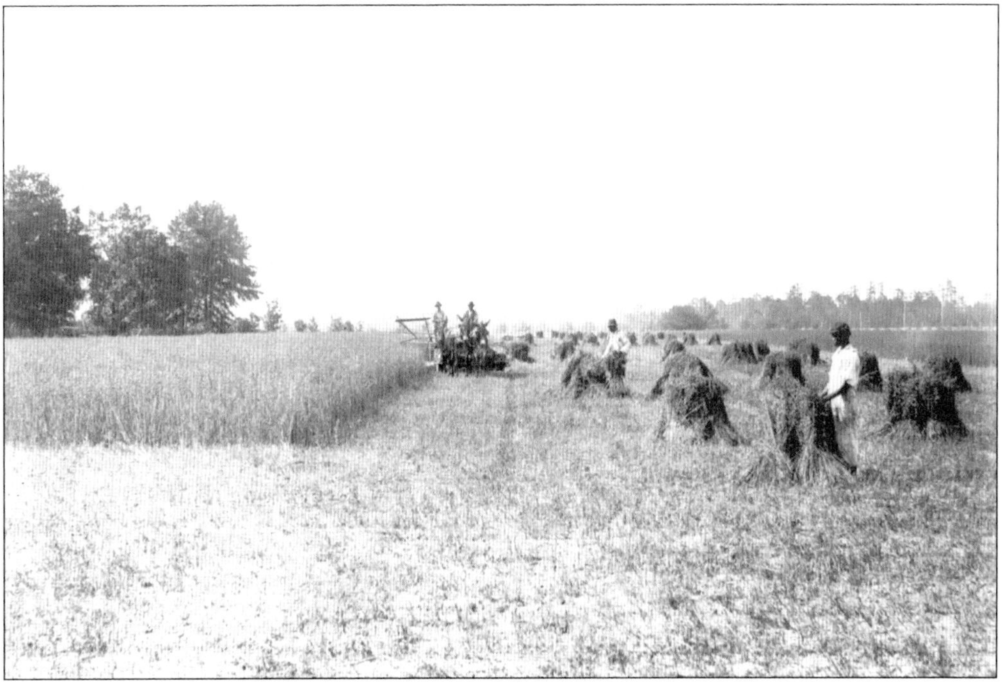

Here a field of oats is harvested in rural Lowndes County early in the 20th century. This photograph is unusual because oat farming was not exactly common in the county at any time.

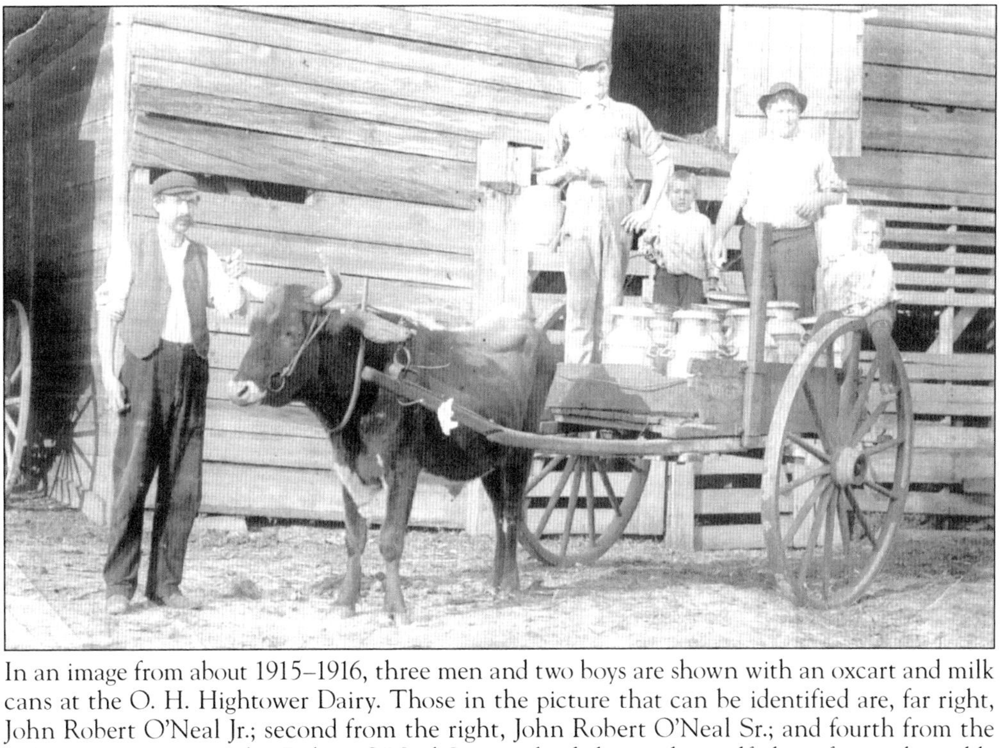

In an image from about 1915–1916, three men and two boys are shown with an oxcart and milk cans at the O. H. Hightower Dairy. Those in the picture that can be identified are, far right, John Robert O'Neal Jr.; second from the right, John Robert O'Neal Sr.; and fourth from the right, Loss Hastings. John Robert O'Neal Sr. was the father and grandfather of several notable Lowndes County athletes.

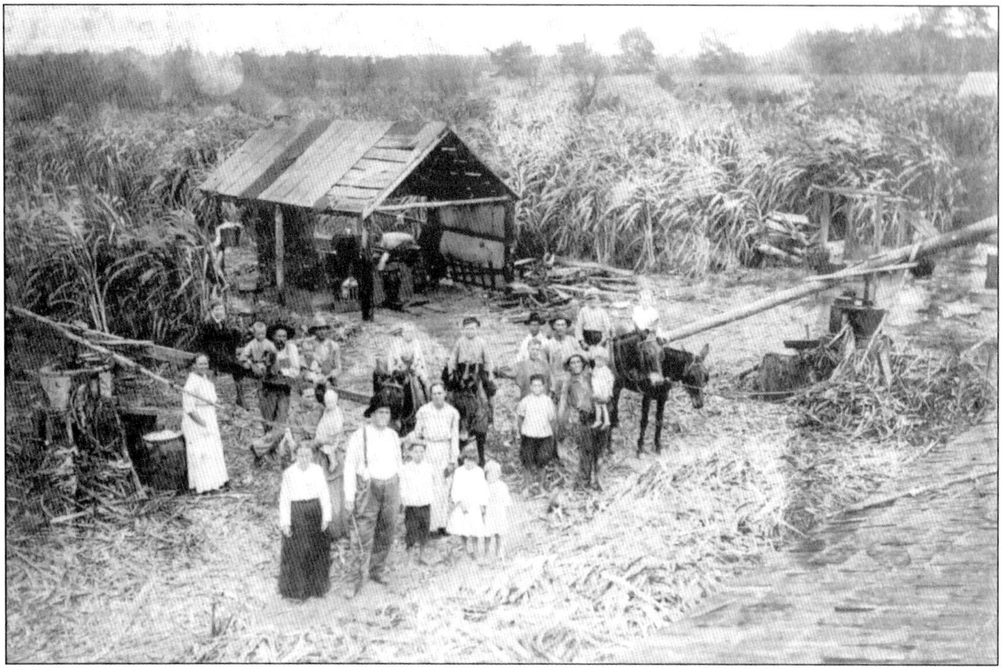

Depicted here is yet another form of agriculture in Lowndes County: the cultivation of sugar cane. The picture is from late in the 19th century or early in the 20th, and it shows the processing of sugar cane to make syrup. The unusual aspects of this operation are, first, the use of two mills at the same time for the grinding of the cane and, second, the use of two mules to turn each of the mills. The cane juice would be cooked in a large kettle, apparently located in the crude shelter in the left middle of the picture.

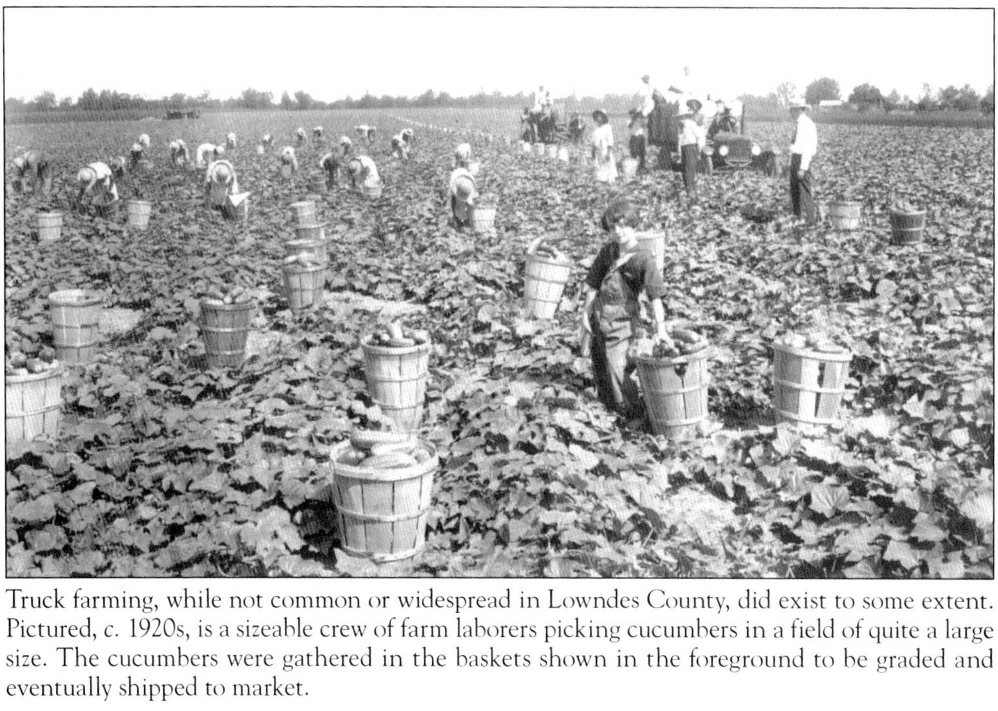

Truck farming, while not common or widespread in Lowndes County, did exist to some extent. Pictured, c. 1920s, is a sizeable crew of farm laborers picking cucumbers in a field of quite a large size. The cucumbers were gathered in the baskets shown in the foreground to be graded and eventually shipped to market.

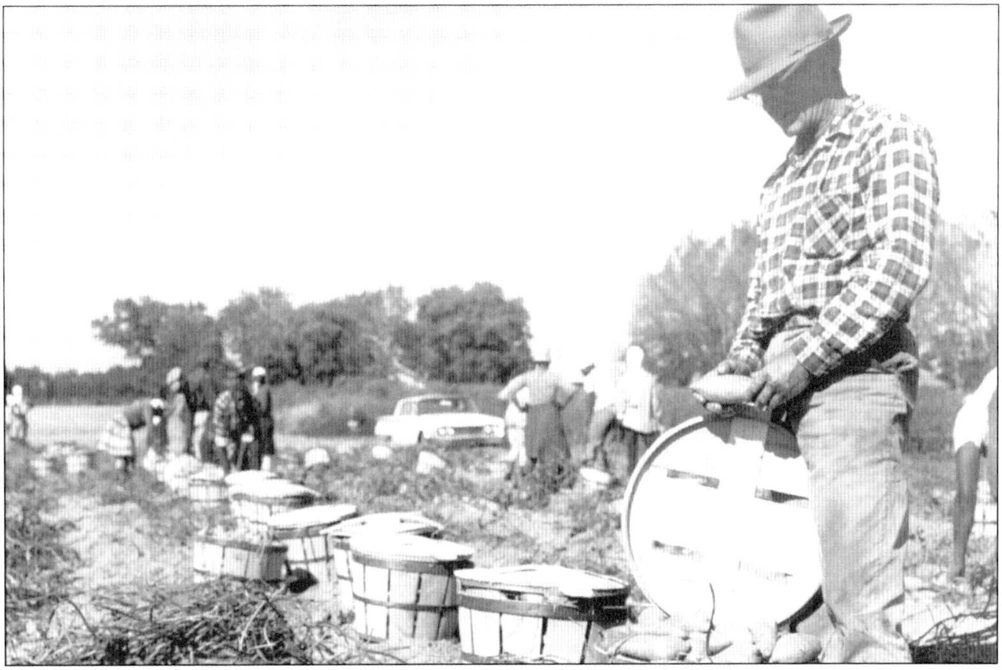

Yet another facet of Lowndes County's agricultural diversity was the growing of sweet potatoes as a food crop. Unlike the cucumbers on the previous page, which are picked from above the ground, sweet potatoes have to be dug from the ground. In this case, the potatoes, having been dug out, also are collected in low baskets for grading and shipping.

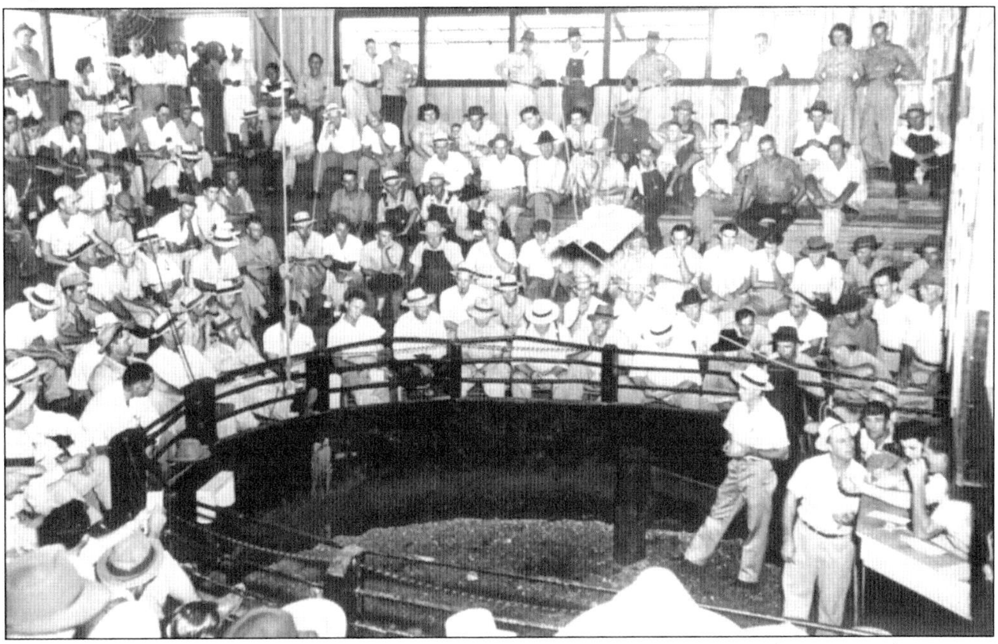

This is a picture of a very crowded cattle auction in Lowndes County in the 1950s. The raising of cattle has been, for many years, a feature of farming in the county, as demonstrated by the longtime yearly fat cattle show. The man standing in the auction ring and facing to the left is Dr. Loyce W. Turner.

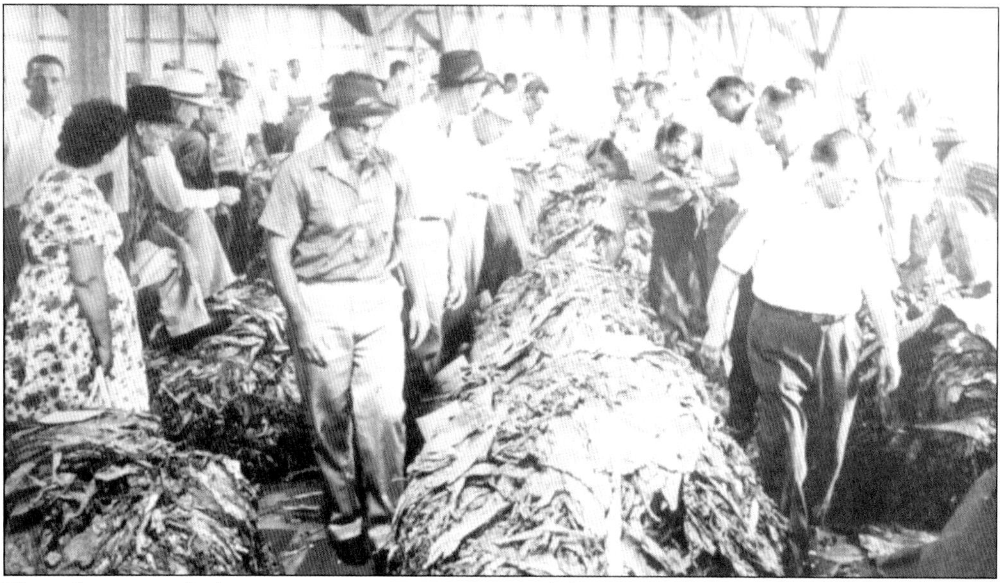

The cultivation of tobacco once was a major aspect of the agricultural scene in Lowndes County. While tobacco continues to be grown in the county, the business has lost some of its appeal because of the accumulation of evidence of tobacco's harmful effects. Traditionally the sale of the crop was by auction at the end of the season. An auction is underway in a Valdosta warehouse in this scene. The buyers and the auctioneer move from basket to basket along the rows, and the auctioneer conducts the sale as the buyers bid on the baskets. The auctioneer, third from the left in the left row and wearing a white hat, is Isaac Gurley.

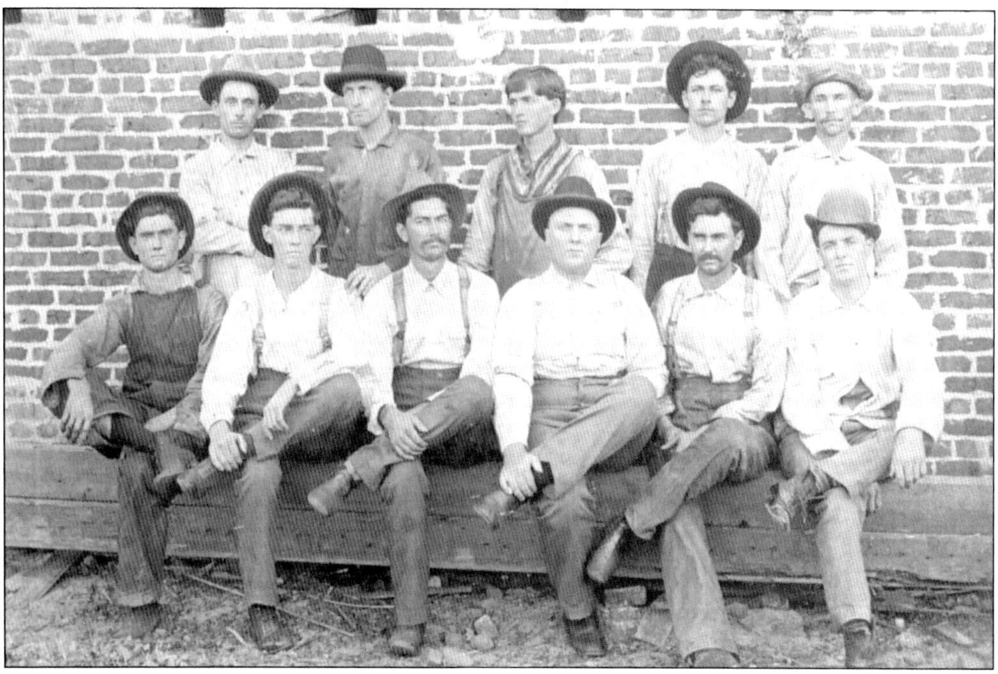

During the period of economic stress for southern agriculture following the Civil War, many farmers felt that it was in their best interest to help themselves by organizing. These 11 men are members of a Lowndes County agricultural society in 1868.

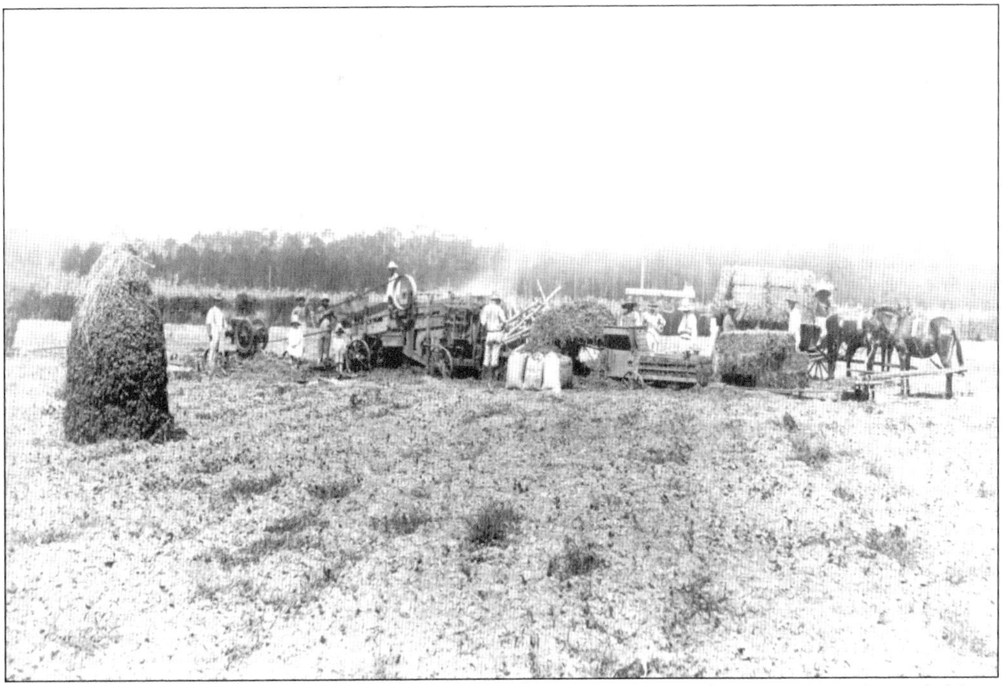

Taking place in this picture is the mechanized harvesting of Spanish peanuts in a large field on a Lowndes County farm, according to information with the photograph. The peanut vines also are stacked like hay for feeding animals.

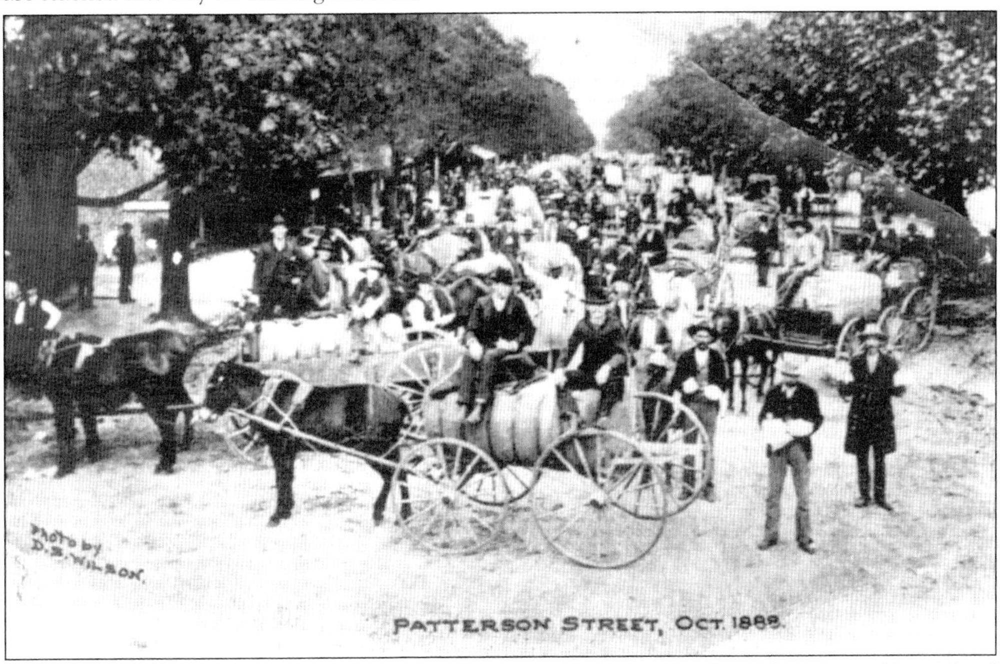

Beginning in the 1880s, some Lowndes County farmers undertook the cultivation of Sea Island or long-staple cotton. Valdosta, the county seat, became a major inland market for the Sea Island cotton, as reflected in the image above, which is of Patterson Street in October 1888, with wagons of cotton completely filling the street.

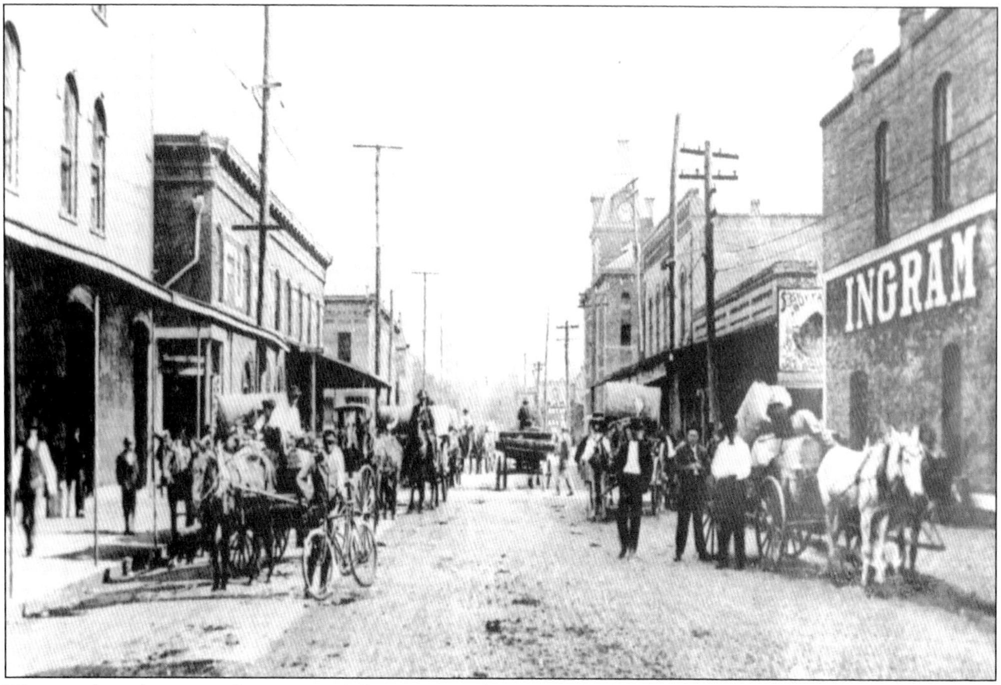

This is a less dramatic depiction of the impact of cotton in Lowndes County than on the preceding page. The location in Valdosta also is different. This is the Cotton Exchange area on West Hill Avenue, looking toward the east, in 1900.

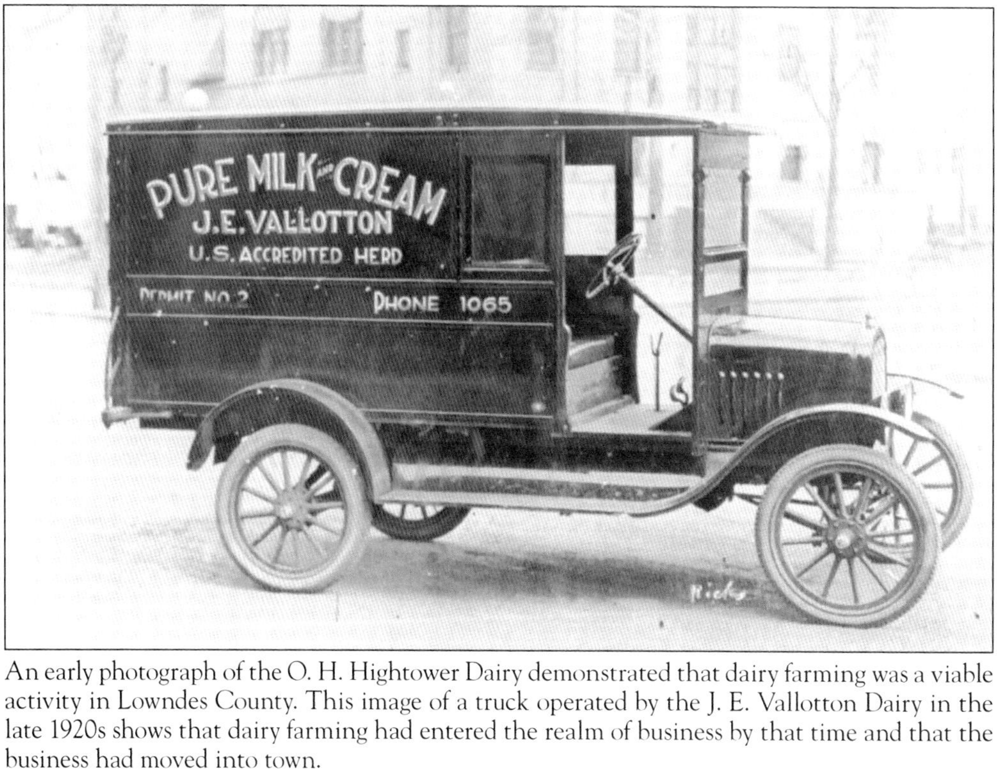

An early photograph of the O. H. Hightower Dairy demonstrated that dairy farming was a viable activity in Lowndes County. This image of a truck operated by the J. E. Vallotton Dairy in the late 1920s shows that dairy farming had entered the realm of business by that time and that the business had moved into town.

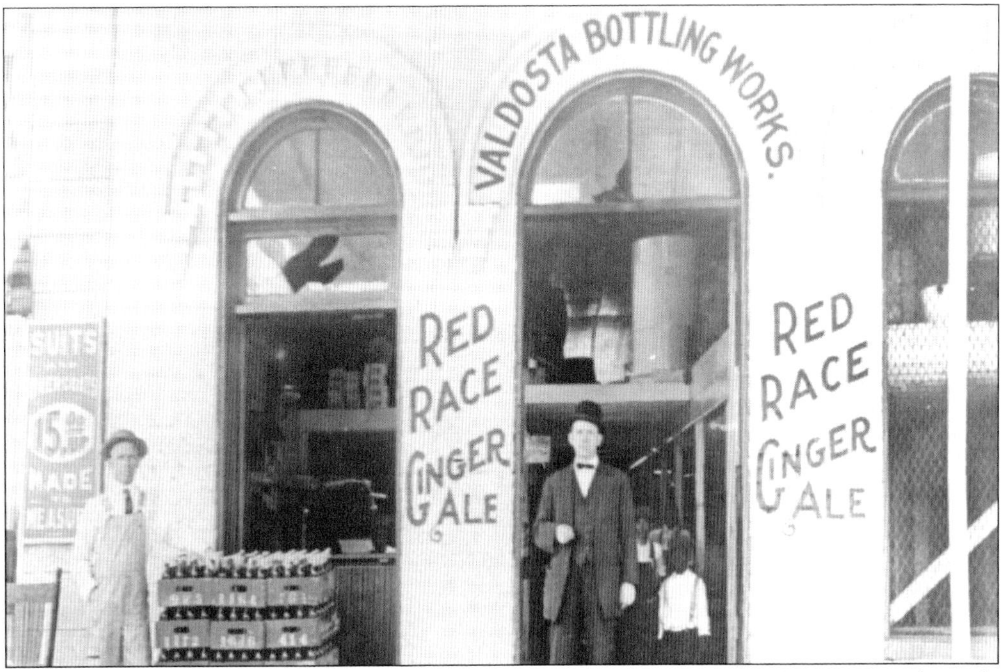

The Valdosta Bottling Works, located at the corner of Ashley Street and Hill Avenue in the early 20th century, advertised Red Race Ginger Ale in this picture. However, the importance of the company went well beyond Red Race Ginger Ale. The Valdosta Bottling Works was the second bottler of Coca-Cola in the world and the first outside Atlanta. The man in the derby standing in the doorway is E. R. Barber, a founder of the business.

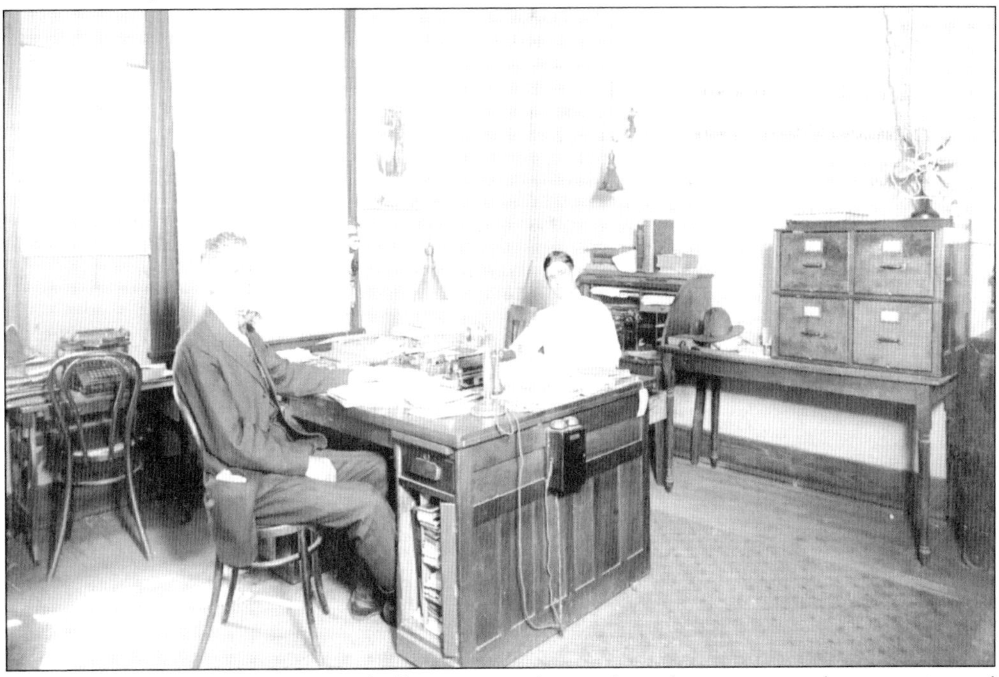

Business and industry both required office personnel to perform the necessary administrative and paper work. Shown here are two male office workers in a Valdosta business in 1917.

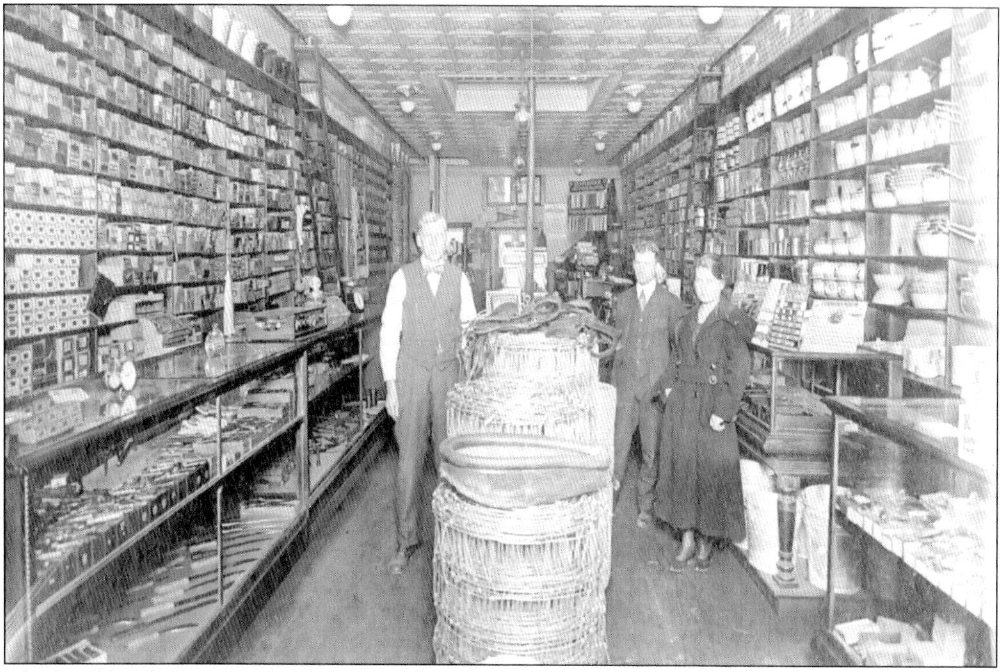

The local hardware store, because of the necessary goods it sold, was a vital part of local business. This picture is of the interior of the Shaw Hardware Company at 108 North Ashley Street in Valdosta in 1925. The figures in the photograph, from left to right, are Will Sims, Roy Shaw, and Clara Darshell Shaw.

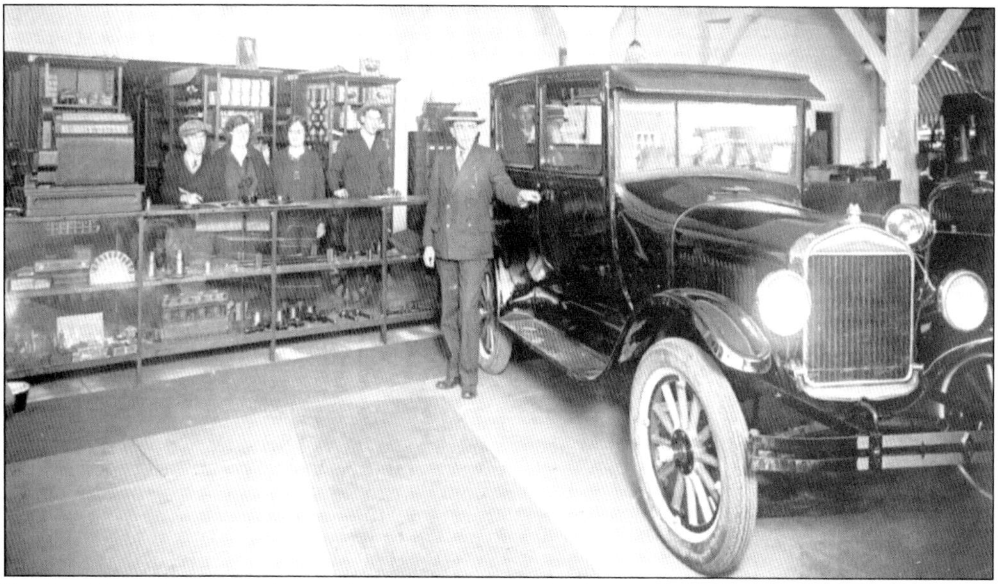

By the 1920s, the automobile industry was among the largest businesses in the United States and the ownership of cars had become widespread. In the circumstances, automobile dealerships proliferated, including in Lowndes County and especially Valdosta. This is the interior of West Motor Company, owned by W. S. West and A. A. Parrish. West Motors sold Lincoln, Ford, and Fordson automobiles and tractors, originally at 123–129 West Central Avenue in Valdosta and later at 311 North Patterson Street.

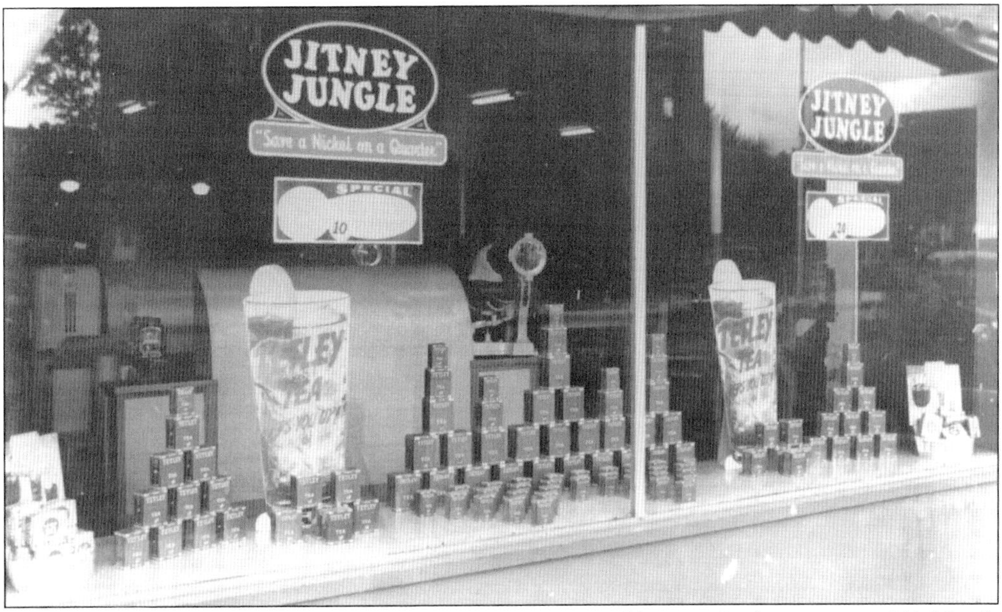

This is an example of the chain store supermarket in Valdosta. The location, at 202 North Patterson Street, housed a Piggly Wiggly grocery store until 1937. After 1937, Jitney Jungle took over the site. The motto of Jitney Jungle, as displayed in the window along with the canned goods, was "Save a nickel on a quarter."

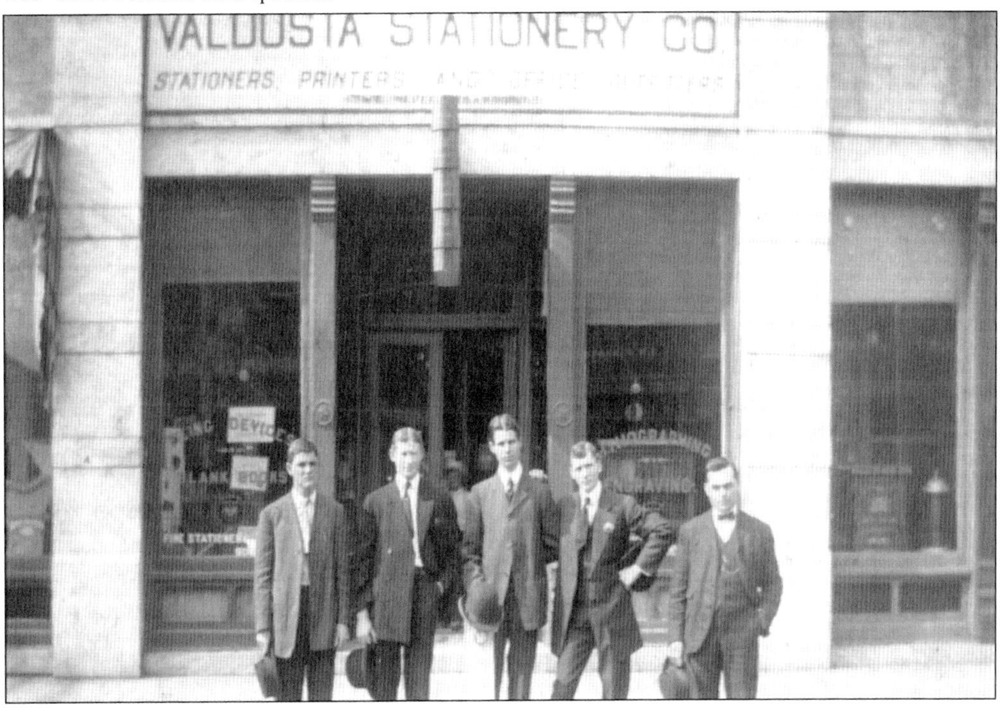

The business portrayed here occupied a building on North Ashley Street for many years and was originally Valdosta Stationery Company. It later became Southern Stationery Company and in time moved to North Patterson Street. The photograph is from the 1920s, and the men shown are, from left to right, unidentified, W. H. Oliver, J. J. (Jules) Newman, ? Ricks, and unidentified.

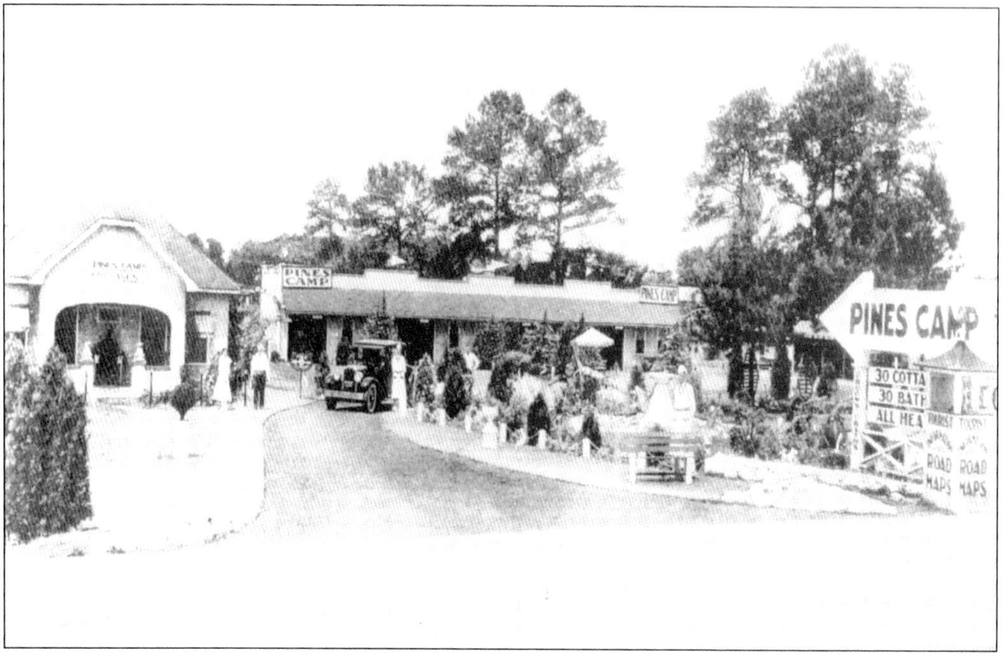

This image points out how much tourism in Lowndes County had grown by the late 1920s with the construction of U.S. Highway 41 through the county. Specifically the picture is of Pines Camp on North Ashley Street in Valdosta, the first so-called tourist camp in the county. Pines Camp advertised itself as providing "hotel accommodations at camp prices."

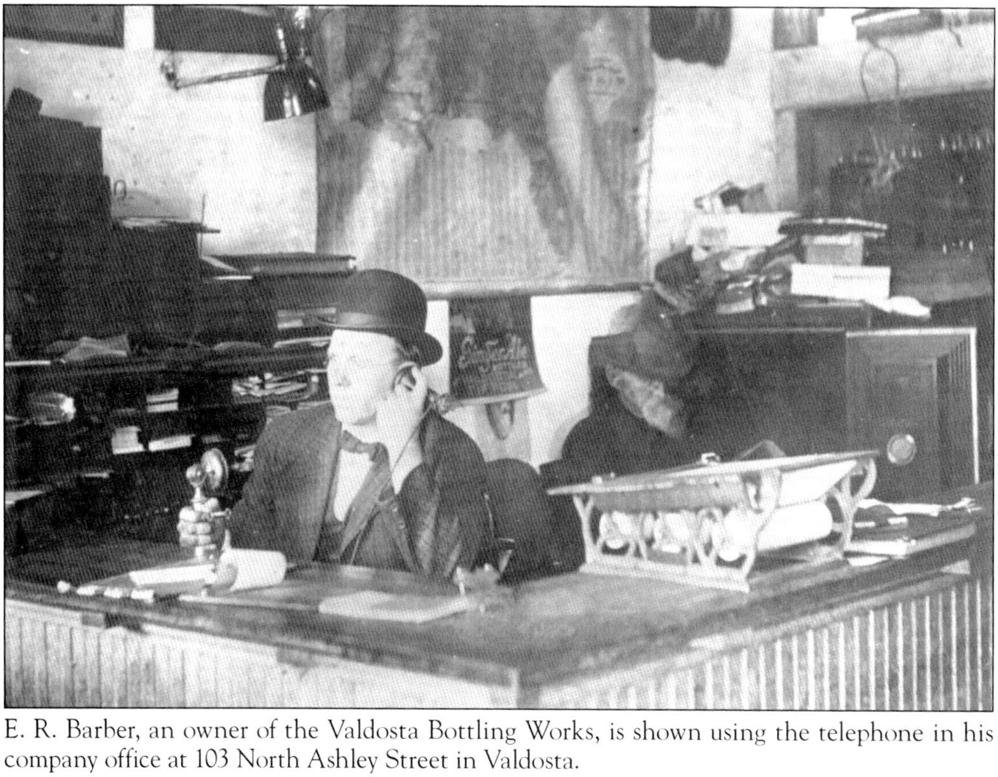

E. R. Barber, an owner of the Valdosta Bottling Works, is shown using the telephone in his company office at 103 North Ashley Street in Valdosta.

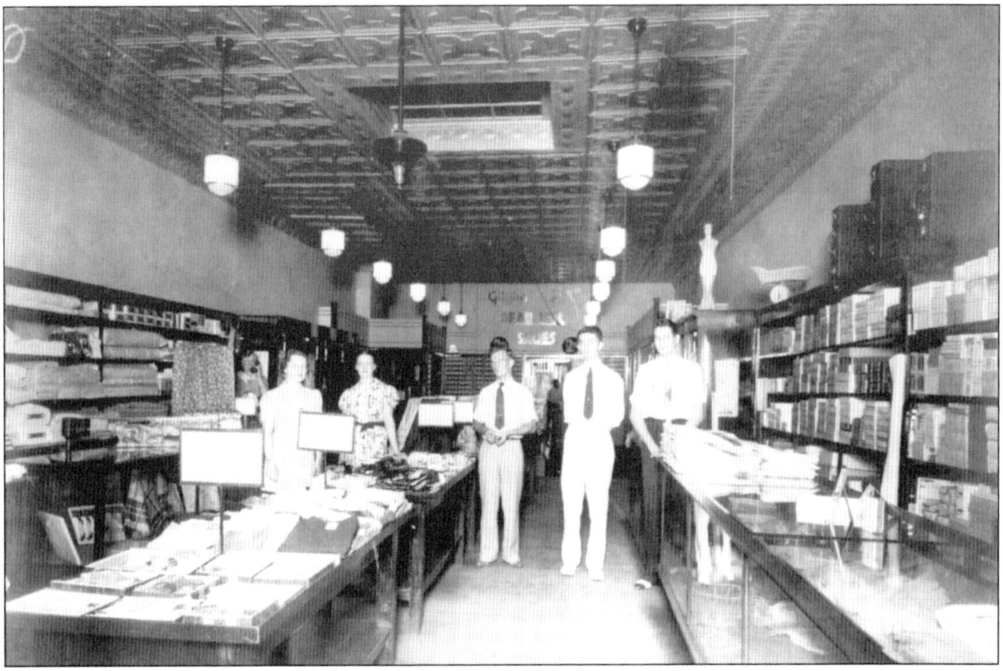

The picture above is of a Valdosta dry goods dealer in the 1930s, the Griffin Company at 127 North Patterson Street. The employees that can be identified are Mrs. Luke and Dorothy Duncan, second and third from the left, and Harry Luke, fifth from the left.

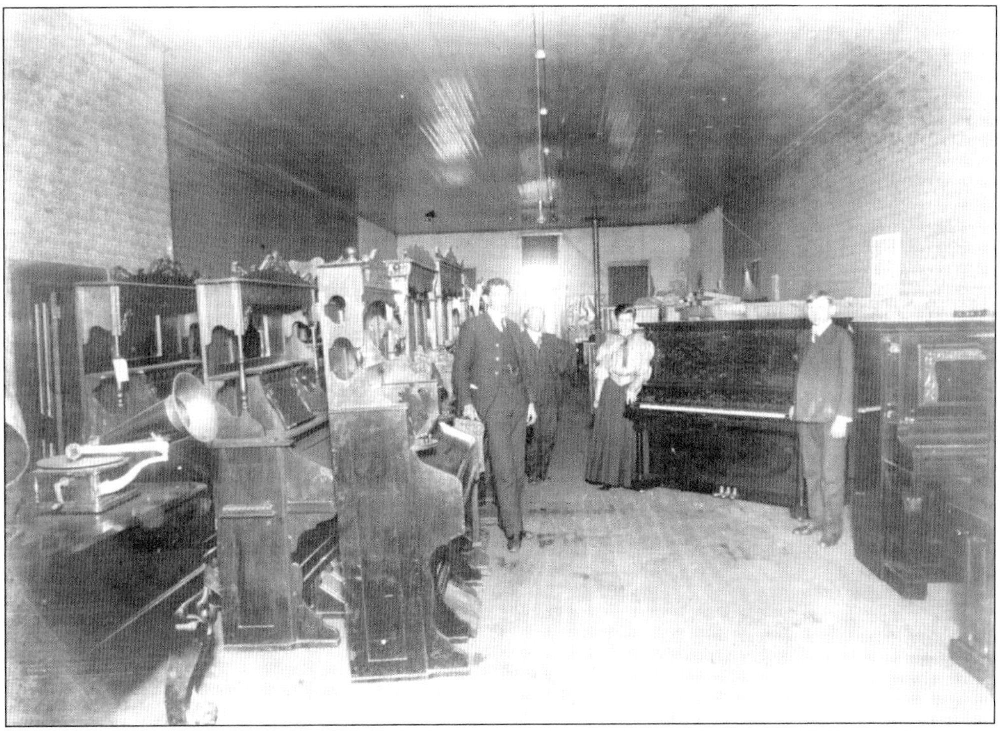

Featured here is the interior of the Mathis and Coleman Music Store at 116 North Patterson Street in Valdosta in 1910. None of the persons in the picture can be identified.

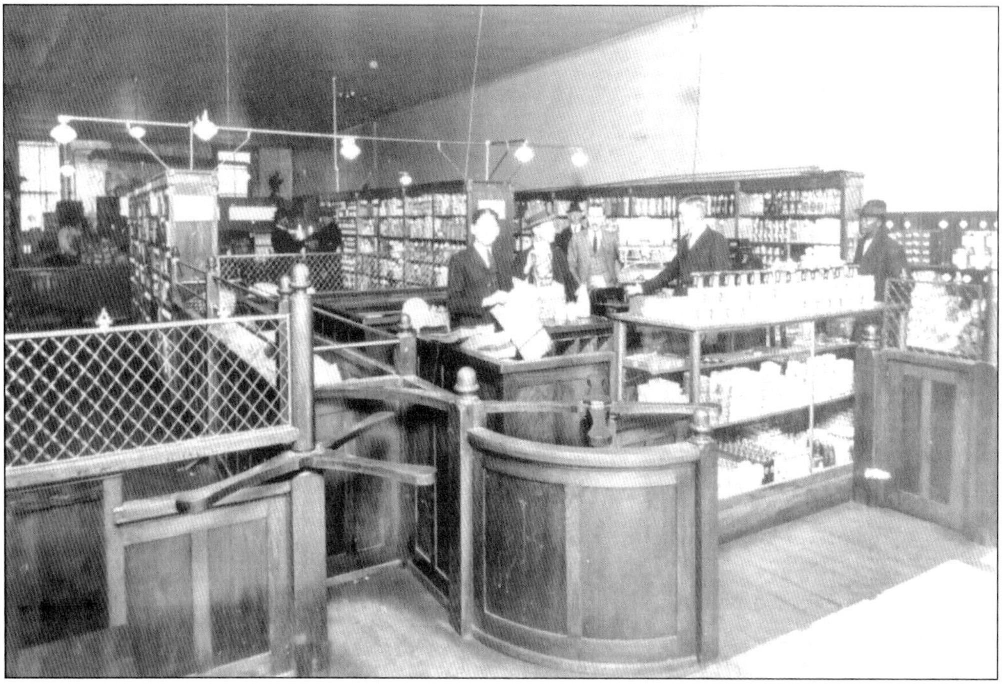

Bondurant Drug Company at 136 North Patterson Street in Valdosta appears in this 1922 image. The only person who can be identified is the man on the left holding the paper bag. He is Denham Huey Lord.

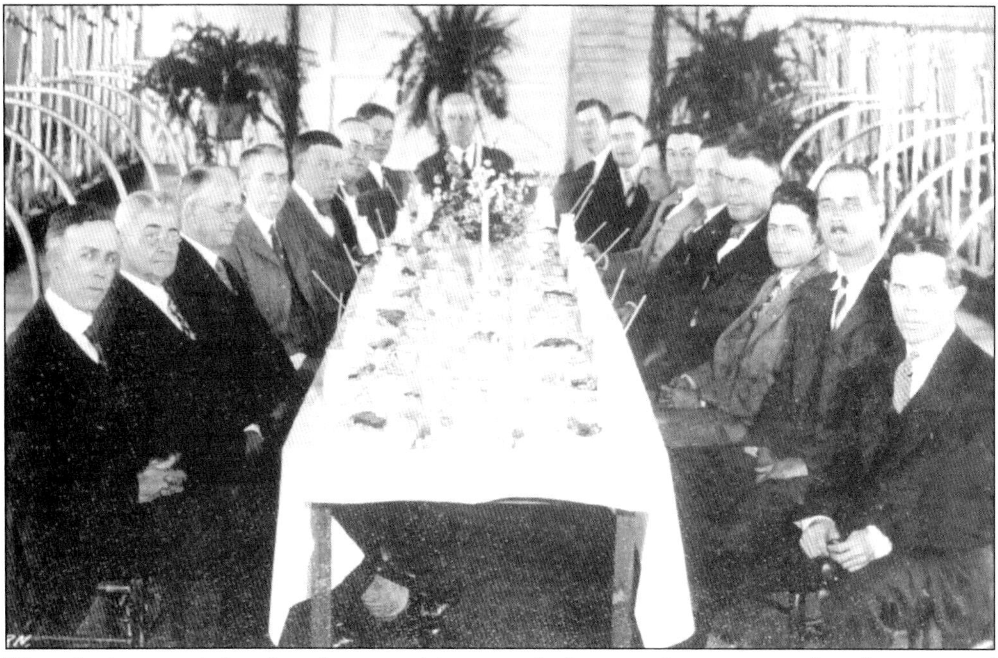

Though the actual date is unknown, this unusual photograph appears to date from around 1920–1930. The event was an effort by the Valdosta–Lowndes County Chamber of Commerce to promote the dairy industry in the county by having the Board of Directors of the chamber dine in the "milking parlor" of the Suitsus Dairy as guests of Jim C. Hunt.

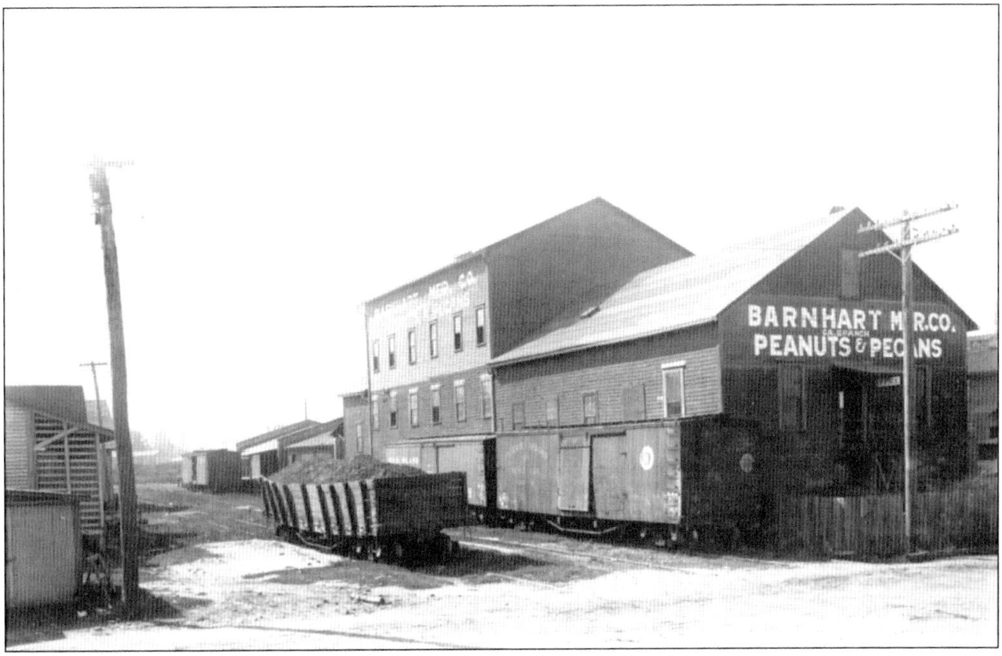

Portrayed in this image is an instance of agriculture-based industry in Lowndes County, the sort of business that often was at the mercy of the vagaries of agriculture. The Barnhart Manufacturing Company, which operated a plant on River Street on the west side of Valdosta, was a processor of peanuts and pecans, both of which were grown extensively in Lowndes County.

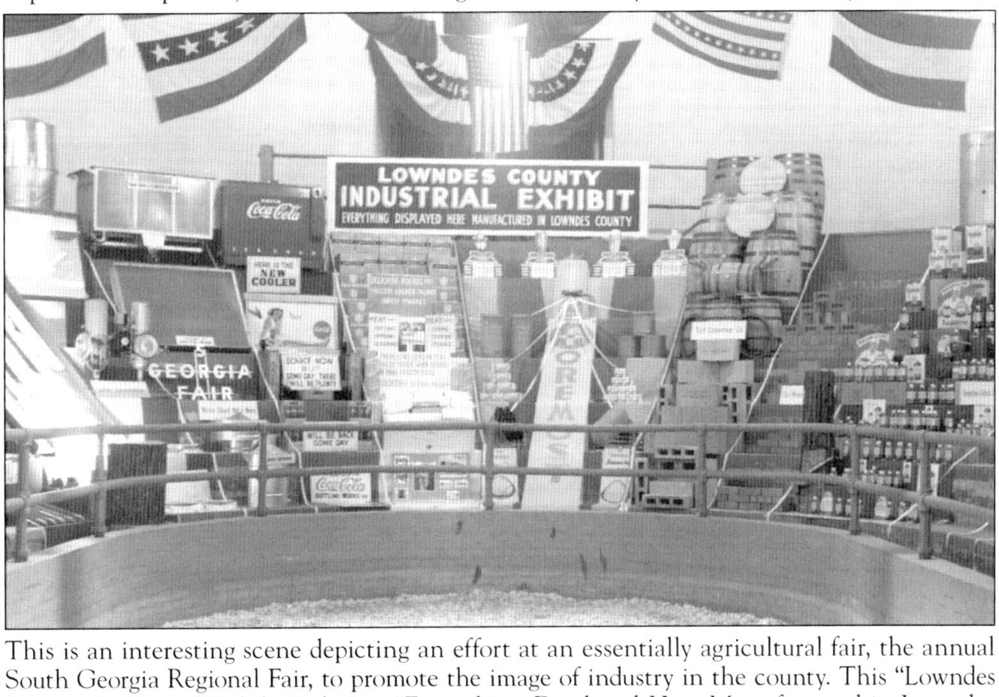

This is an interesting scene depicting an effort at an essentially agricultural fair, the annual South Georgia Regional Fair, to promote the image of industry in the county. This "Lowndes County Industrial Exhibit" claims, "Everything Displayed Here Manufactured in Lowndes County." Evidence within the photograph indicates that the display is probably from the 1940s. (Valdosta–Lowndes County Chamber of Commerce.)

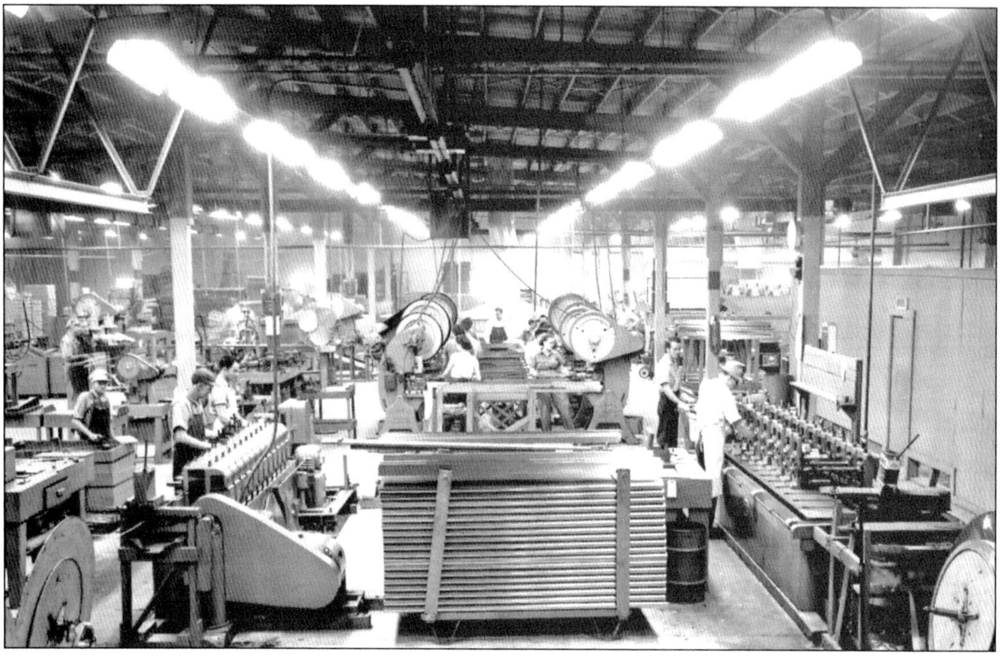

The photograph above features the manufacturing process underway at the Metal Products Division of Thompson Industries in Valdosta in the 1950s. Metal Products fabricated automobile trim components for various automobile manufacturers. (Valdosta–Lowndes County Chamber of Commerce.)

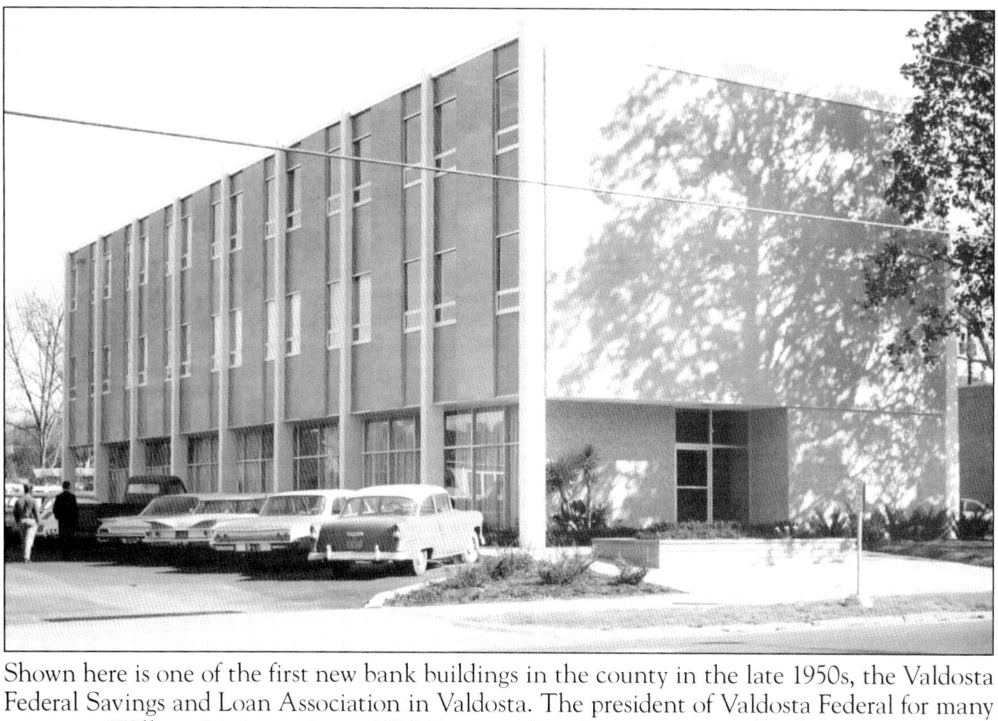

Shown here is one of the first new bank buildings in the county in the late 1950s, the Valdosta Federal Savings and Loan Association in Valdosta. The president of Valdosta Federal for many years was William M. Lester Jr.; as BB&T, it is still in business at another location on North Ashley Street. (Valdosta–Lowndes County Chamber of Commerce.)

Four

CHURCHES AND RELIGIOUS LIFE

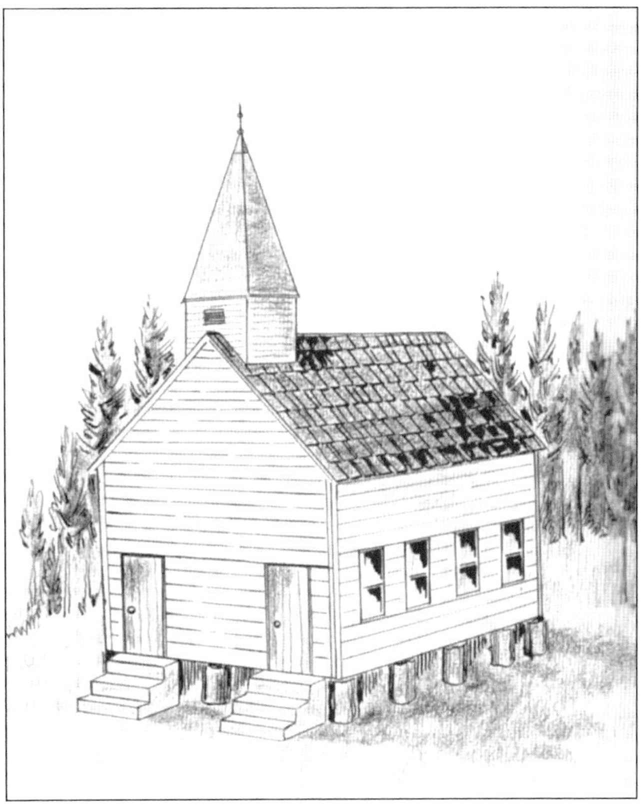

This is one of the very few depictions of a church that existed at Troupville prior to the abandonment of that town as the county seat and the creation of the new county seat of Valdosta. The sketch is of the Troupville Baptist Church as it presumably appeared in 1860 or earlier.

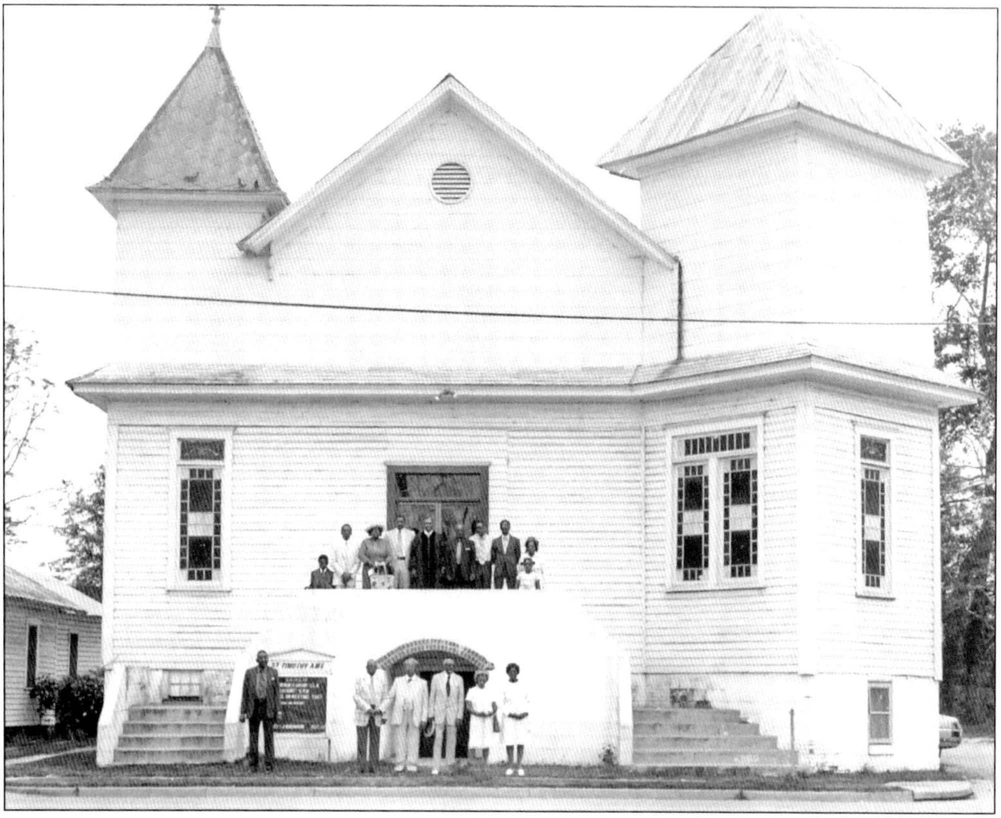

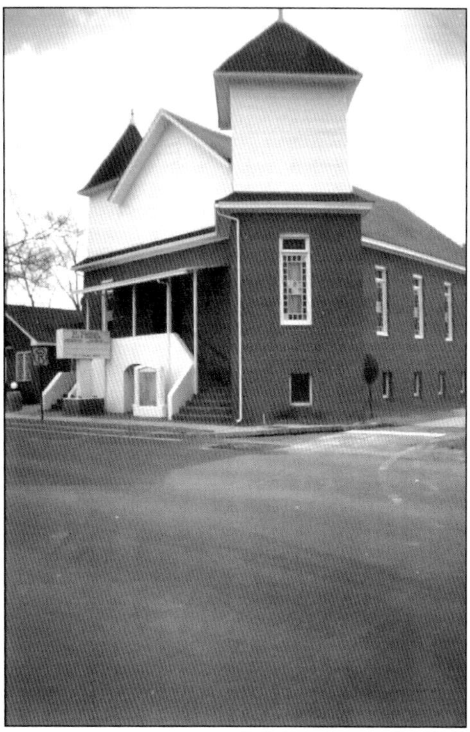

The two photographs on this page provide contrasting views of one of Valdosta's historic churches, St. Timothy's African Methodist Episcopal Church on West Hill Avenue. The image at the top is of St. Timothy's with its original wooden siding. The picture at the bottom shows the building after bricks were placed as the exterior covering.

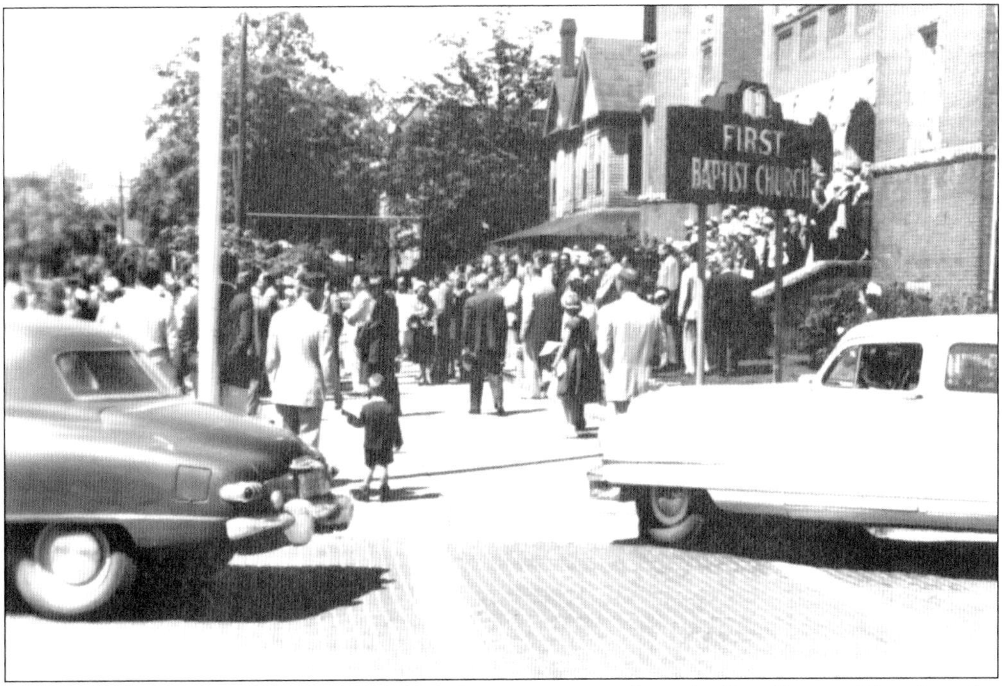

On a Sunday morning, a large group of worshippers emerges from the First Baptist Church at the end of a service. The location is West Central Avenue in Valdosta, and the image dates from the very early 1950s, judging from the automobiles caught in the picture.

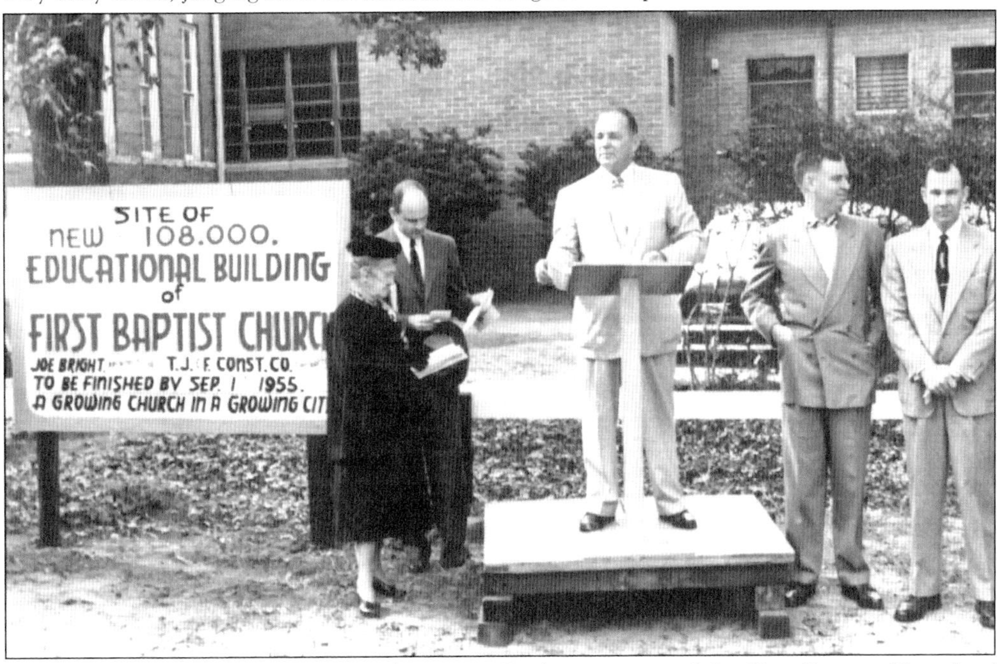

In a 1954 photograph, the Reverend James P. Rodgers, pastor of the First Baptist Church of Valdosta, dedicates the site of a new educational building. Other than Reverend Rodgers, the persons in the picture that can be identified are John W. Langdale, second from the left standing next to the sign, and Jack Gayle, standing at the far right.

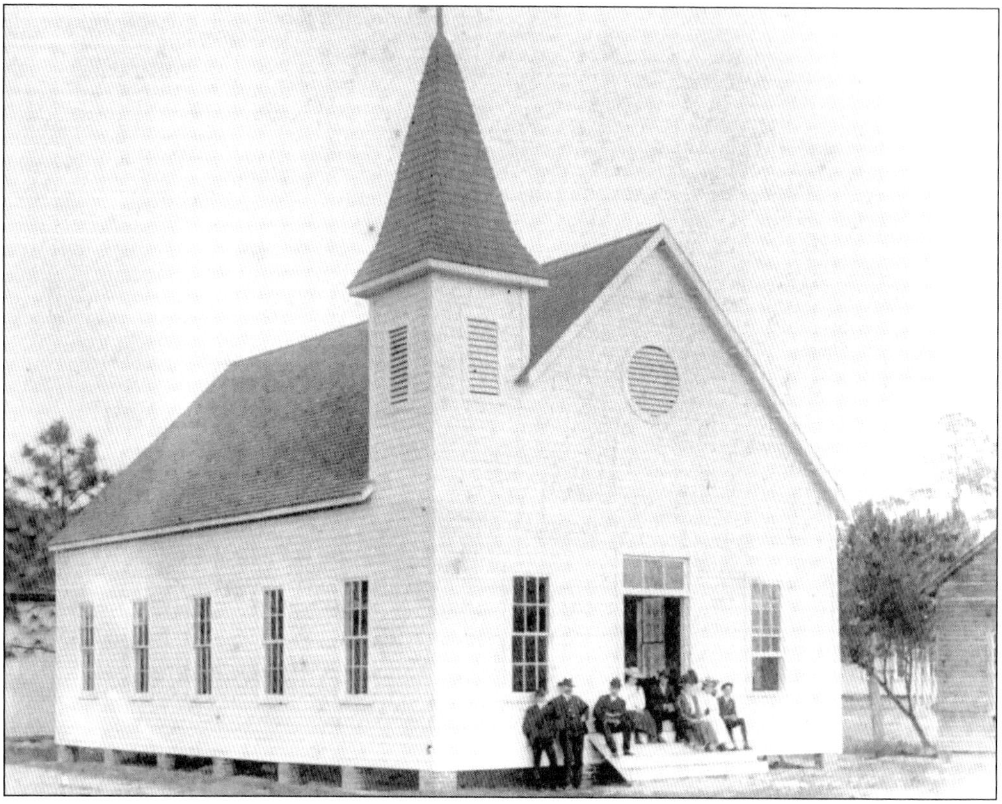

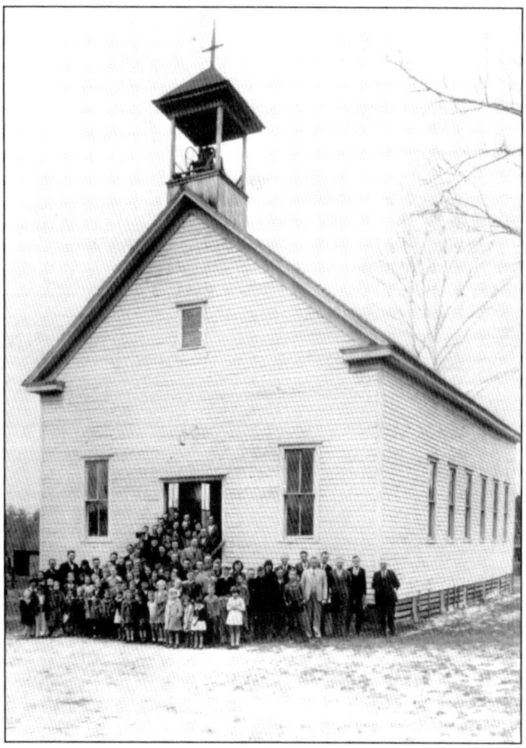

The beautiful little white church in the picture above is the Naylor Baptist Church in eastern Lowndes County in the 1890s.

This is the Remerton Baptist Church, located in the Strickland Cotton Mill's village of Remerton, shown with the congregation in the 1920s or 1930s.

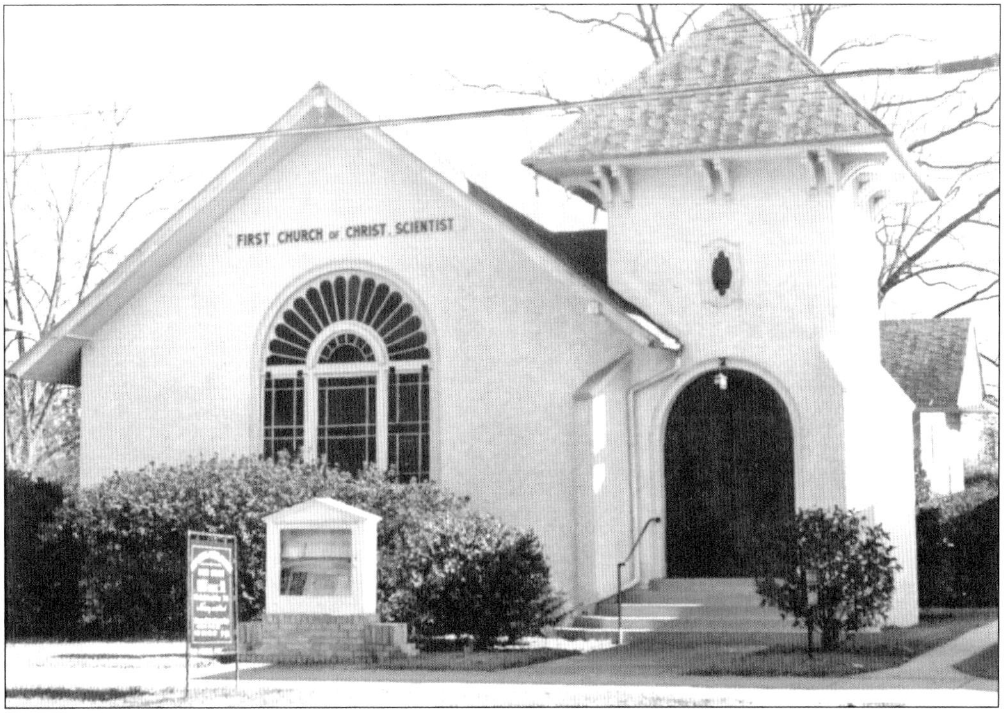

The structure shown here from both inside and outside was, until 1949, Christ Episcopal Church. When Christ Church moved to a newly constructed building on North Patterson Street, the old church was sold to the Christian Scientists. The two views are, respectively, of the exterior of the building after the 1949 departure of the Episcopalians and of the interior after being renovated by the Christian Scientists.

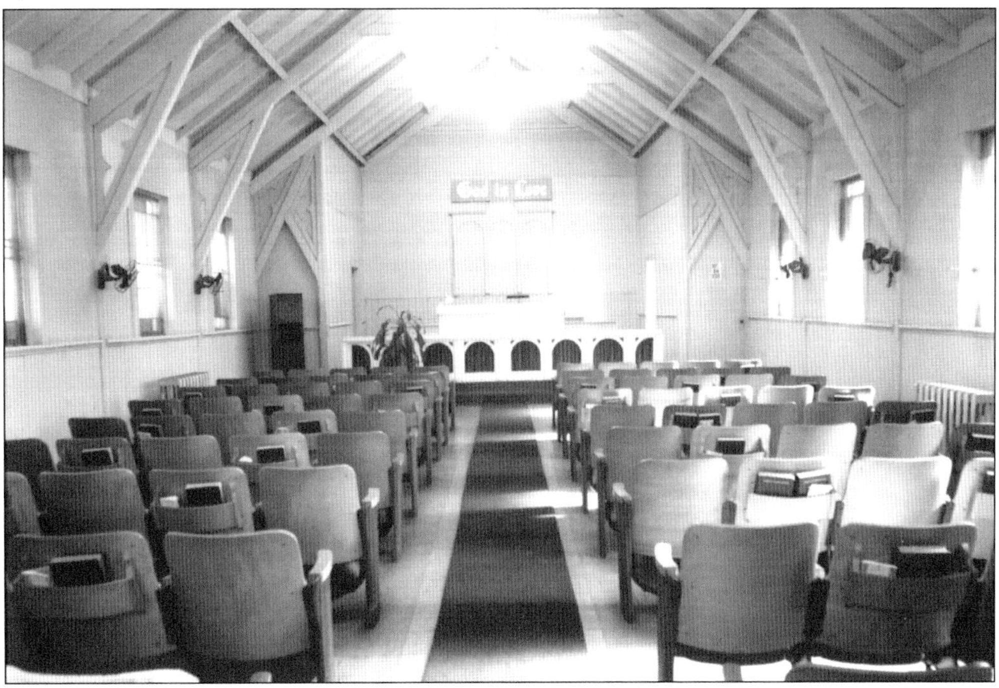

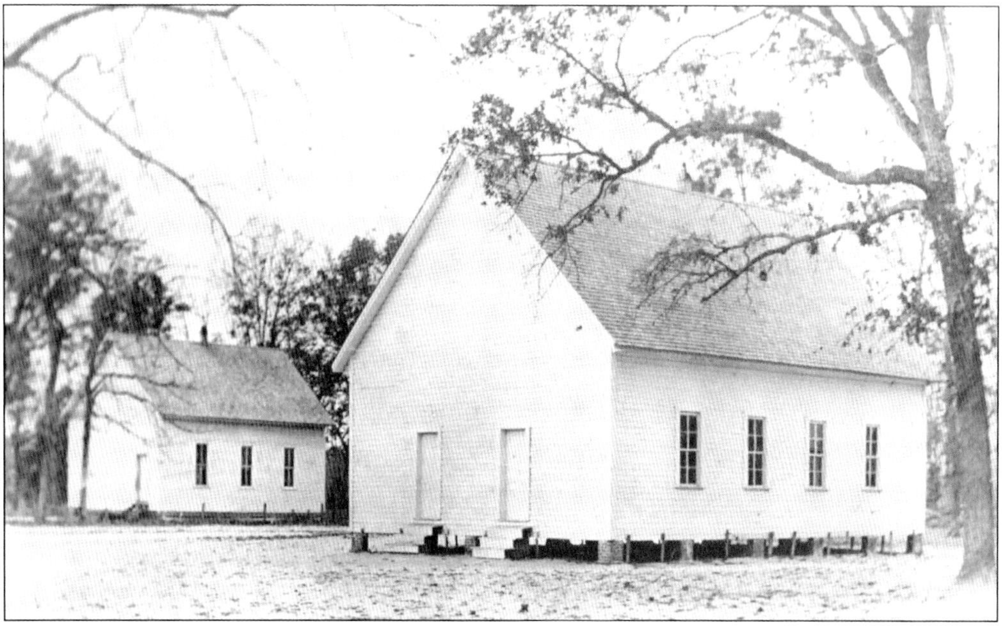

These are two very neat, very plain buildings of an unidentified church in Lowndes County at an unknown time. Given the severely plain appearance of the structures, the church is likely to have been Primitive Baptist or Missionary Baptist. Primitive Baptist seems to be the most plausible choice, except for one salient point, which is that the buildings are painted, and many Primitive Baptists ordinarily have not favored even the application of paint.

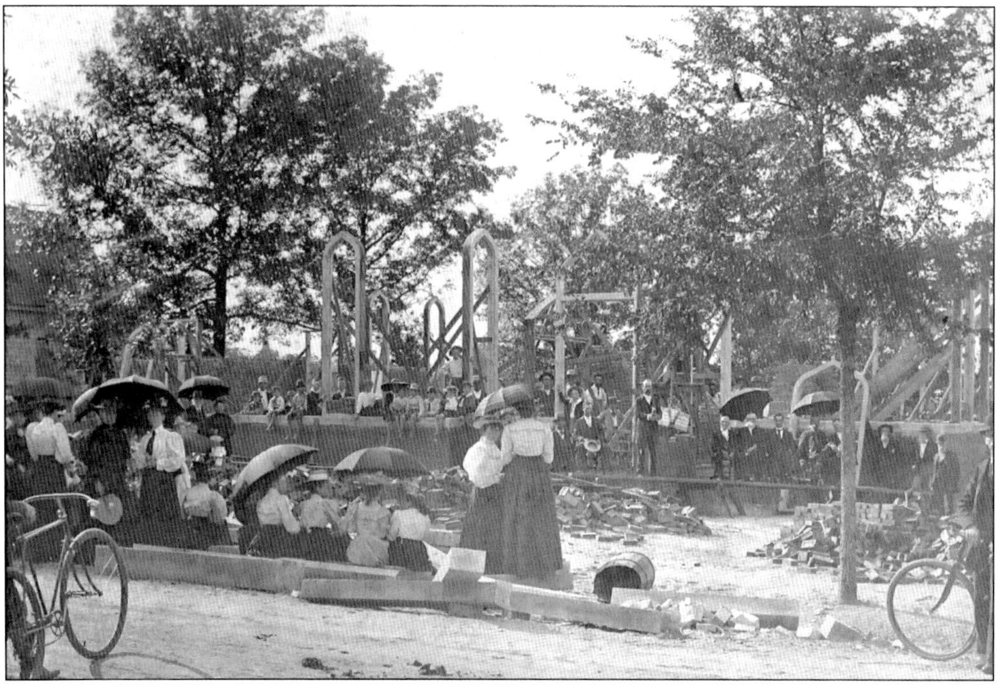

The scene above is of the dedication of a church in Lowndes County, perhaps in Valdosta at some time in the 1890s. This may have been the dedication of the First Baptist Church of Valdosta in 1895, except that the window frames appear to be set too low in the walls.

The two pictures here demonstrate vast differences in church architecture between a historic downtown church and a Hispanic Catholic church in southern Lowndes County. At the top is an aerial view of the First Methodist Church of Valdosta from a vantage point in the Lowndes County Courthouse on the east side of Patterson Street early in the 20th century. Here is a handsome building with a large, stained-glass window facing the street and a soaring tower and steeple at its northeast corner. In stark contrast is Iglesia Catolica San Jose in the southern part of the county, with its plain and utilitarian structure and its stark cross in the front.

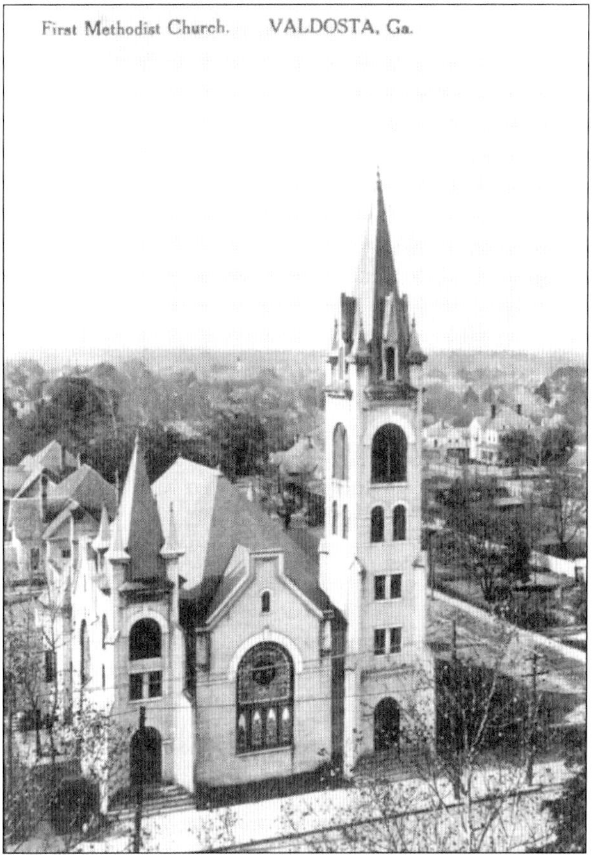

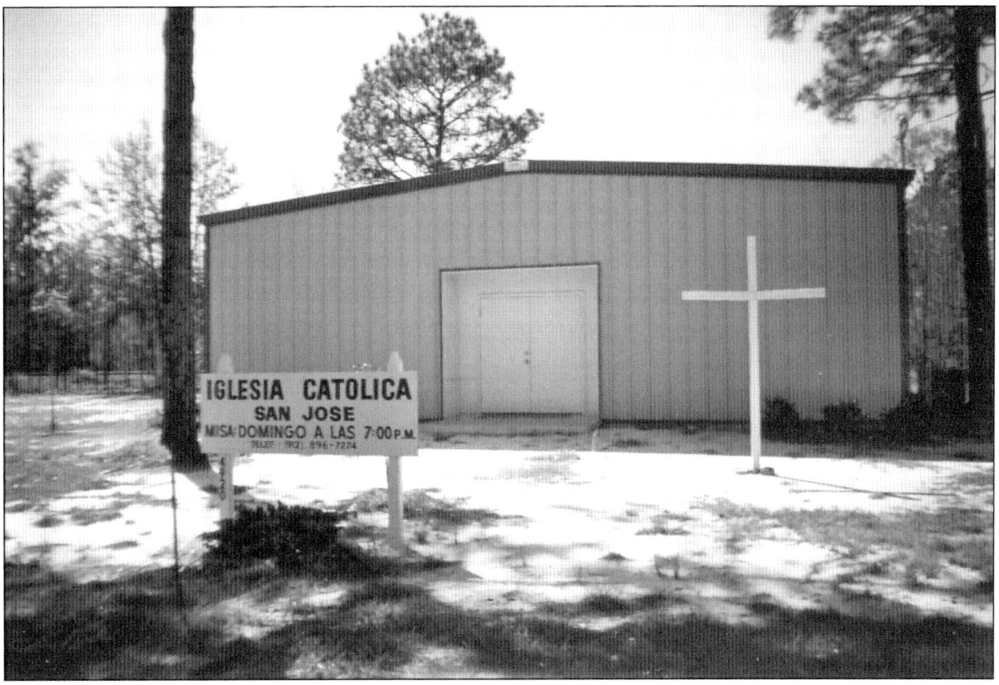

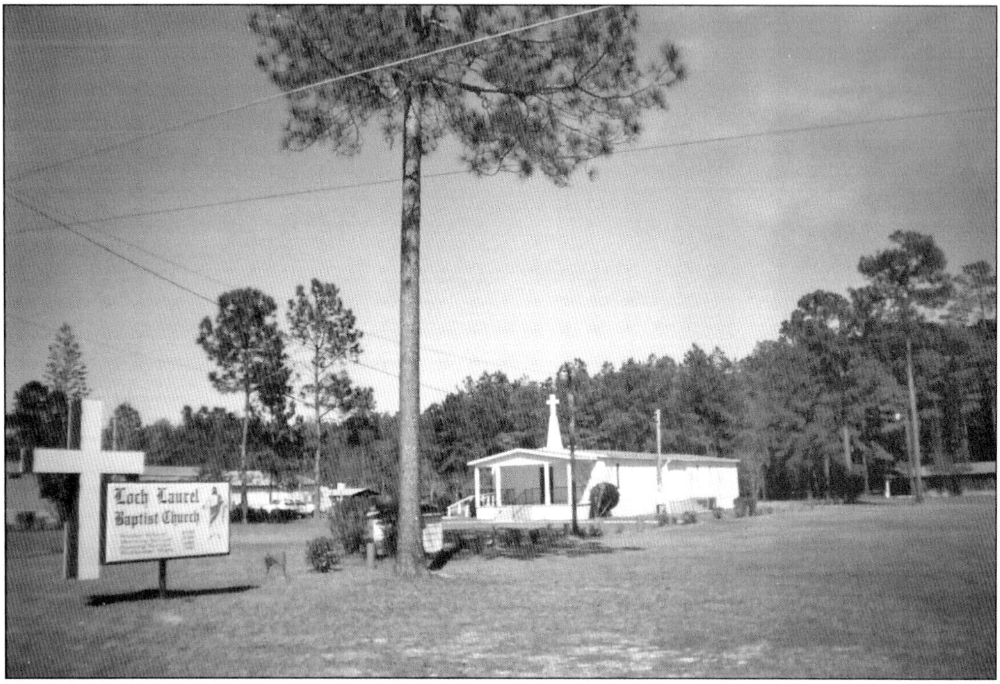

Pictured above is a small country Baptist church, the Loch Laurel Baptist Church on Loch Laurel Road in southern Lowndes County.

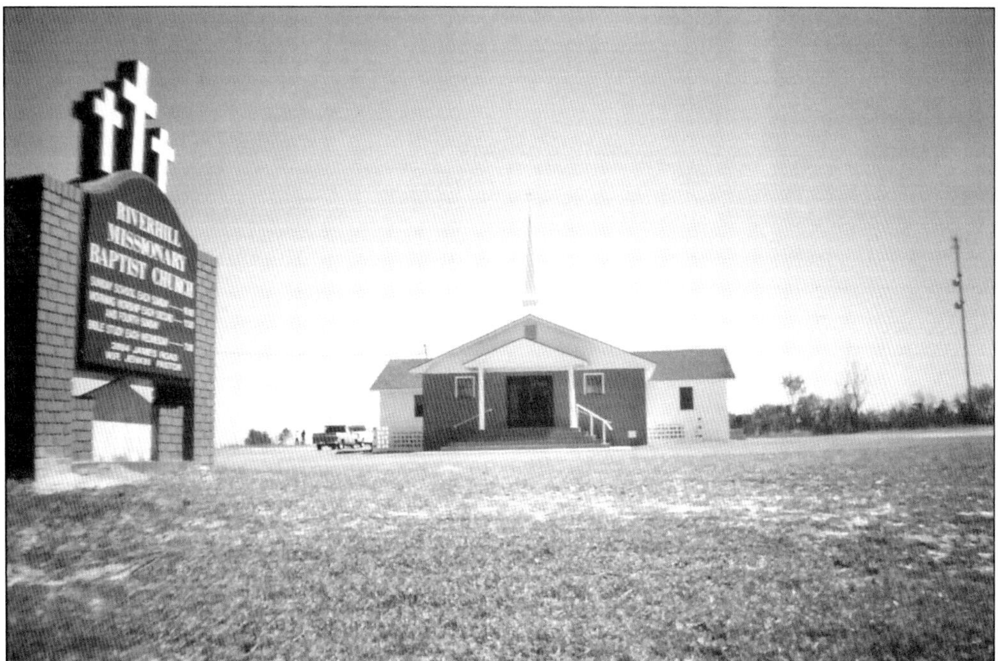

This is the Riverhill Missionary Baptist Church on the Morven Road in northern Lowndes County.

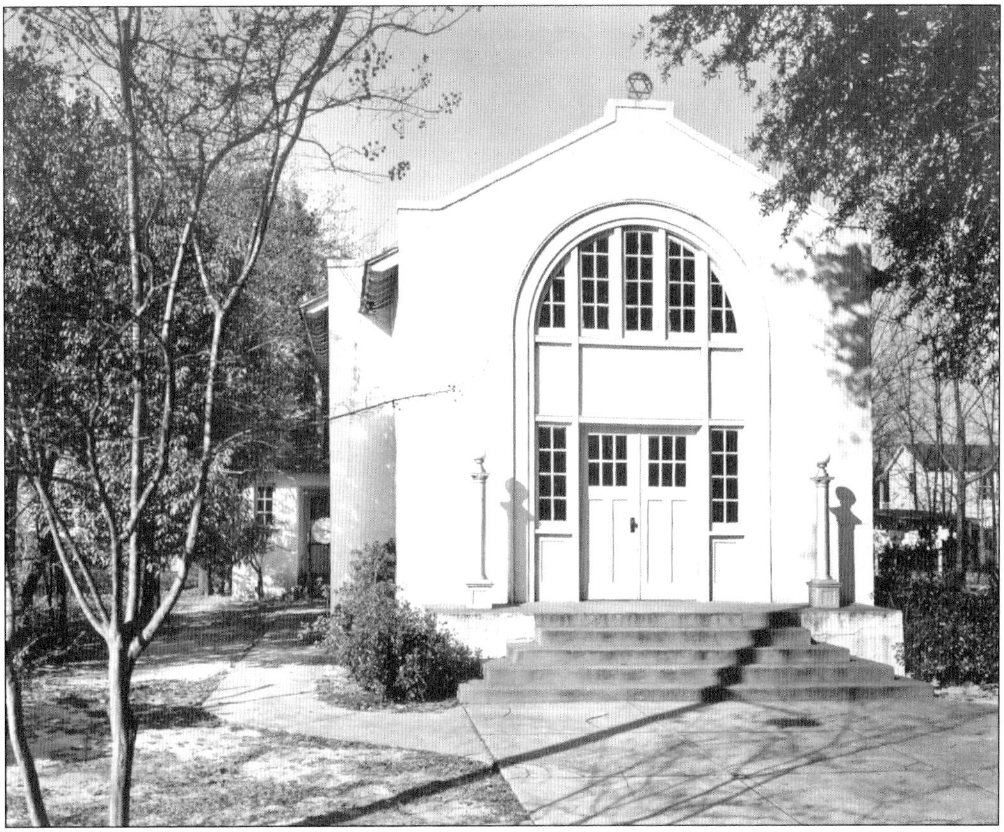

The structure shown above is the earlier Valdosta synagogue, Temple Israel, which was on Smithland Place near downtown Valdosta and was in service until the late 1960s. At that point, a new synagogue, also named Temple Israel, was constructed on Baytree Road in northwest Valdosta and remains in use to the present. (Above: Valdosta–Lowndes County Chamber of Commerce.)

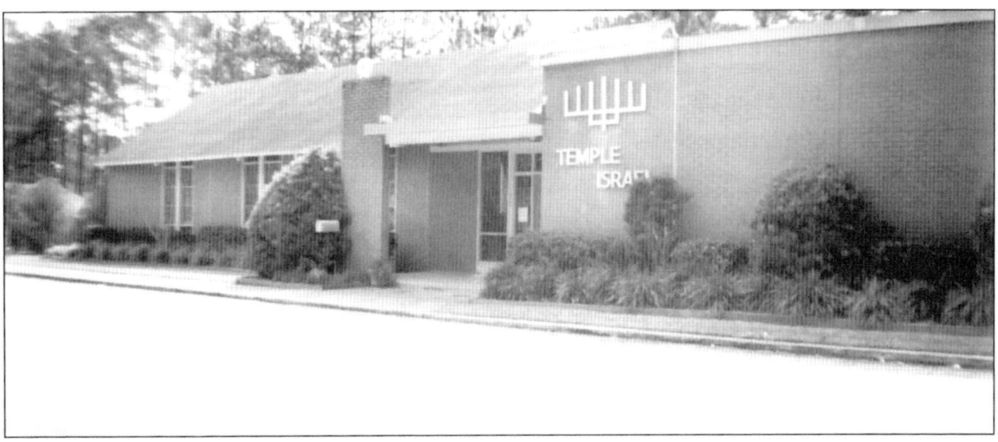

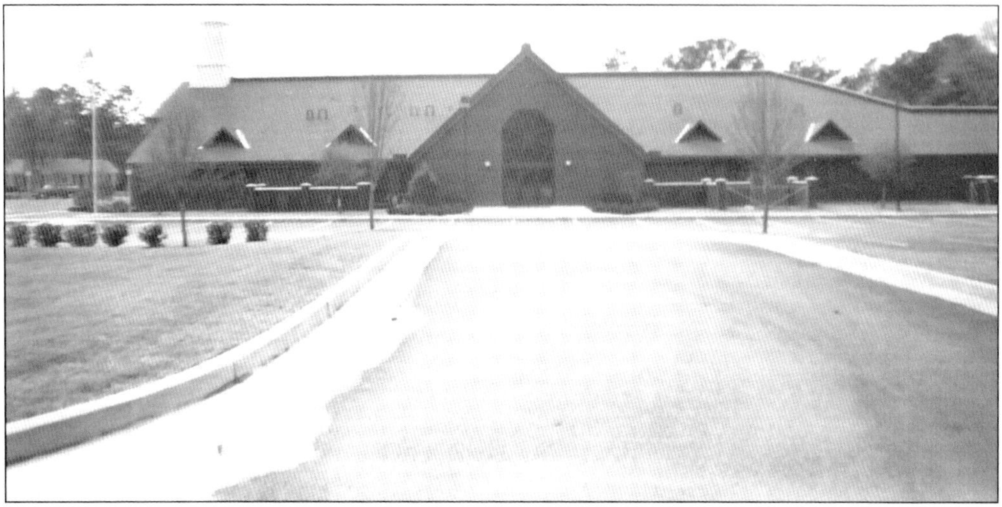

The previous home of the Church of Jesus Christ of Latter-Day Saints was near the western end of Alden Avenue in Valdosta. That structure is now a preschool and day care center. The new Latter-Day Saints church is at the corner of Jerry Jones Drive and Gornto Road on land that previously was the site of the Jerry Berry Jones plantation house and of many majestic oaks that no longer stand.

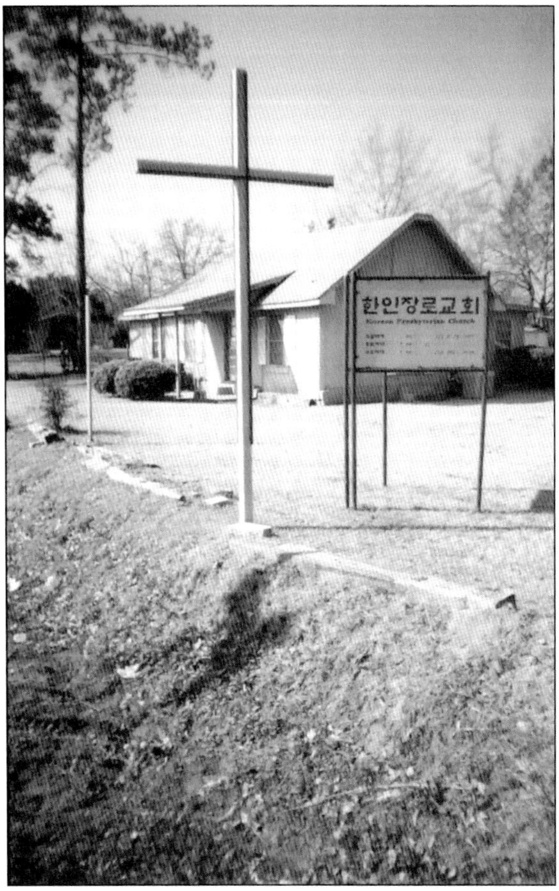

Just as the presence of Iglesia Catolico San Jose in south Lowndes symbolizes some of the growing religious diversity of the county, so also does the presence of the Korean Presbyterian Church on Bemis Road on the northern edge of Valdosta.

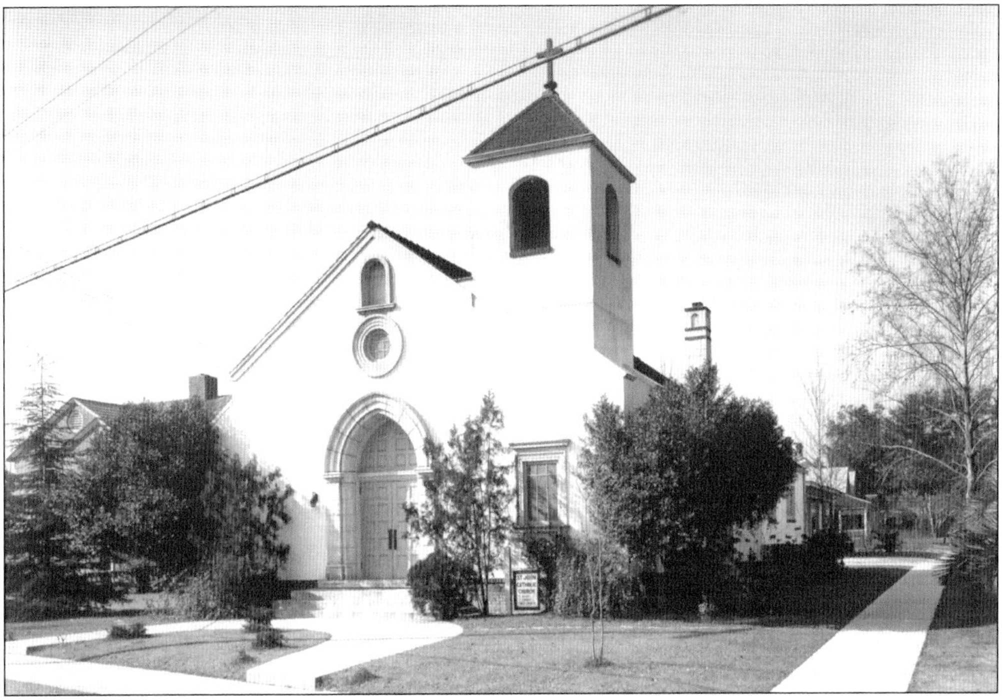

Pictured above is the former location of St. John the Evangelist Catholic Church at the corner of North Ashley Street and East Adair Street in Valdosta. After the congregation moved to the new building on Gornto Road in northwest Valdosta, the old structure became the home of the Unitarian Universalist Church for a number of years. Below is the later version of St. John the Evangelist Church. At this site, the congregation has carried out major construction programs to expand the parochial school and other facilities in recent years. (Above: Valdosta–Lowndes County Chamber of Commerce.)

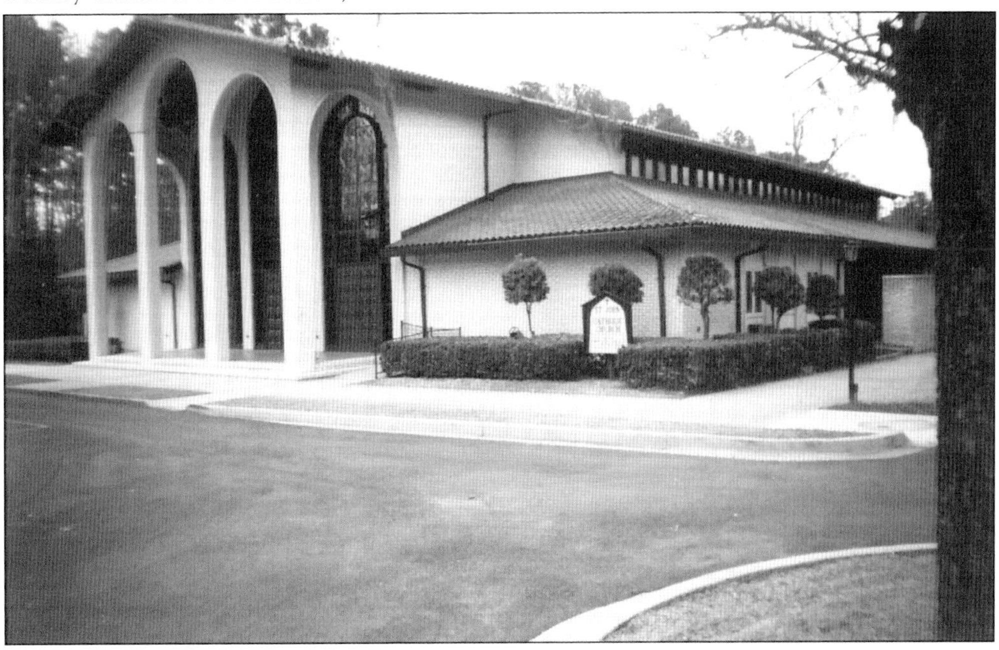

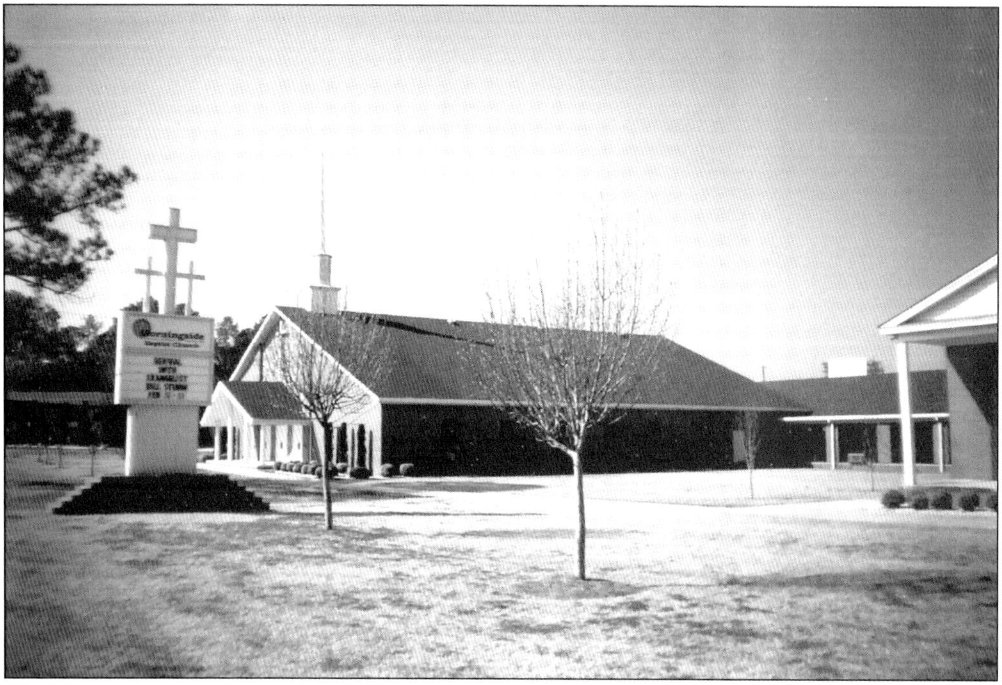

The impression created by this picture is somewhat misleading because it makes Morningside Baptist Church on Bemis Road look rather small. In truth, Morningside is anything but small, as it has for many years been the home of a very large and very active congregation.

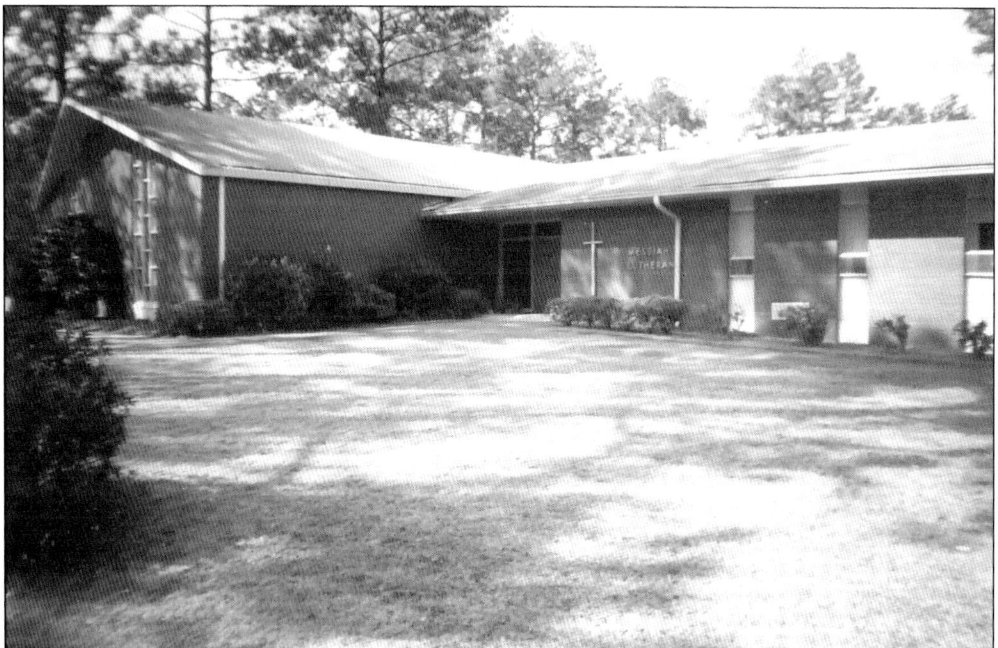

The Lutheran Church historically was almost a nonexistent Christian group in Lowndes County, until the establishment of Messiah Lutheran Church in 1956. Messiah Lutheran Church, as shown above, is in Valdosta at the corner of Baytree Road and McLeod Road.

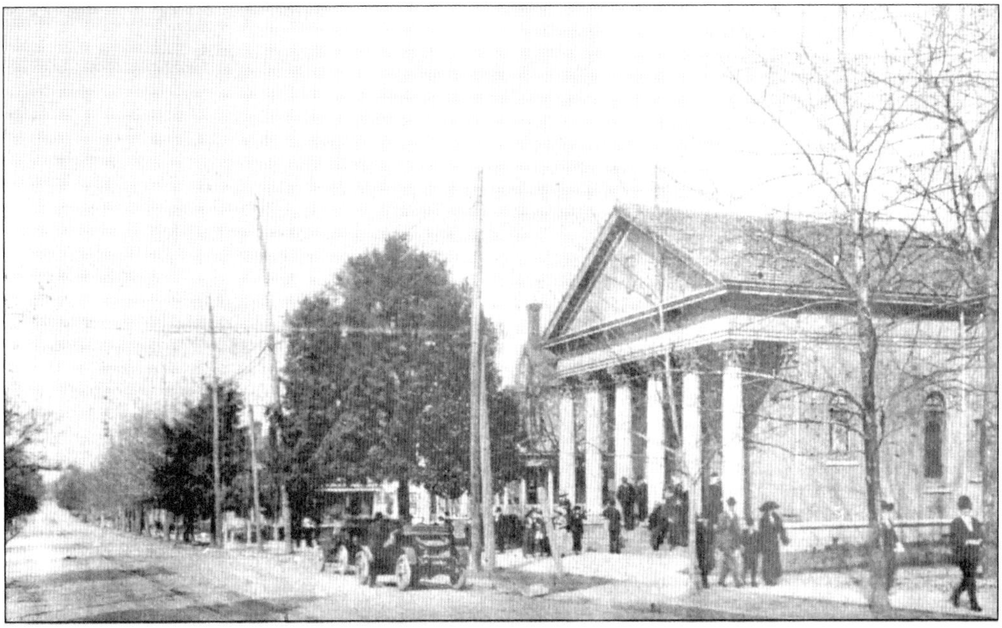

The images on this page offer two different views of the First Presbyterian Church, one of the historic churches of downtown Valdosta. This church has been at its present location, at the corner of North Patterson Street and East Magnolia Street, since the early part of the 20th century. In the picture above, the congregation is seen leaving a Sunday service around 1920 with only two automobiles present in front of the church. The image below is from the 1960s prior to the construction of the new federal building next door. The appearance is very much the same as 40 years earlier but amazingly with no automobiles in sight. (Below: Valdosta–Lowndes County Chamber of Commerce.)

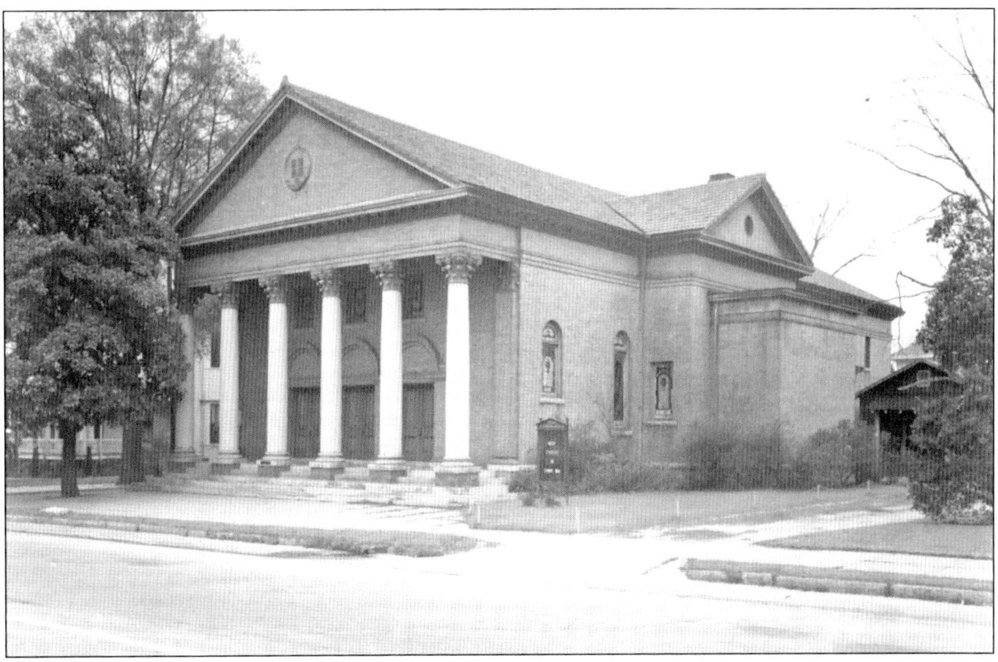

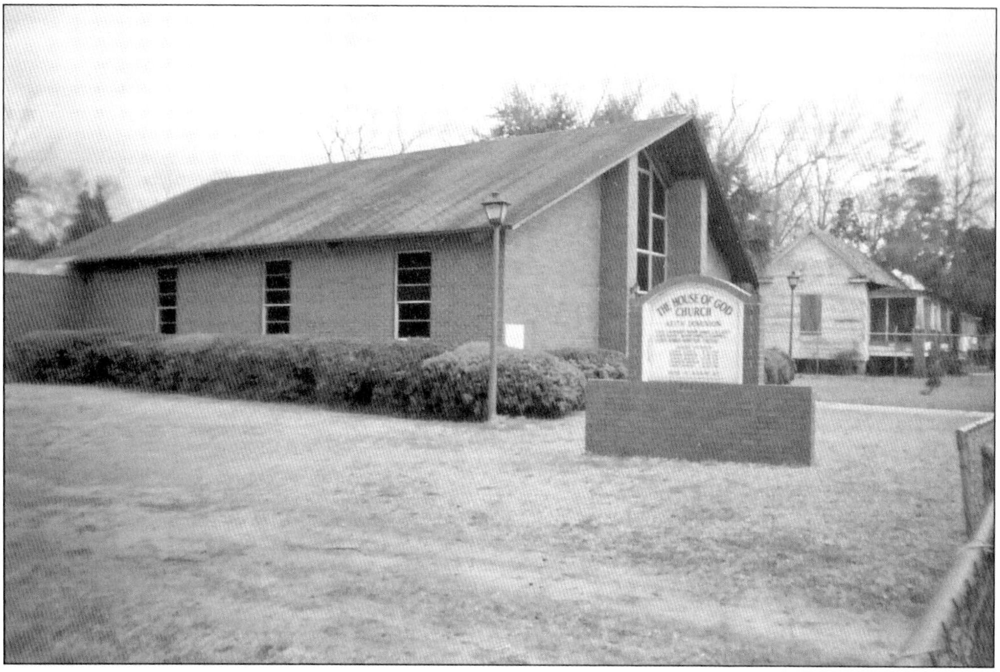

Shown above is a small, primarily African American church in Valdosta, the House of God Church on West Adair Street.

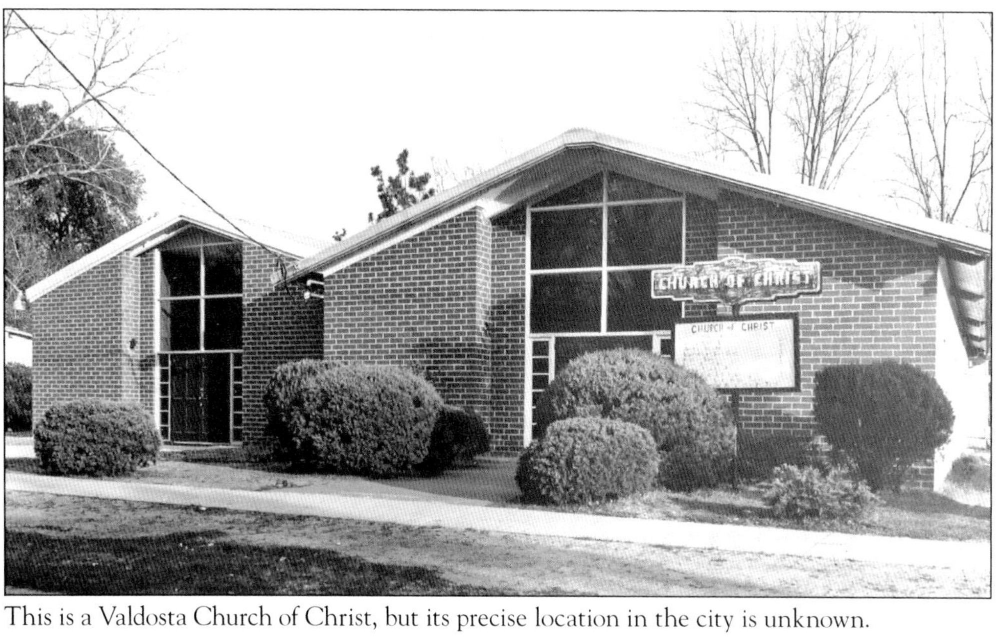

This is a Valdosta Church of Christ, but its precise location in the city is unknown.

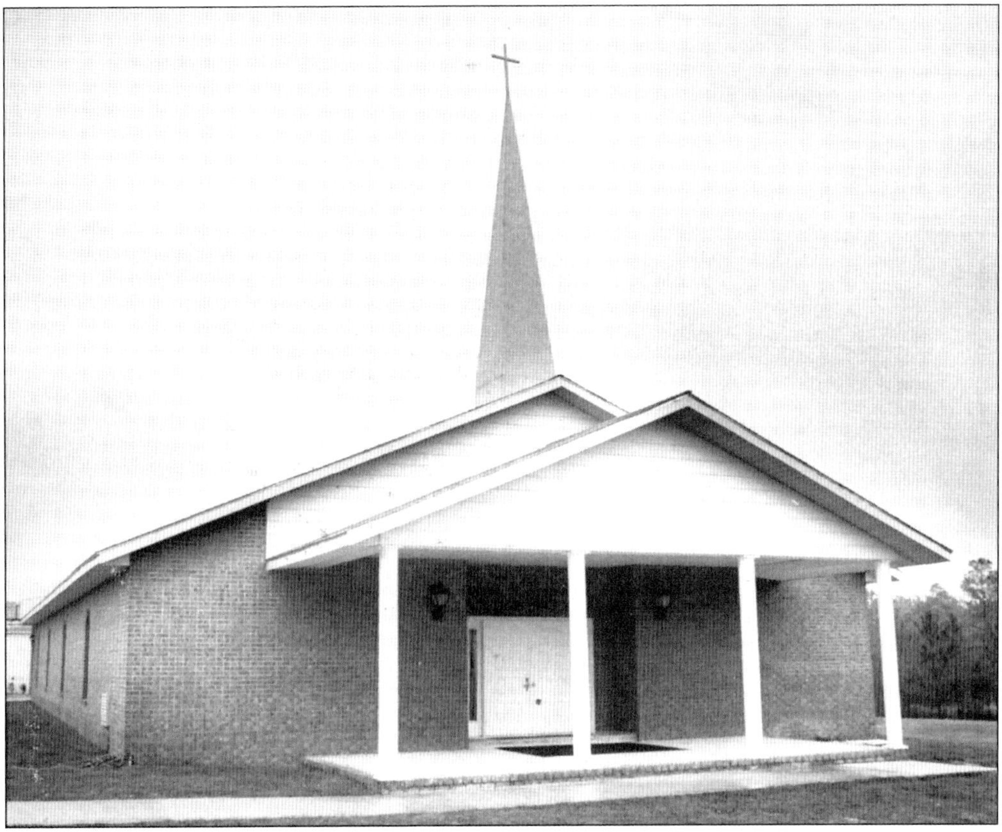

This image is of a very modern rural Baptist church in Lowndes County, namely Gateway Baptist Church on Georgia Highway 94 in the county.

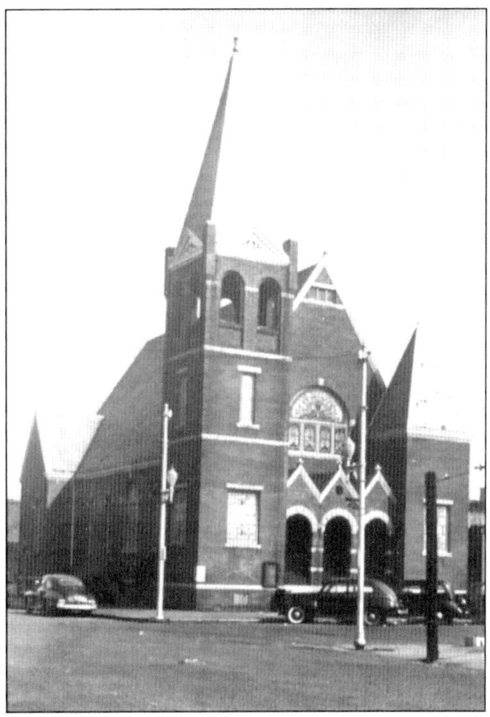

The very striking church edifice shown to the right no longer exists. This building was the original First Christian Church at 124 West Hill Avenue, on the northeast corner of West Hill and North Toombs. When the First Christian congregation constructed a new church on North Patterson Street at the end of the 1950s, this structure was taken down.

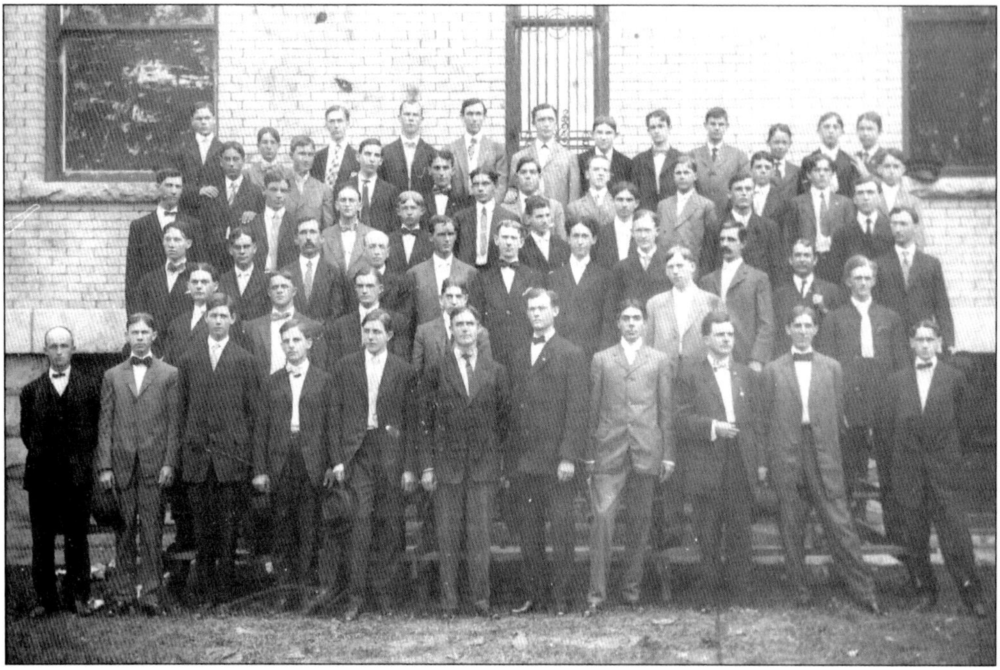

These pictures are, respectively, of a men's Sunday school class and a women's Sunday school class of what was originally the Tabernacle Baptist Church of Valdosta and then the Lee Street Baptist Church. Both are from the 1920s. The image above is of the Baraca men's class and is impressive because of the size of the group. The site of the photograph was the Lowndes County Courthouse. Below is the Philathea women's class, pictured in front of the church, and this image too is striking because of the number of class members shown.

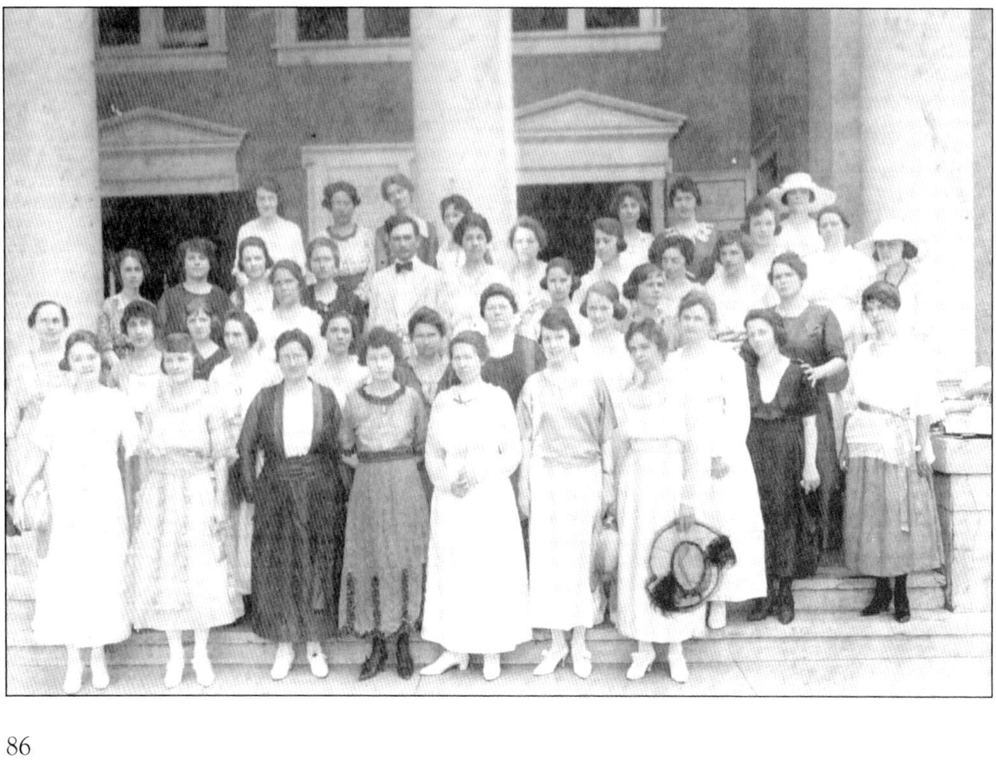

The picture above is of another of the historic African American churches in Valdosta, in this instance the Macedonia Baptist at 715 J. L. Lomax Drive in the western part of the city.

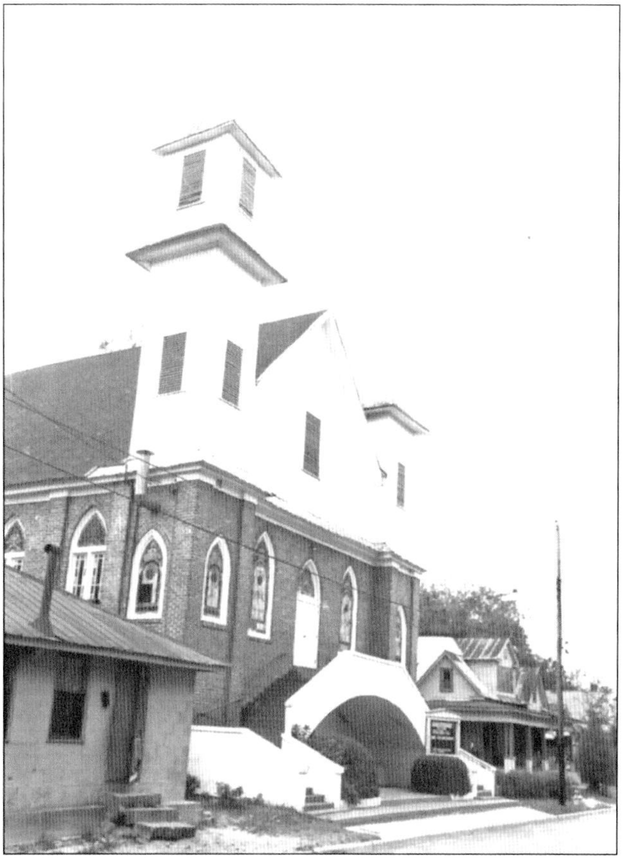

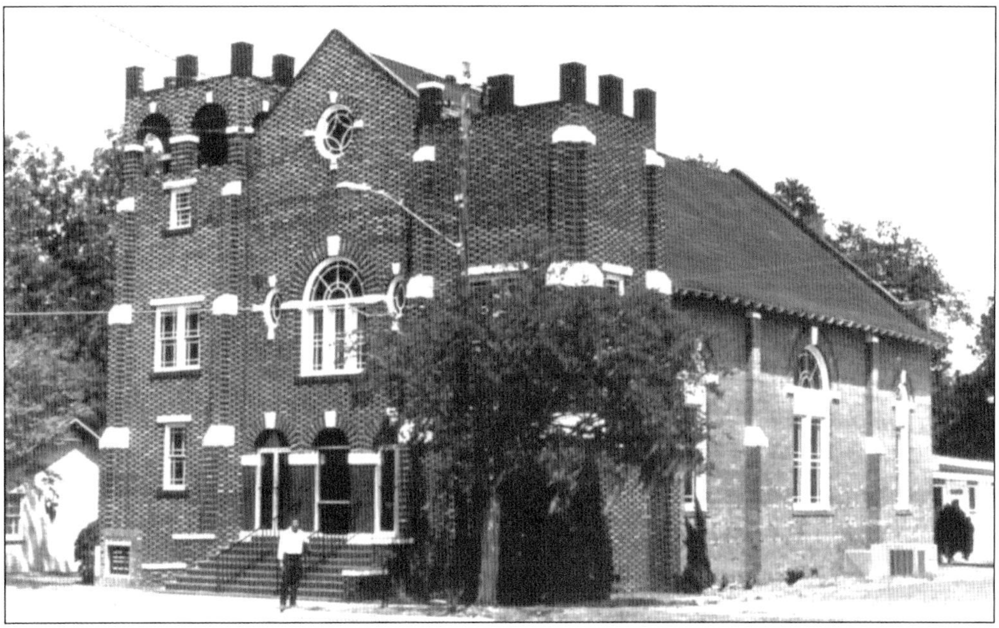

Shown here also is a historic African American church in Valdosta, the First Antioch Baptist Church at 517 North Oak Street.

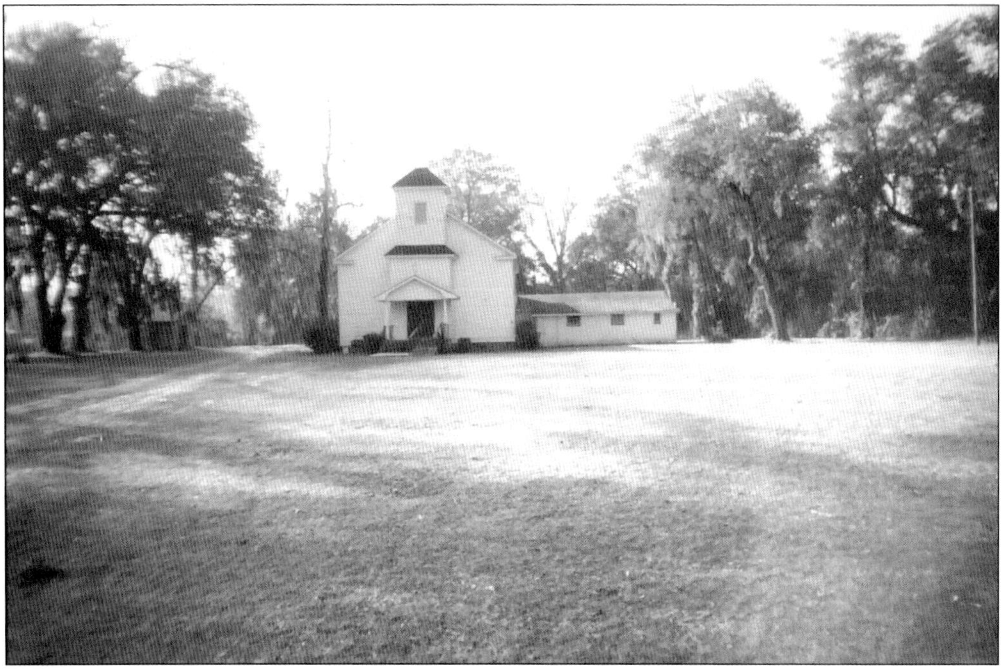

This church in a woodsy setting is Mount Zion African Methodist Episcopal Church on Mount Zion Road in Lowndes County.

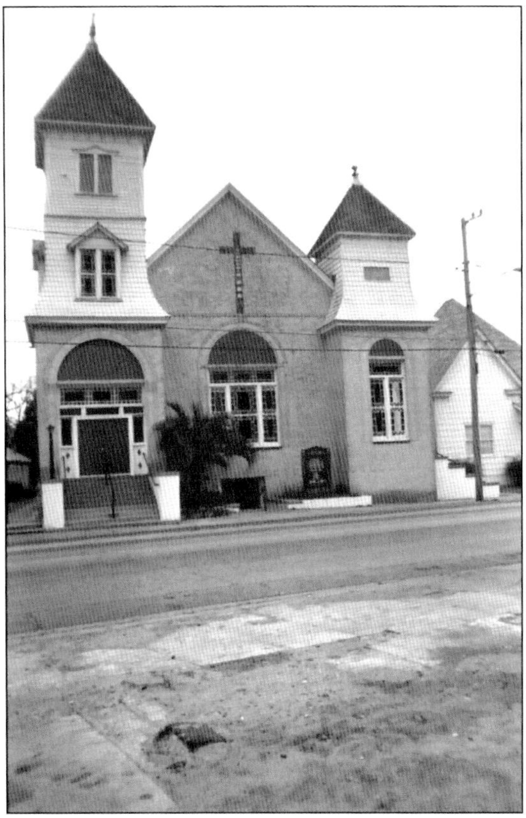

Pictured to the left is another of the historic African American churches in Lowndes County, which dates from the 1890s. St. Paul's African Methodist Episcopal Church, for most of its long history, has been situated on South Ashley Street in Valdosta.

This scene is of an outdoor baptism by immersion in a pond or lake in Lowndes County in the 1940s–1950s. The exact date and location are unknown.

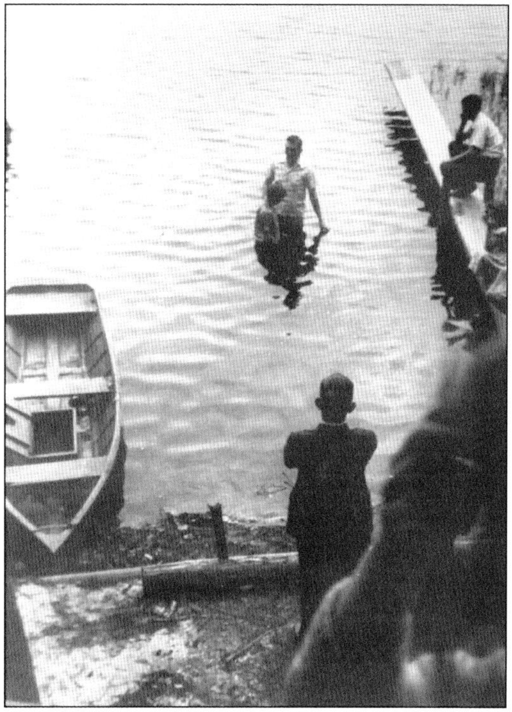

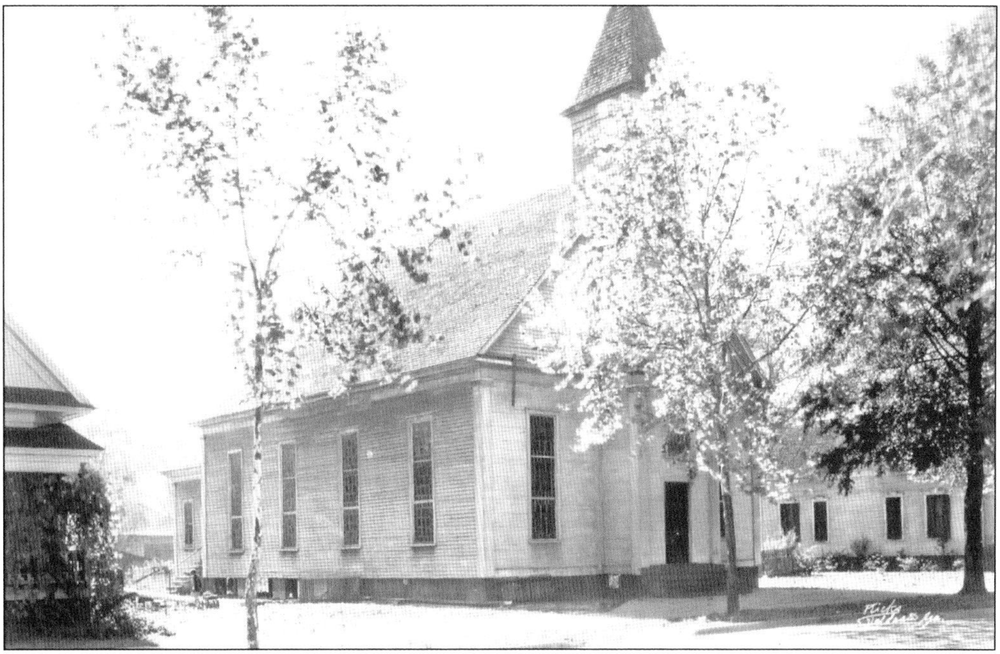

This building on East Central Avenue was originally the Valdosta First Baptist Church. After First Baptist constructed its new sanctuary on West Central Avenue in 1895, the building was purchased by the Valdosta Primitive Baptist Church, which explains why a Primitive Baptist church structure happened to have a steeple and stained-glass windows. For many decades, the Primitive Baptists remained in this building, and when they finally moved, it became a Pentecostal church. (Valdosta–Lowndes County Chamber of Commerce.)

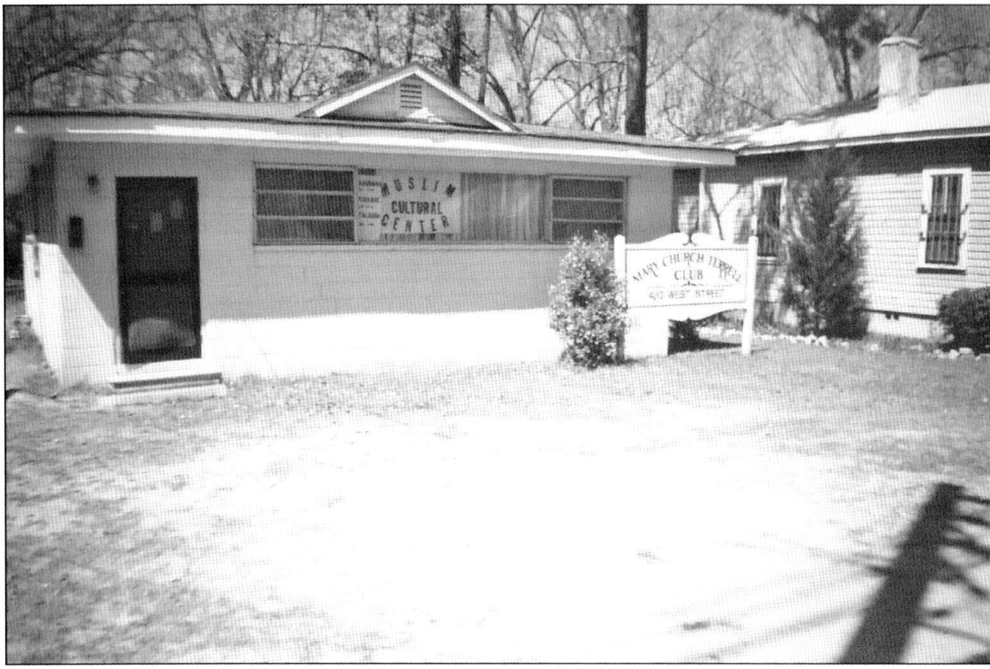

The two images on this page prove that religious activity does not necessarily require a large building. At the top is the Valdosta Muslim Cultural Center on West Street. The small structure shown in the bottom image is a country church in the vicinity of Cat Creek in northern Lowndes County. (Below: Valdosta–Lowndes County Chamber of Commerce.)

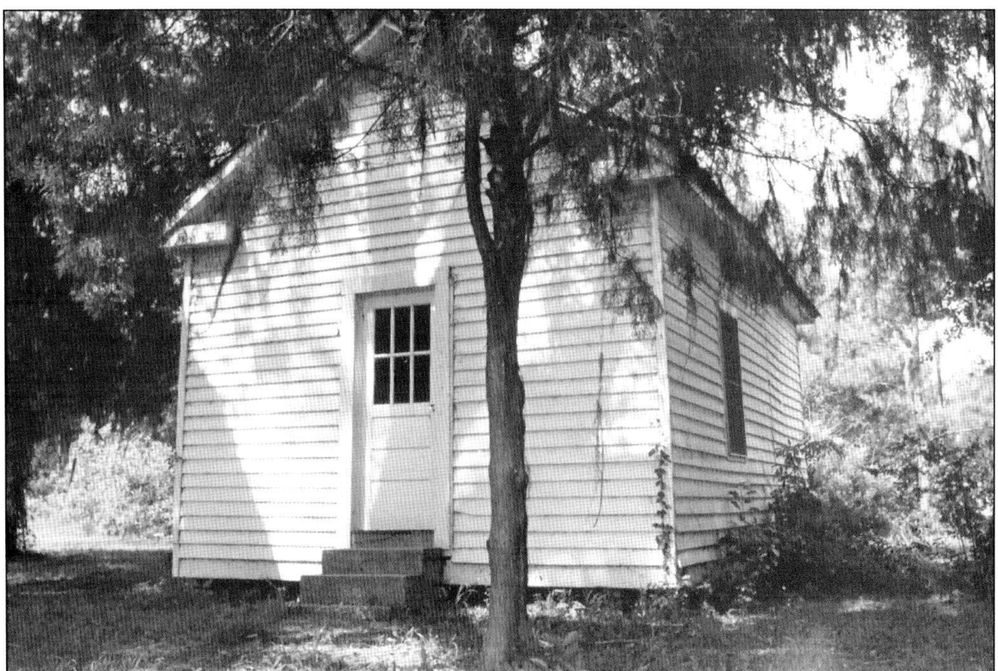

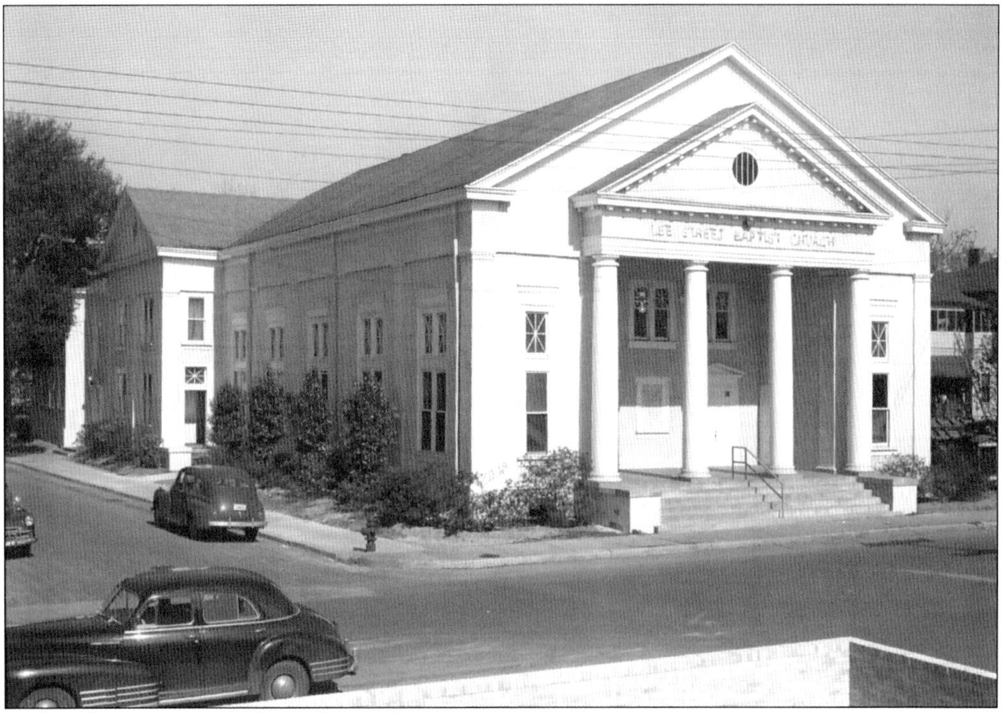

The picture above is the first Lee Street Baptist Church, formerly the Tabernacle Baptist Church, at the corner of North Lee Street and Smithland, the site of the onetime Valdosta Opera House. The time is in the late 1940s. This building preceded the new church built later, which was sold to the Central Avenue Church of Christ in 1997–1998. The building below is the Lee Street Baptist Church's Sunday School Annex and offices, which now houses City of Valdosta administrative offices. (Valdosta–Lowndes County Chamber of Commerce.)

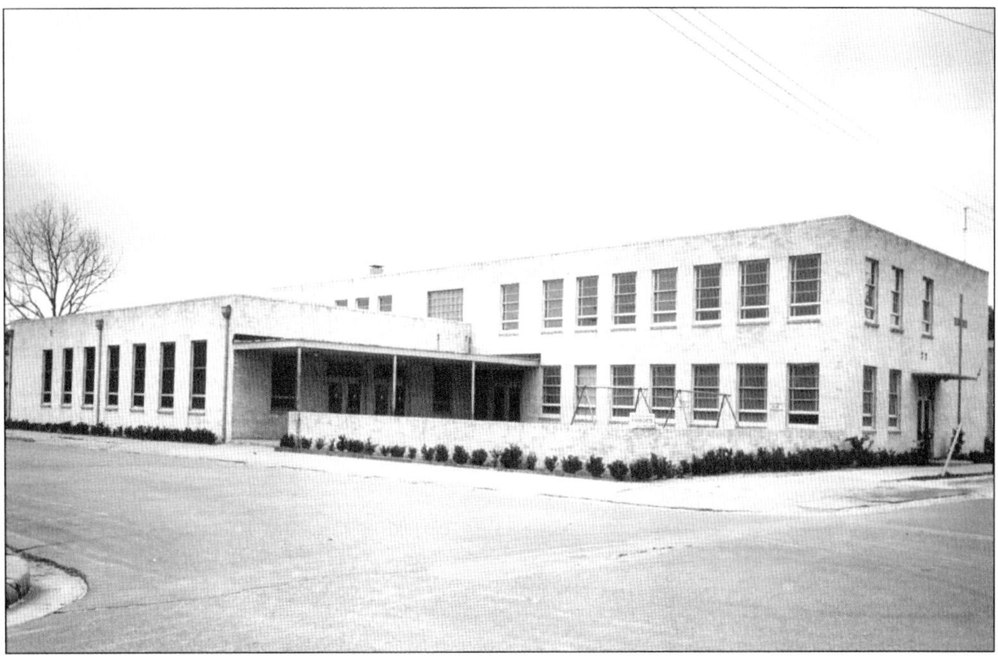

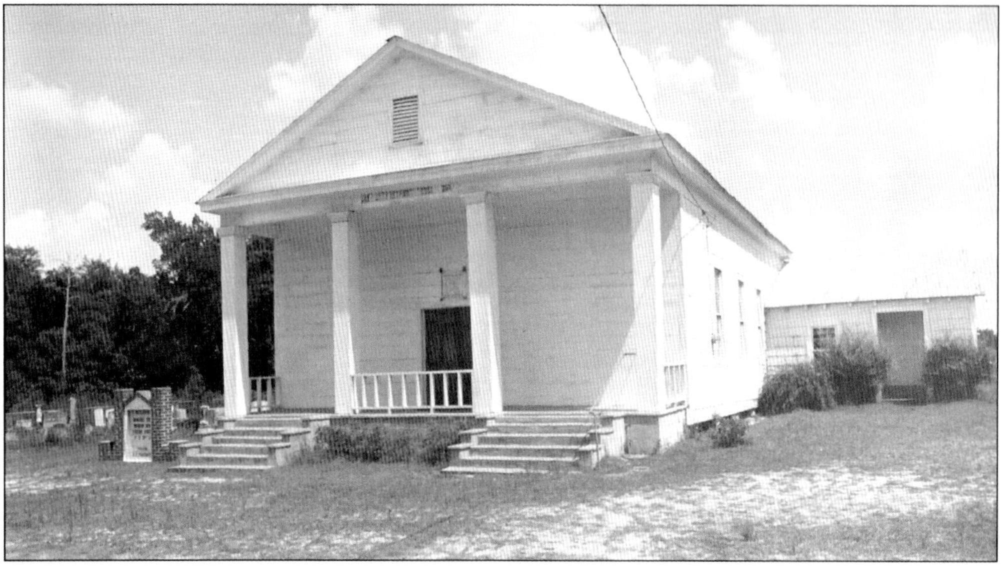

The image at the top is Salem Methodist Church, northwest of Hahira, in rural Lowndes County. Dating from 1856, it is a beautiful, old country church of classical appearance that has endured to the present. In contrast is the Gonwood Church of Christ on Canna Drive, with its unusual modern architectural style. Though the building itself still exists, the church is now defunct. (Valdosta–Lowndes County Chamber of Commerce.)

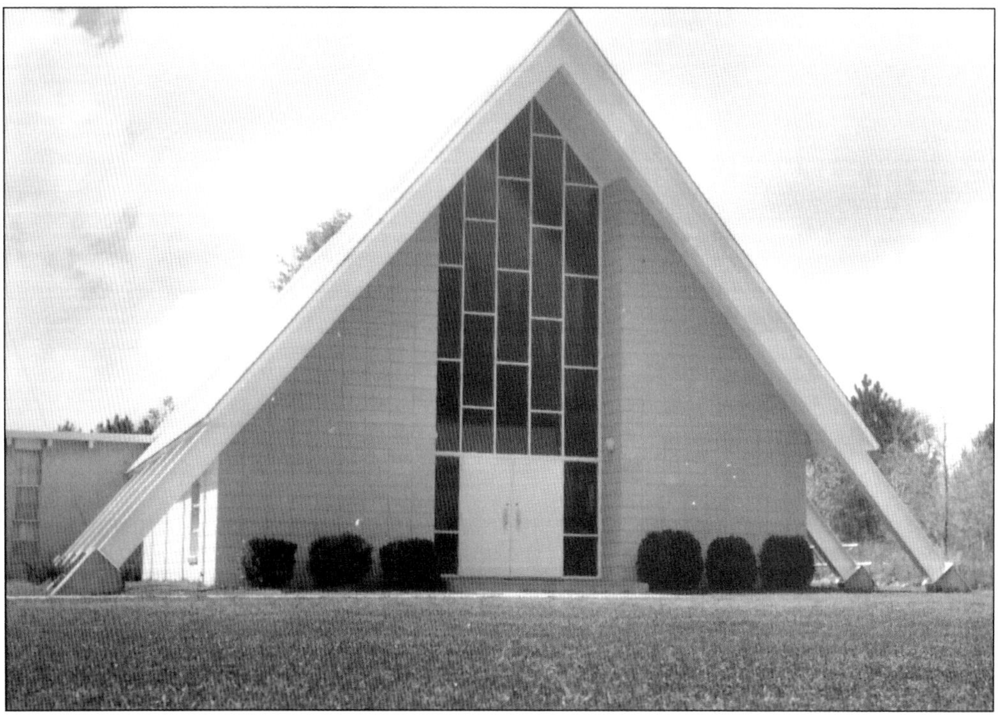

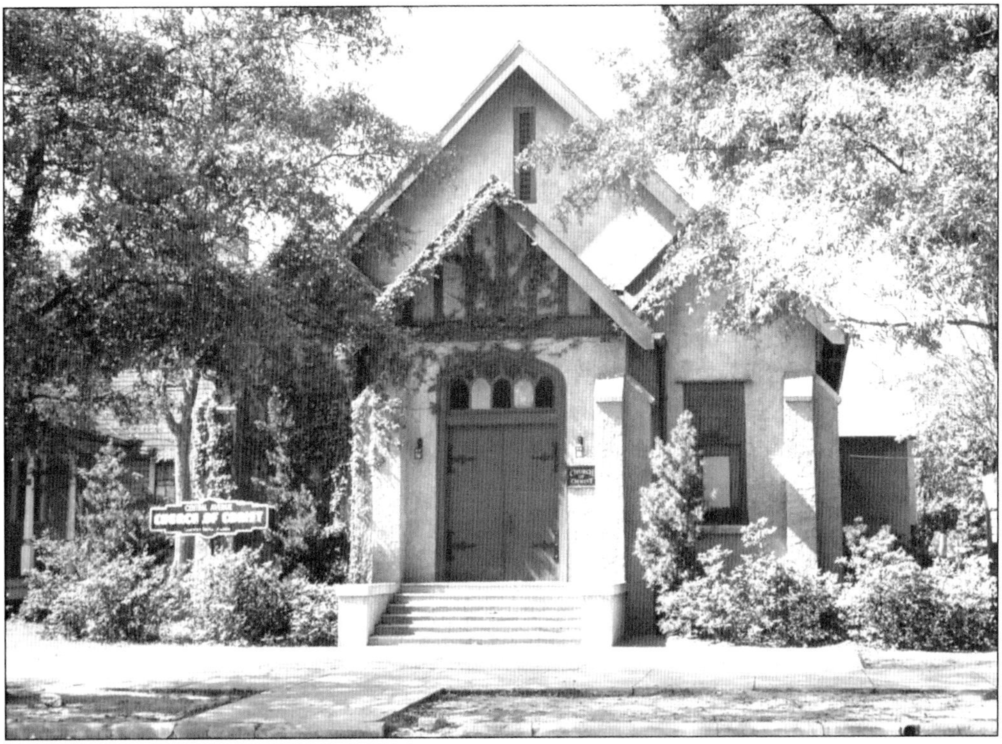

Shown above is the original sanctuary of the Central Avenue Church of Christ on East Central Avenue in Valdosta. After many years at this location, the congregation in 1997 purchased the facilities of the Lee Street Baptist Church around the corner on Lee Street and moved into those buildings while continuing to own the old site. (Valdosta–Lowndes County Chamber of Commerce.)

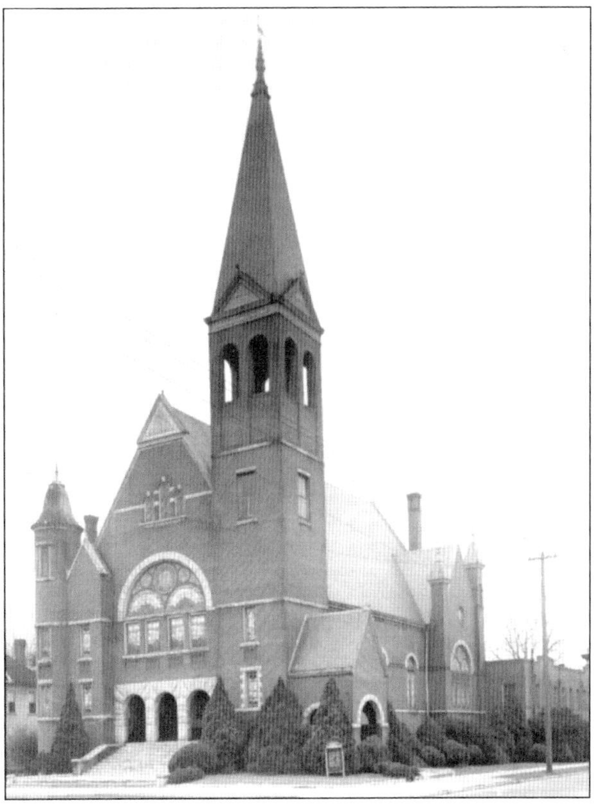

With its high tower at its southeast corner and its huge stained-glass windows facing West Central Avenue, this is the First Baptist Church of Valdosta, which was constructed and occupied in the mid-1890s. The interior of the church also is strikingly attractive. The educational building at the rear was dedicated in 1954 and began being used in 1955. (Valdosta–Lowndes County Chamber of Commerce.)

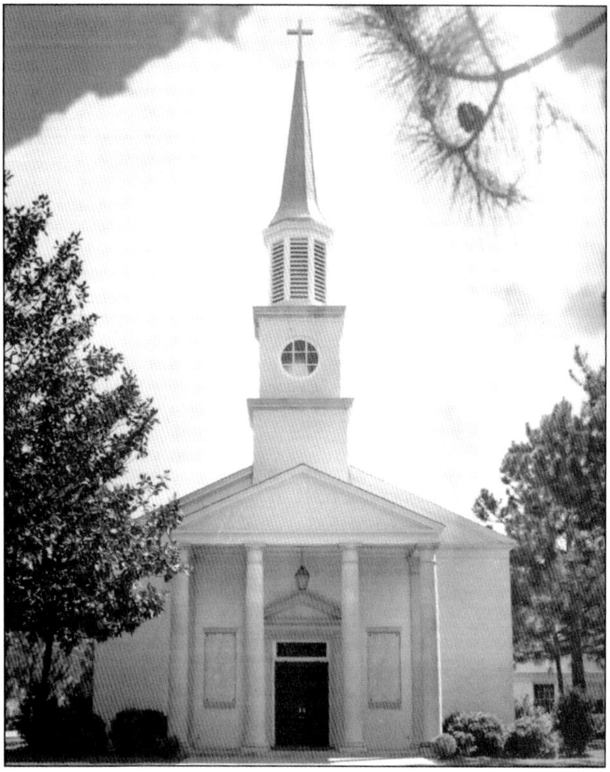

Positioned on the southeast corner of North Patterson Street and East Alden Avenue in Valdosta, the "new" First Christian Church has been at the present site since the end of the 1950s. This structure replaced the original First Christian, which had been in the downtown area of Valdosta on West Hill Avenue. (Valdosta–Lowndes County Chamber of Commerce.)

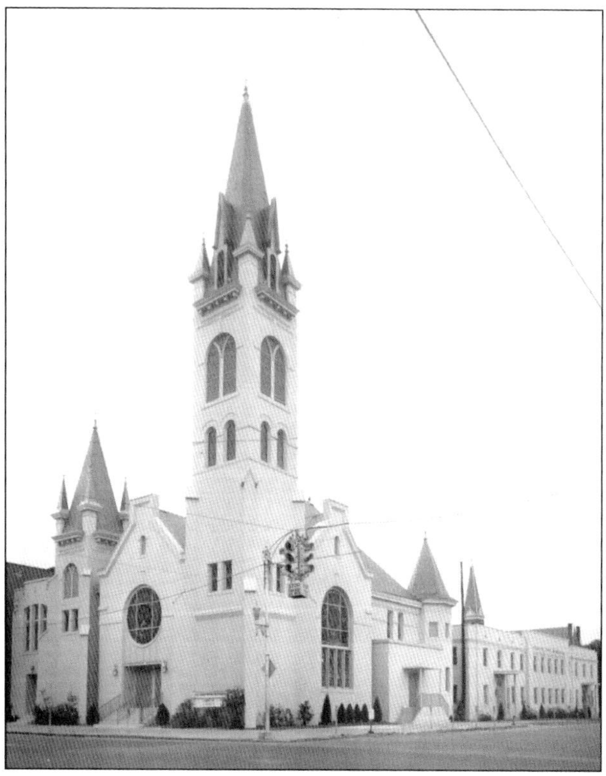

This is a comprehensive view of the First United Methodist Church, one of the historic downtown churches of Valdosta on North Patterson Street at West Valley Street. The image shows something of the size of the structure, along with the Strickland Memorial Building to the rear, facing West Valley Street. (Valdosta–Lowndes County Chamber of Commerce.)

Shown to the right is the "new" Lee Street Baptist Church, which replaced the church building in the top picture on page 91. Originally the Tabernacle Baptist Church, Lee Street Baptist in 1997–1998 merged with the congregation of the Azalea City Baptist Church to form Crossroads Baptist Church and sold the sanctuary to the Central Avenue Church of Christ. The Sunday School Annex, just barely visible on the left, was sold to the City of Valdosta. (Valdosta–Lowndes County Chamber of Commerce.)

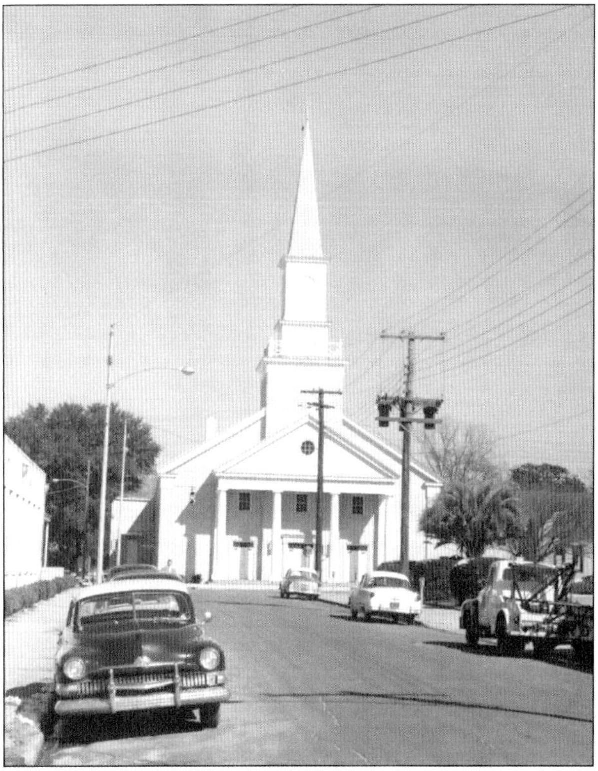

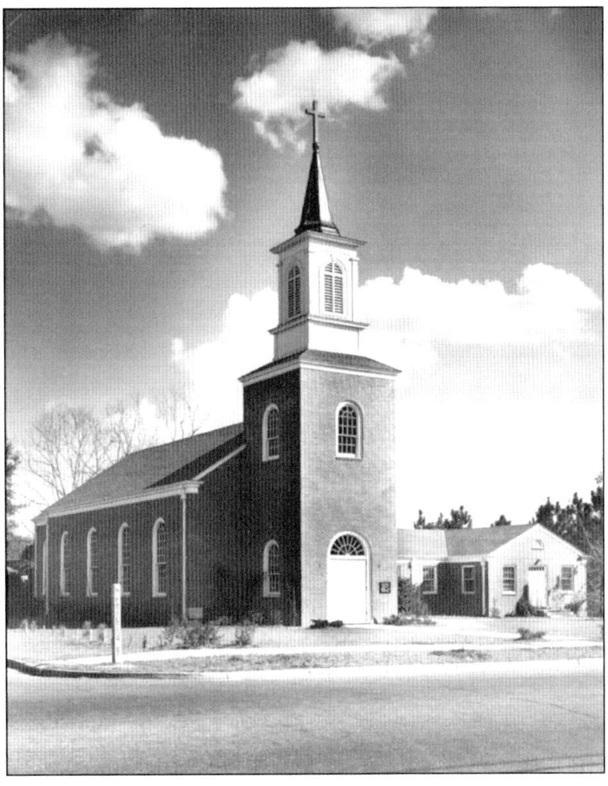

This image, from 1949, is the newly built Christ Episcopal Church on North Patterson Street across from what was then Georgia State Woman's College, now Valdosta State University. The sanctuary and parish hall to the right, whose architectural style is based on the historic Bruton Parish Episcopal Church in Williamsburg, Virginia, replaced a much smaller building on East Central Avenue that became the Christian Scientist Church. (Valdosta–Lowndes County Chamber of Commerce.)

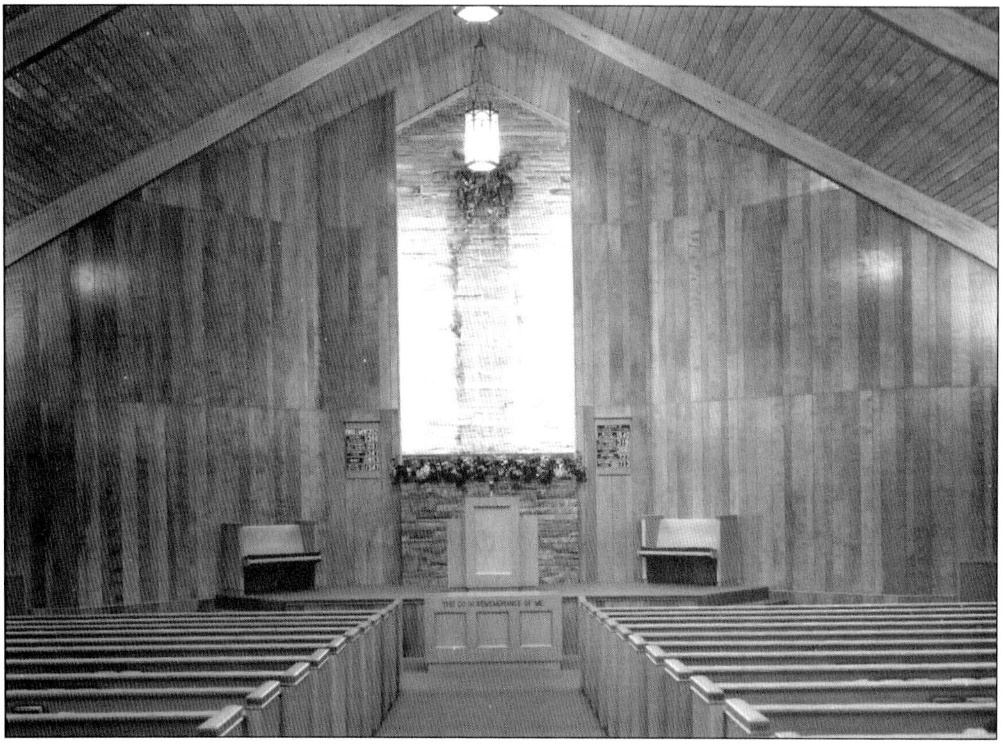

Displayed in the image above is the starkly modernistic interior of an unidentified Lowndes County Church. Also in the modern mode is the architectural style of the original sanctuary of the Azalea City Baptist Church at the corner of County Club Road and Eager Road in Valdosta. Since the merger of Azalea City Baptist with Lee Street Baptist in the late 1990s, the vastly expanded congregation has constructed a new, larger, and more traditional sanctuary to the left of the structure shown, facing Country Club Road. (Valdosta–Lowndes County Chamber of Commerce.)

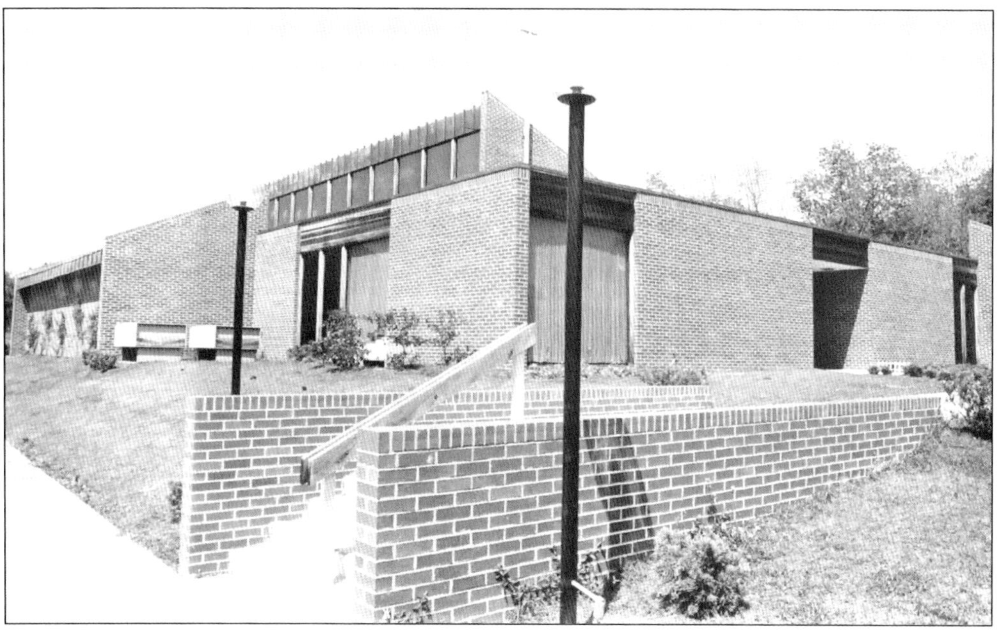

Five

People, Homes, and Life in the Community

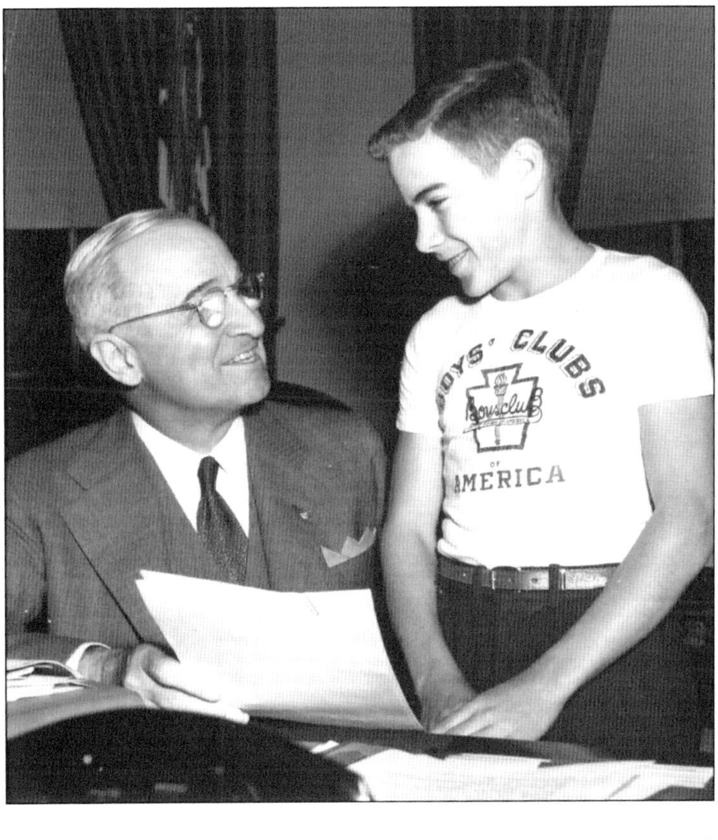

Pictured on the right with Pres. Harry S. Truman is Frankie Harrison of Valdosta, who was a member of the Valdosta Boys Club and National Boy of the Year for 1948.

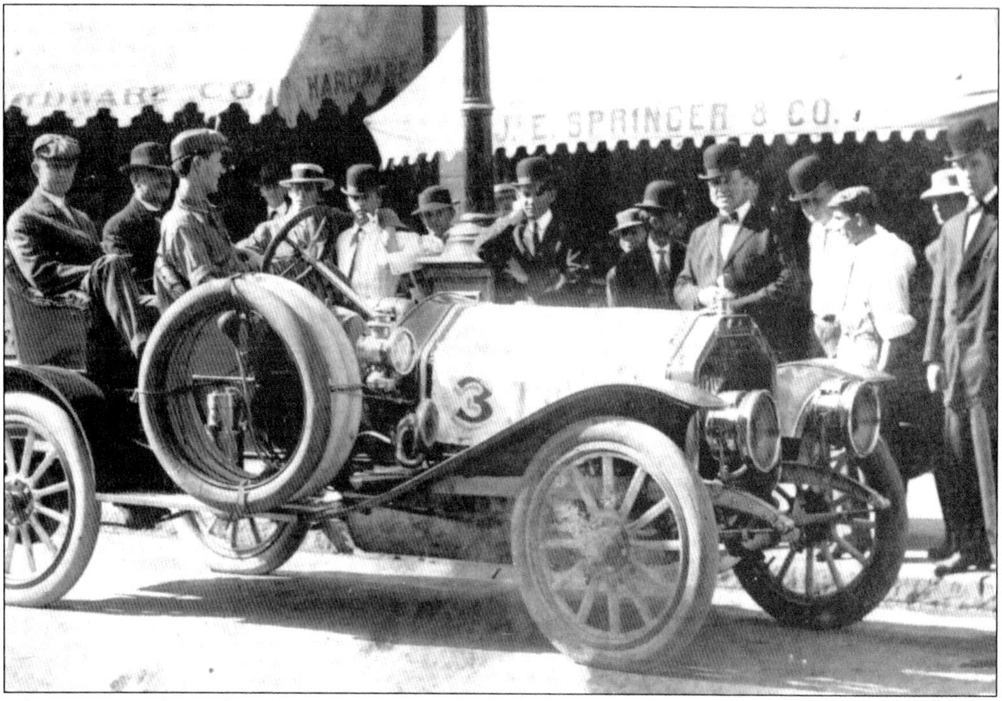

The sports roadster above is shown at 124 North Patterson Street in front of J. E. Springer and Company, a Valdosta jeweler. The exact time of the image is not certain, but it must date from before 1923. By 1923, Springer and Company was no longer in operation. The appearance of the vehicle, with the number painted on the right side, indicates that it was involved in a road race.

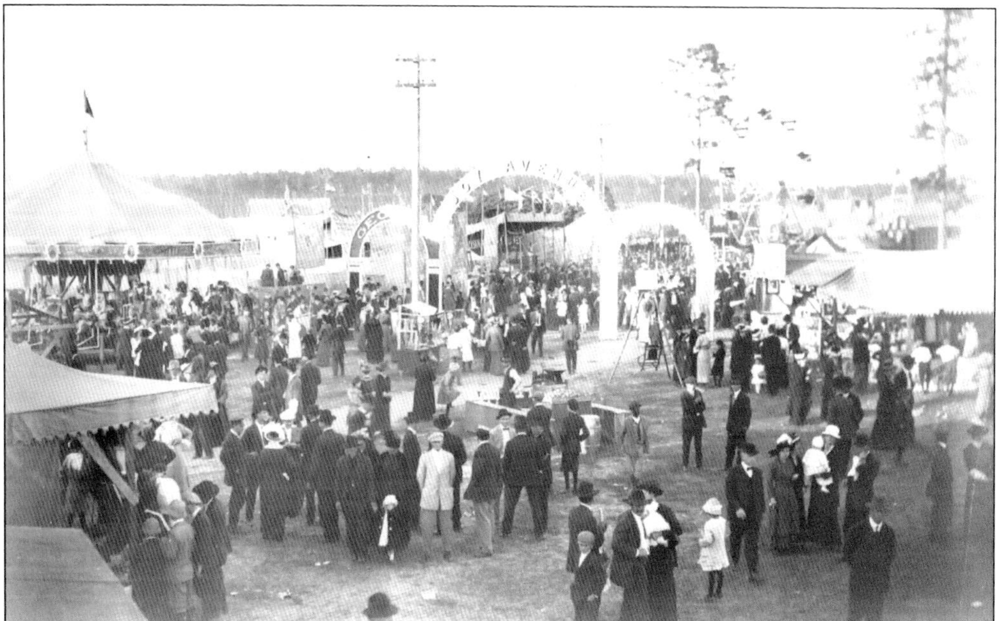

A momentous event in Lowndes County's history was the state fair, held at Pine Park on the north side of Valdosta, in October 1900. The picture shows something of the size of the crowd that the fair attracted.

Here a group of affluent and well-dressed young people pose in a wagon in front of the clubhouse at Ocean Pond in southern Lowndes County near Lake Park in the 1890s.

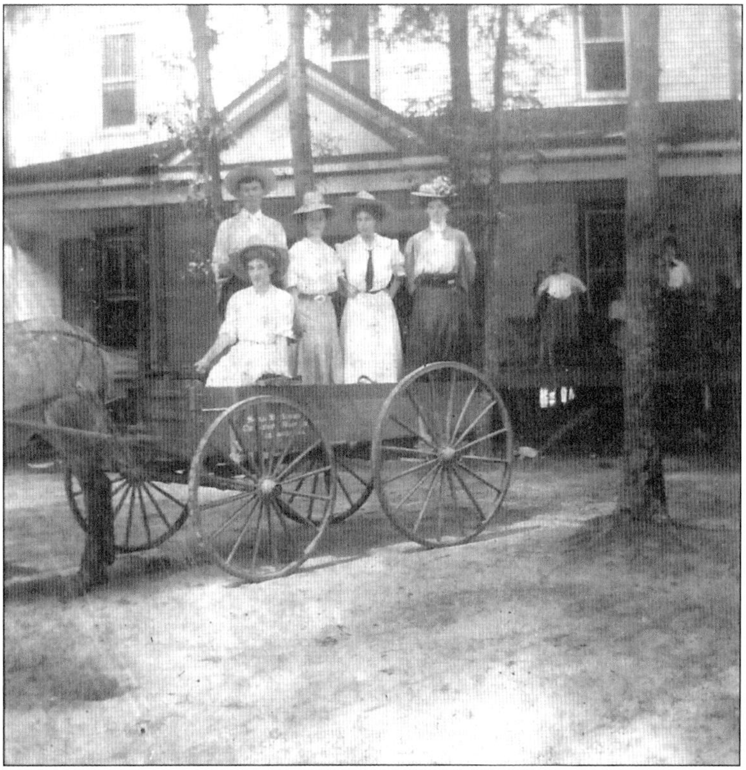

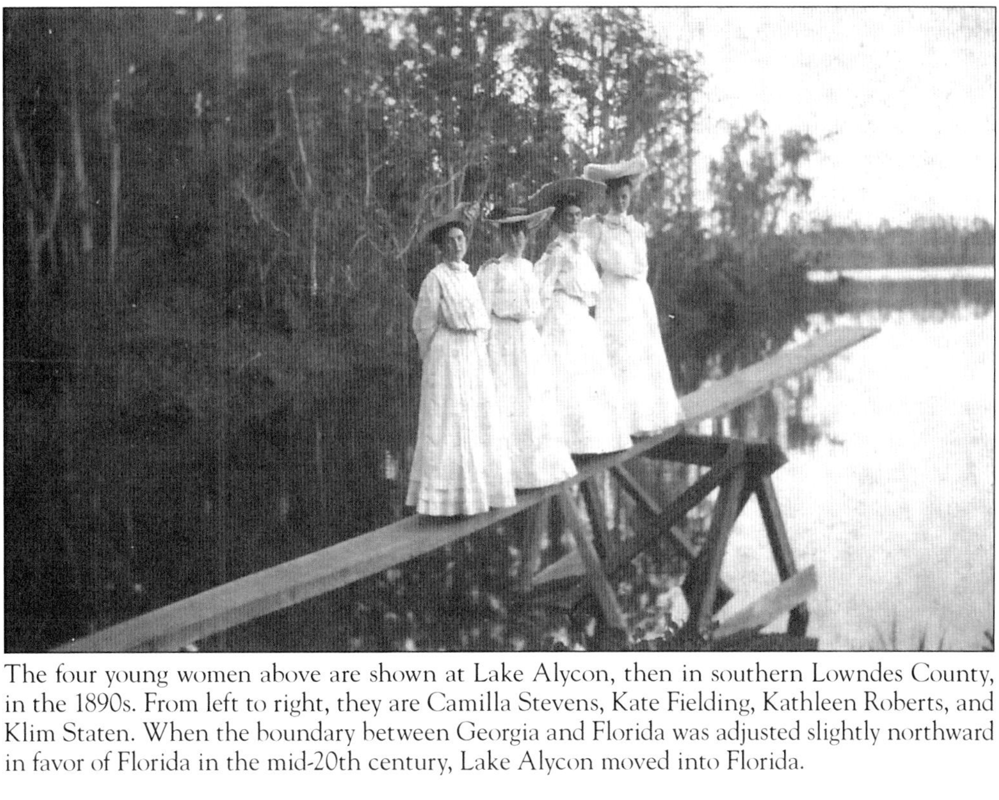

The four young women above are shown at Lake Alycon, then in southern Lowndes County, in the 1890s. From left to right, they are Camilla Stevens, Kate Fielding, Kathleen Roberts, and Klim Staten. When the boundary between Georgia and Florida was adjusted slightly northward in favor of Florida in the mid-20th century, Lake Alycon moved into Florida.

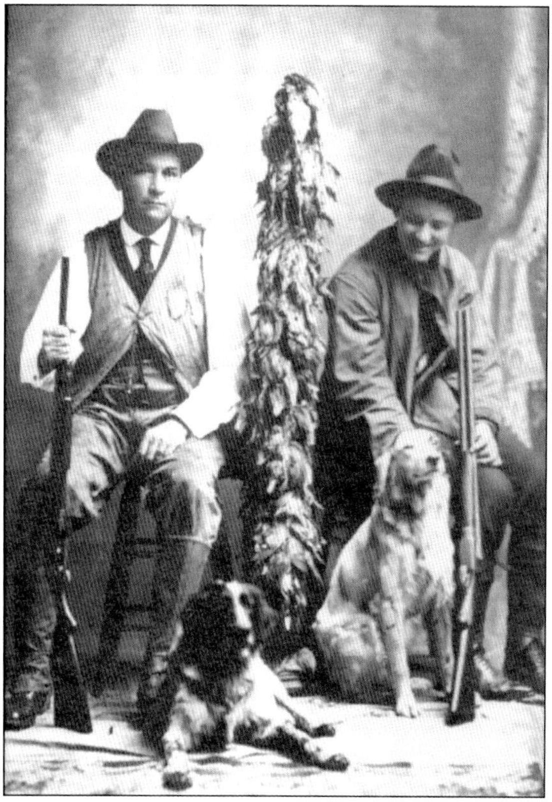

In 1917, a pair of Lowndes County quail hunters poses with their shotguns and their kill. The hunt was for a good purpose: to provide quail for a dinner at a Shriner ceremonial occasion. The hunters are George Feagle on the left and Alex Malloy on the right.

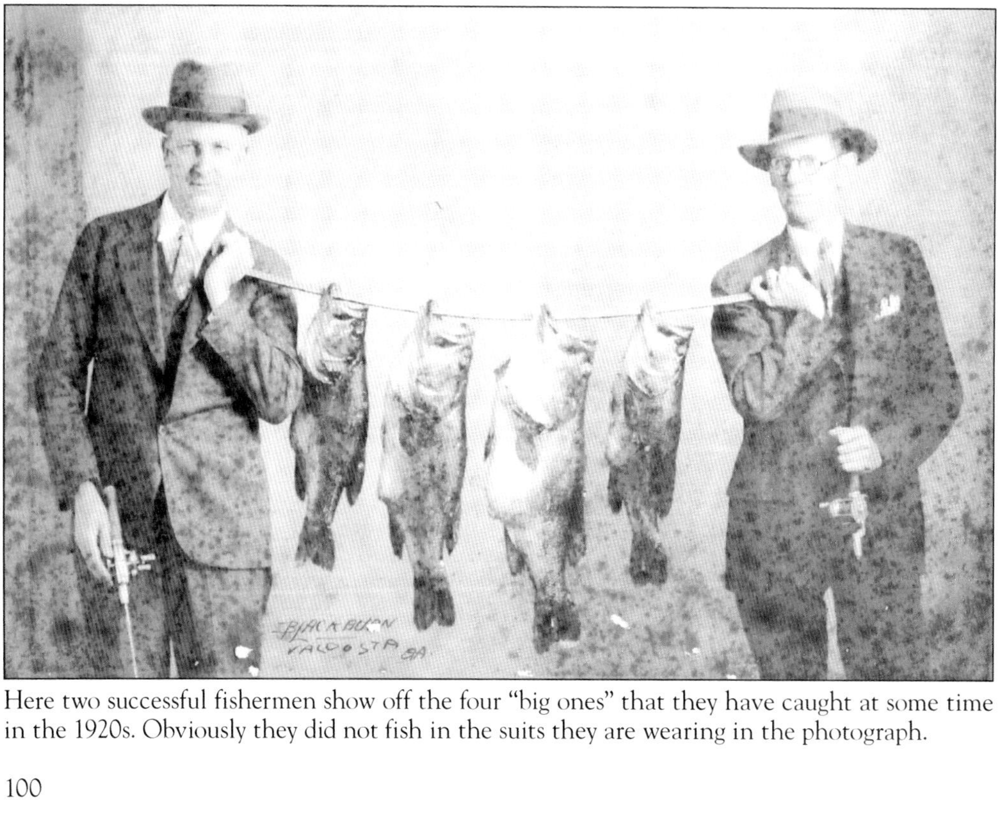

Here two successful fishermen show off the four "big ones" that they have caught at some time in the 1920s. Obviously they did not fish in the suits they are wearing in the photograph.

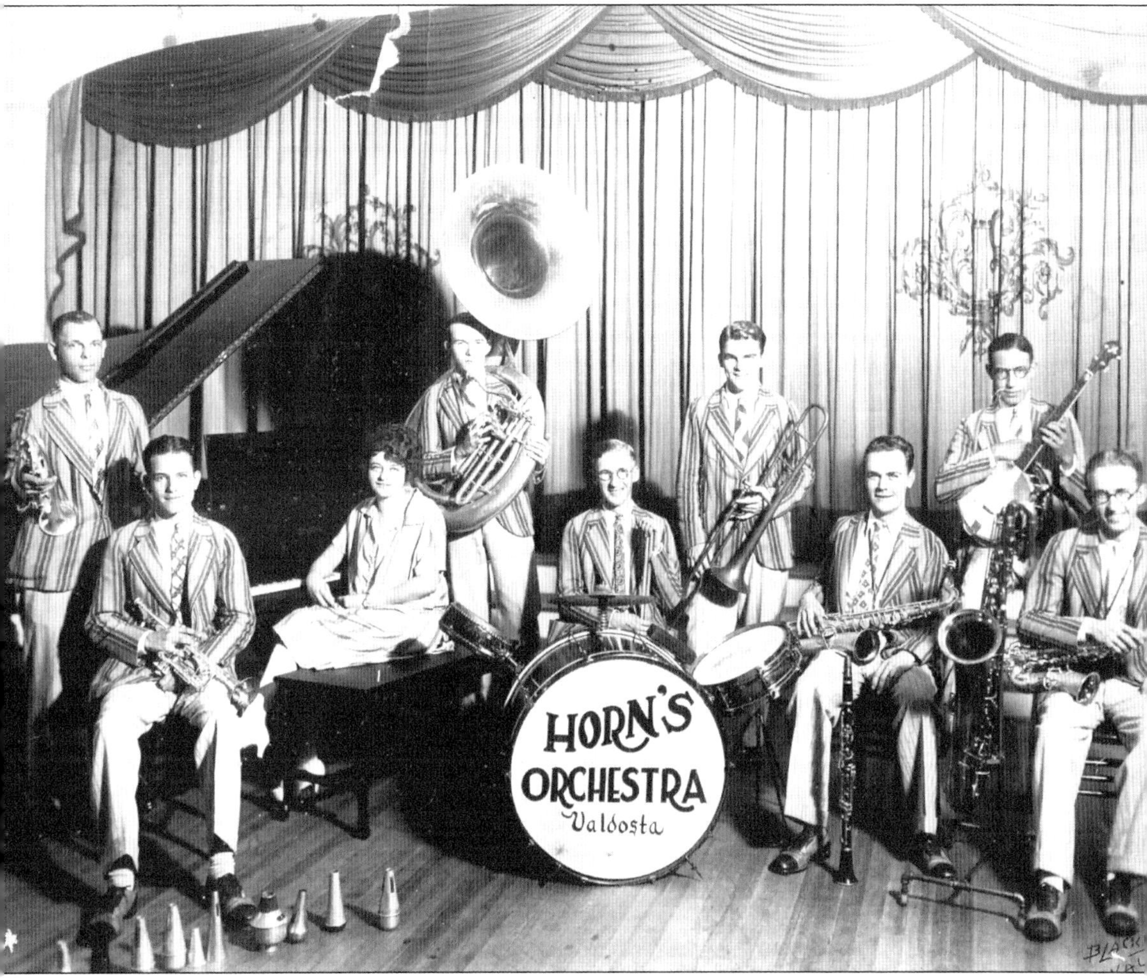

Pictured above is the Elsa Horn Orchestra of Valdosta in the mid-1920s. The musicians from left to right are O. B. Williams, trumpet; Leon Cowart, trumpet; Elsa Horn, piano; Cecil Barker, bass horn; Jack Mixer, drums; unidentified, trombone; Charlie Joyner, saxophone and clarinet; Weenie Bramlett, banjo; and J. R. McGowan, saxophone. The Horn Orchestra was a mainstay of the local popular music scene for much of the 1920s.

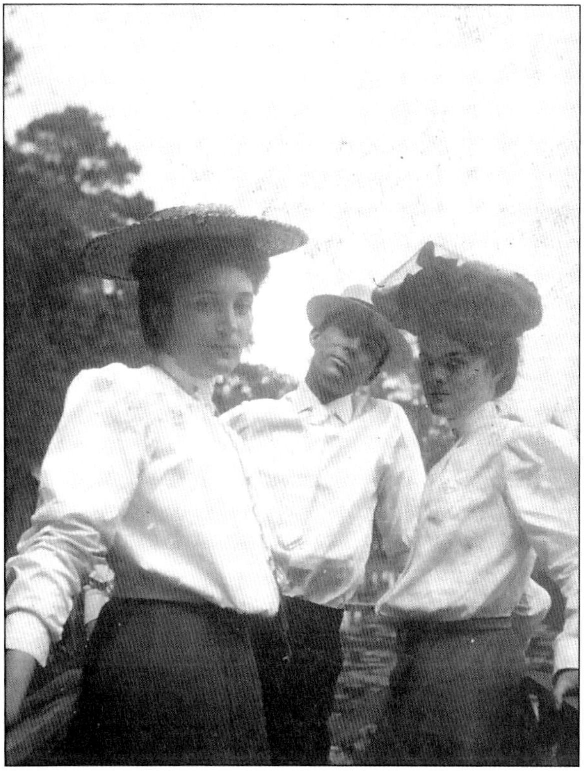

Three stylish young people of the 1890s are shown in southern Lowndes County at the Ocean Pond clubhouse. They are, from left to right, Emma Joe, Walin Davis, and Kathleen Winn.

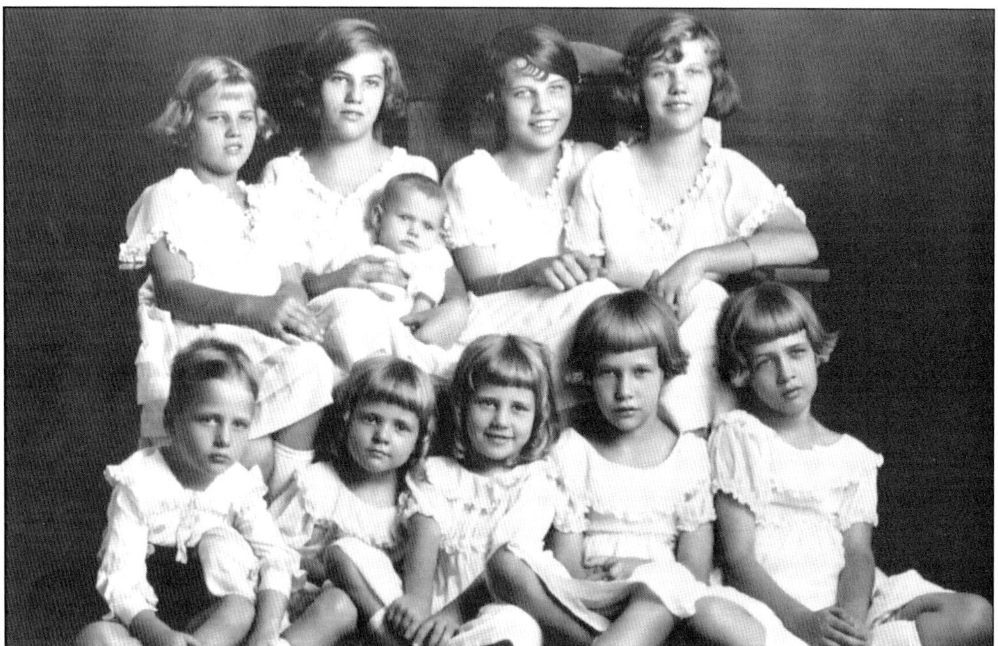

These beautiful youngsters, nine girls and one boy, are the children of the Oscar D. Dalton family of Valdosta. From left to right are (first row) Oscar Jr. and Dorothy, 5; Margaret, 7; Lacy, 9; and Adelma, 10; (second row) Virginia, 12; Vallie, 13; Gloria, 14 months; Emily, 14; and Ferrell, 15.

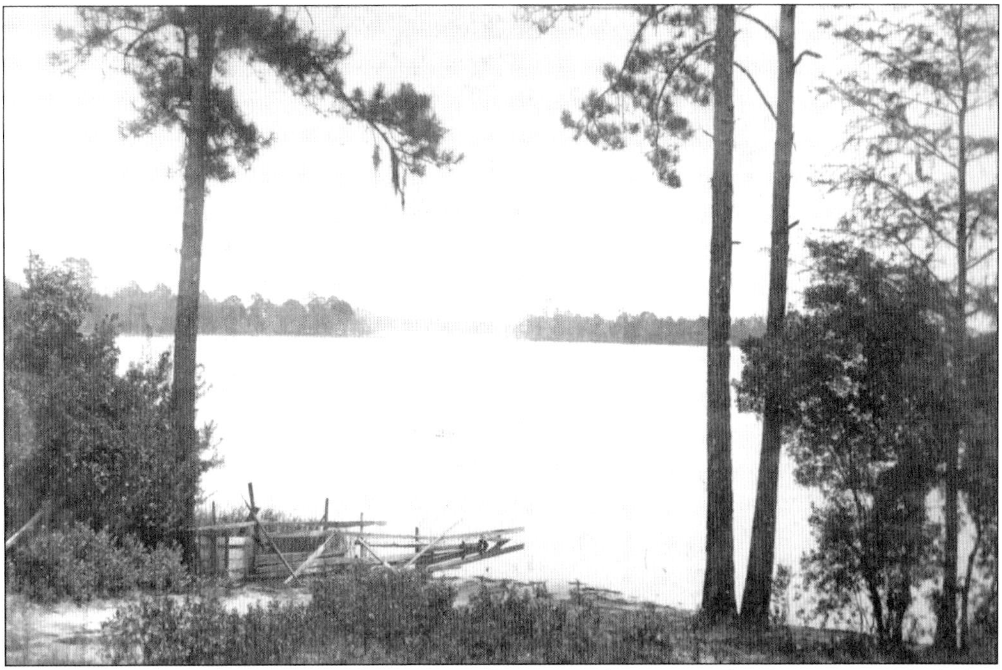

The top image depicts Long Pond or Twin Lakes in southern Lowndes County in 1922 before large-scale development destroyed the pristine appearance of the site. Below is the Twin Lakes Pavilion at Long Pond in the mid- to late 1920s, when development had commenced. As the picture indicates, the pavilion attracted large crowds, especially on weekends for swimming and socializing. One old-fashioned feature of the scene is provided by the split-rail fence in the background to the right of the pavilion building.

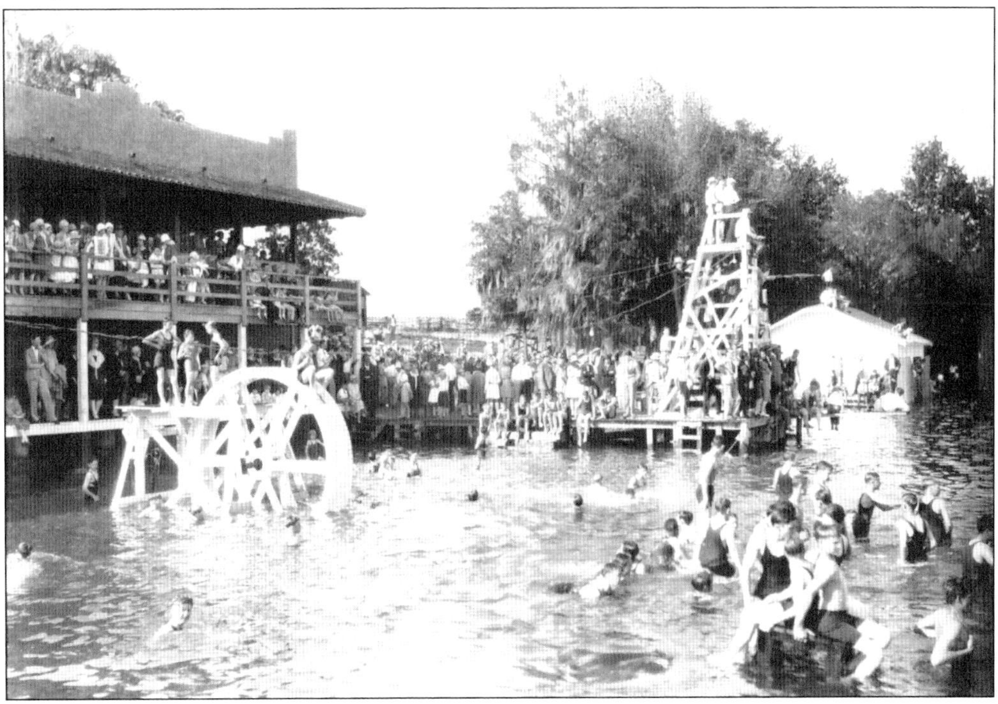

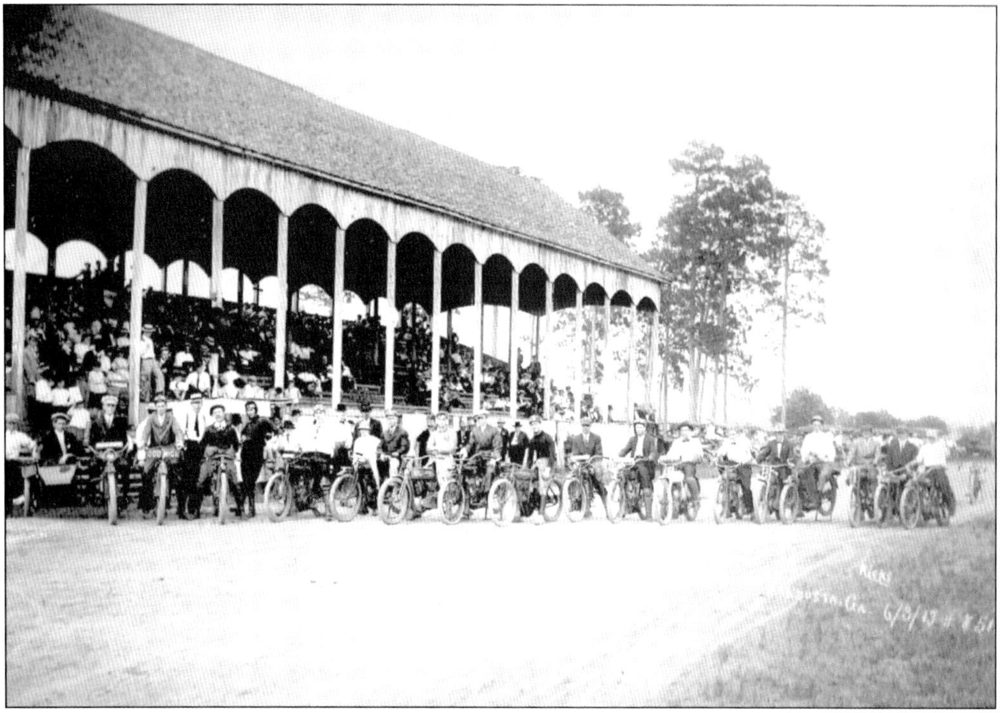

Racing of almost any type has long been popular in the South. Here motorcycle riders pose with their machines on the racetrack at Pine Park in northern Valdosta on June 13, 1913.

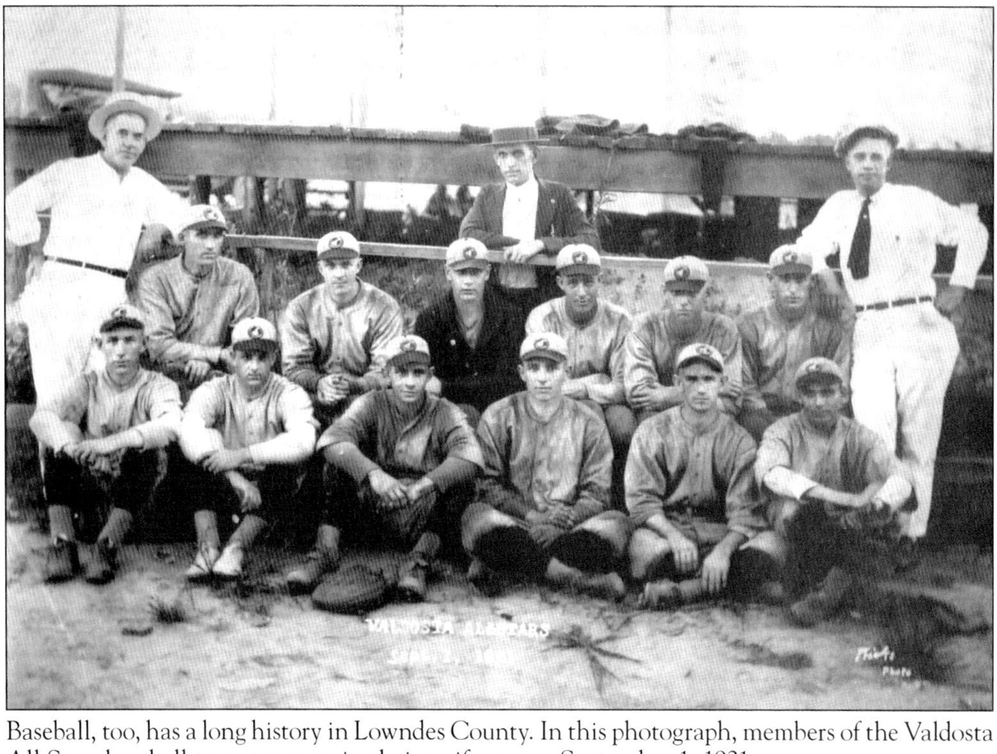

Baseball, too, has a long history in Lowndes County. In this photograph, members of the Valdosta All-Stars baseball team are seen in their uniforms on September 1, 1921.

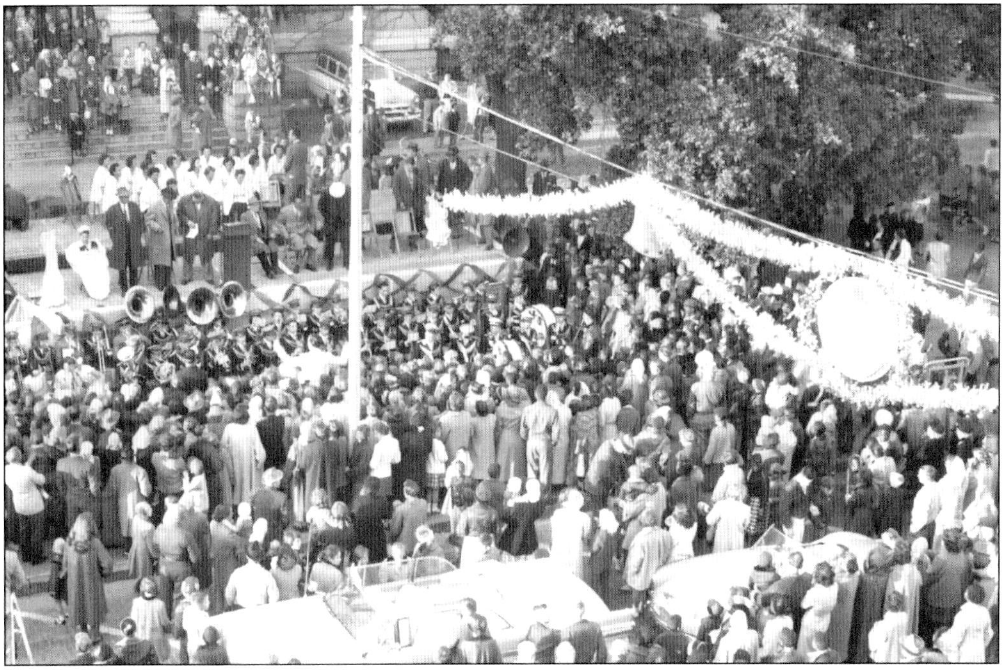

A very large assembly of local resident on the south side of the Lowndes County Courthouse spills over onto East Central Avenue. The time is the late 1950s, and the occasion may well be the annual Christmas parade, traditionally held on the evening of Thanksgiving Day. The man standing just to the left of the speaker's podium is Noah Langdale Jr.

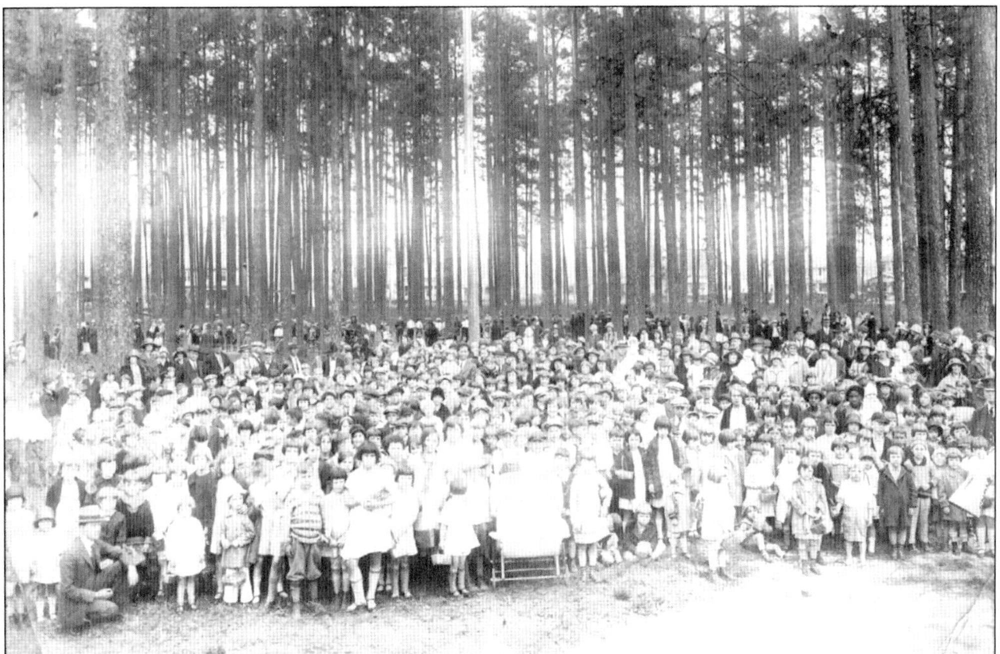

The event pictured here is a community Easter egg hunt in 1927 on the campus of Georgia State Woman's College in Valdosta. The site appears to be approximately at Georgia Avenue and North Patterson Street at the north end of the campus.

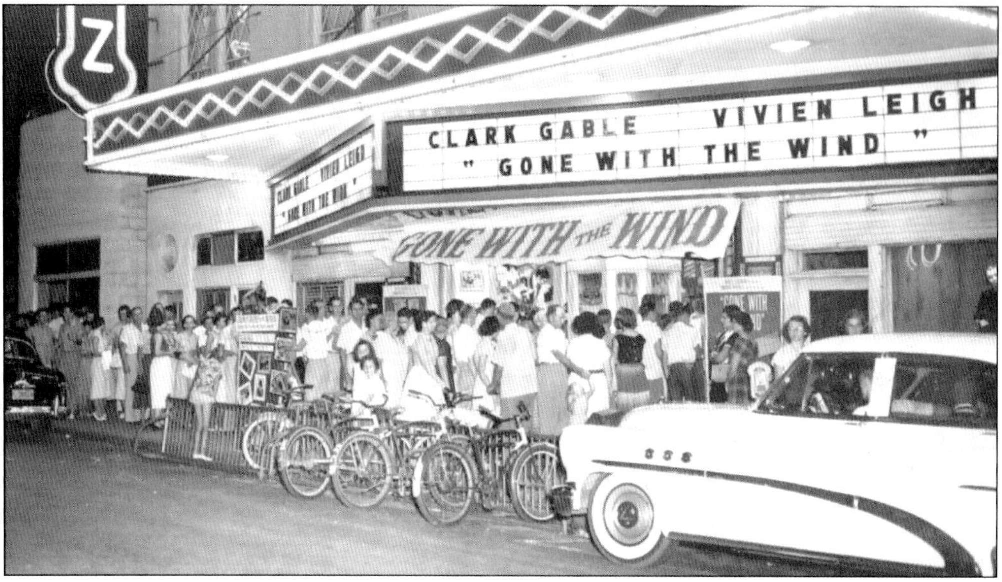

In the 1950s, the Ritz Theater on North Patterson Street in Valdosta presented a re-release of the exceptionally popular 1939 motion picture *Gone With the Wind.* The size of the crowd of patrons waiting to purchase tickets emphasizes the movie's continuing popularity. The ticket prices shown, ranging from 25¢ for children to 75¢ for adults, make certain that large audiences will attend each showing, while the advertising assures viewers that the motion picture is "COMPLETE! INTACT!"

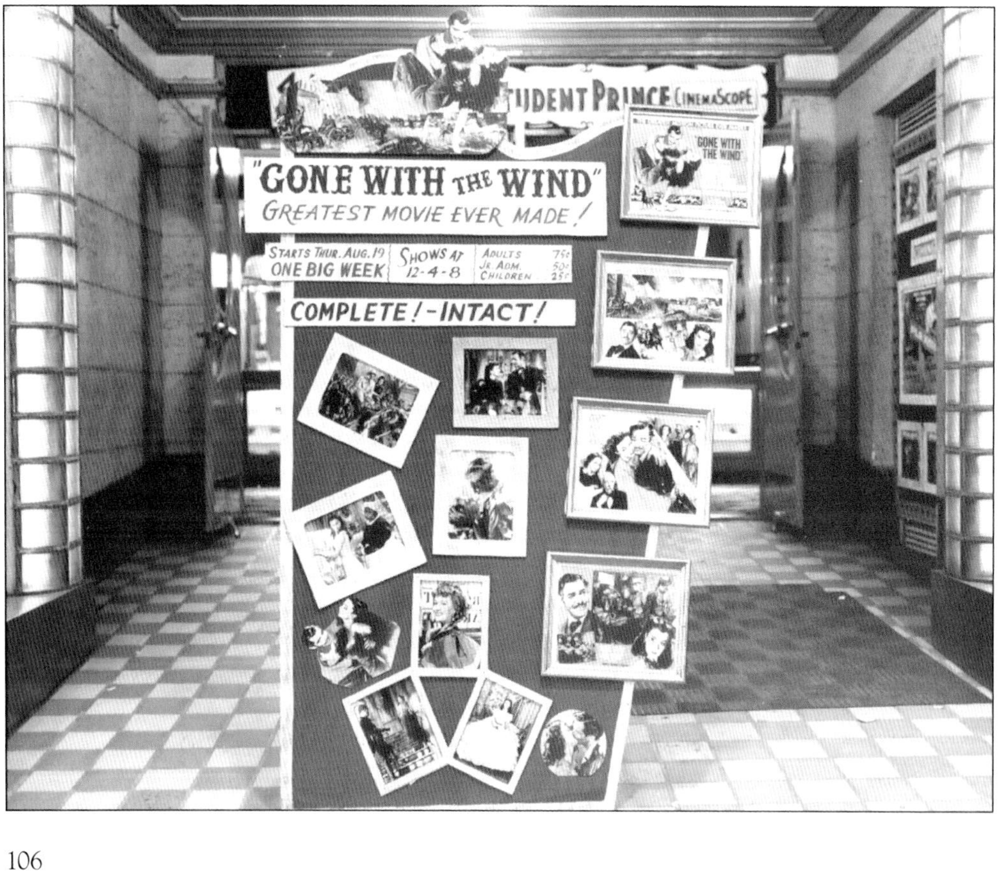

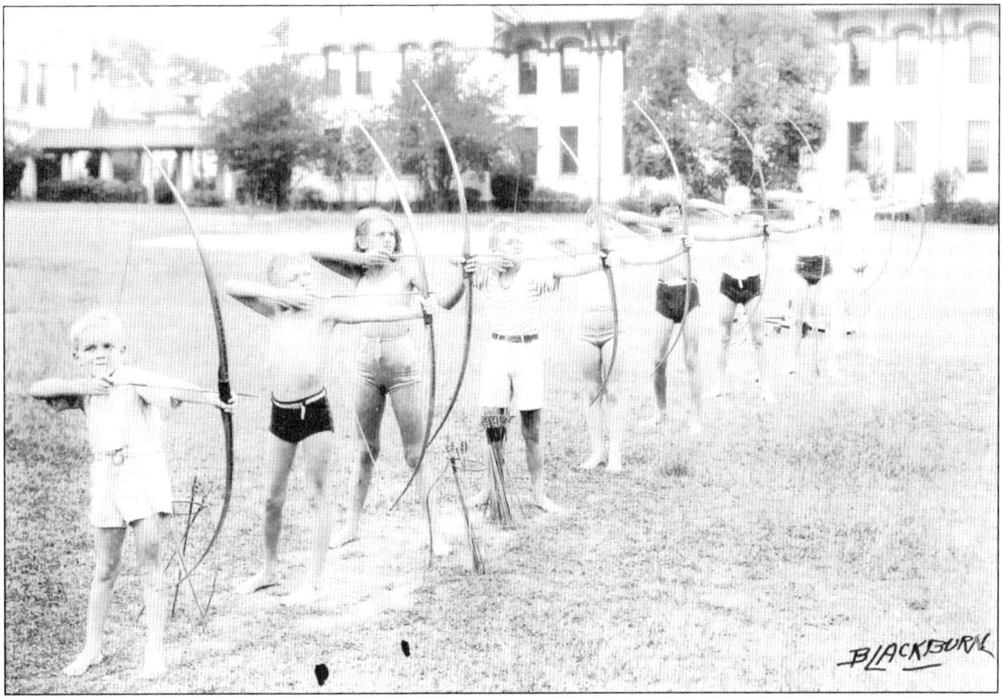

The young people in the picture above are attending a YMCA summer camp on the campus of Georgia State Woman's College in Valdosta in August 1938.

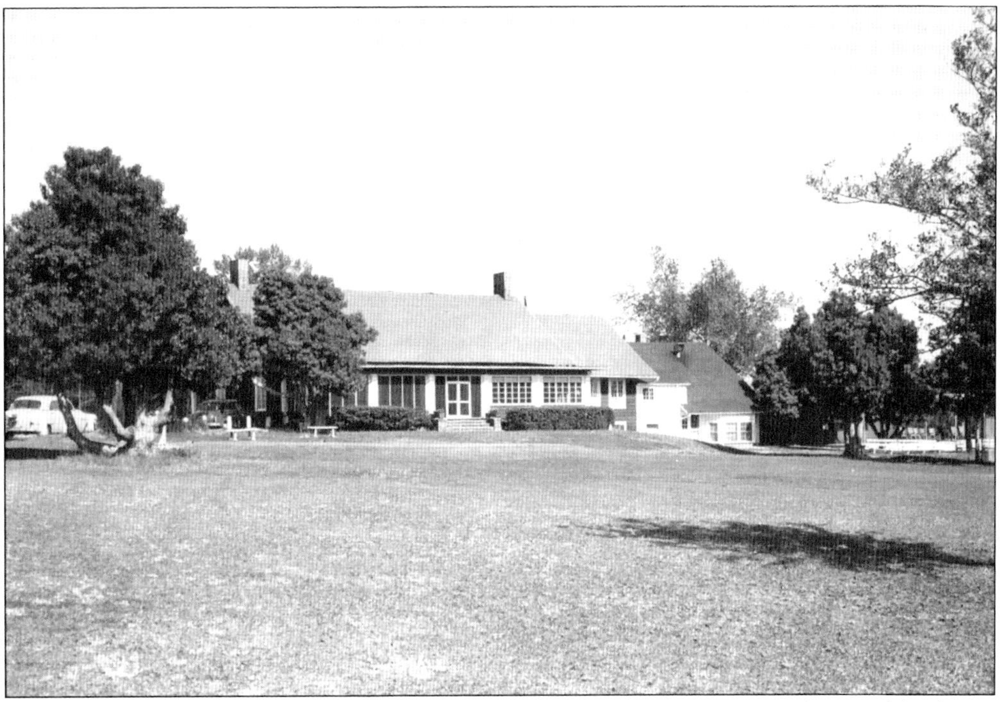

This is the old clubhouse at the Valdosta County Club. The structure was destroyed by fire in 1958 and subsequently replaced by a new and much larger building. The image apparently dates from the mid-1950s.

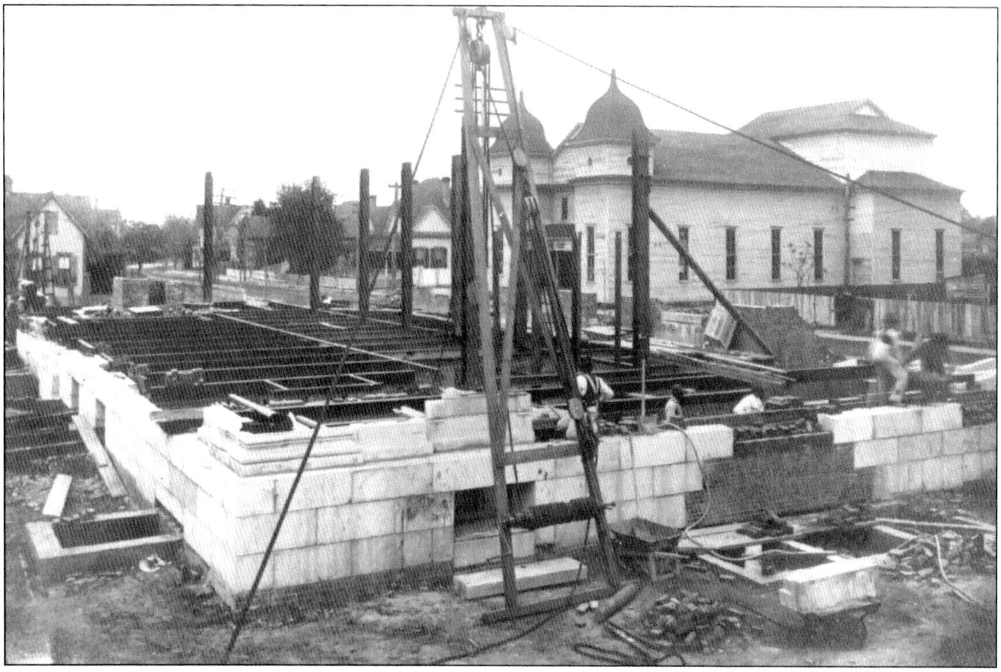

The two pictures show the progress of the 1908 construction of the Valdosta Post Office and Federal Building on Lee Street between East Valley Street and East Central Avenue. The top photograph, made at a very early stage of the construction, includes in the area to the right the old Valdosta Opera House, which became the first home of the Tabernacle Baptist Church. The lower photograph shows the building with the walls virtually completed. This structure was the post office and Federal Building from 1908 until 1969, when a new Federal Building opened on North Patterson Street. The old Federal Building then became Valdosta's city hall in 1970.

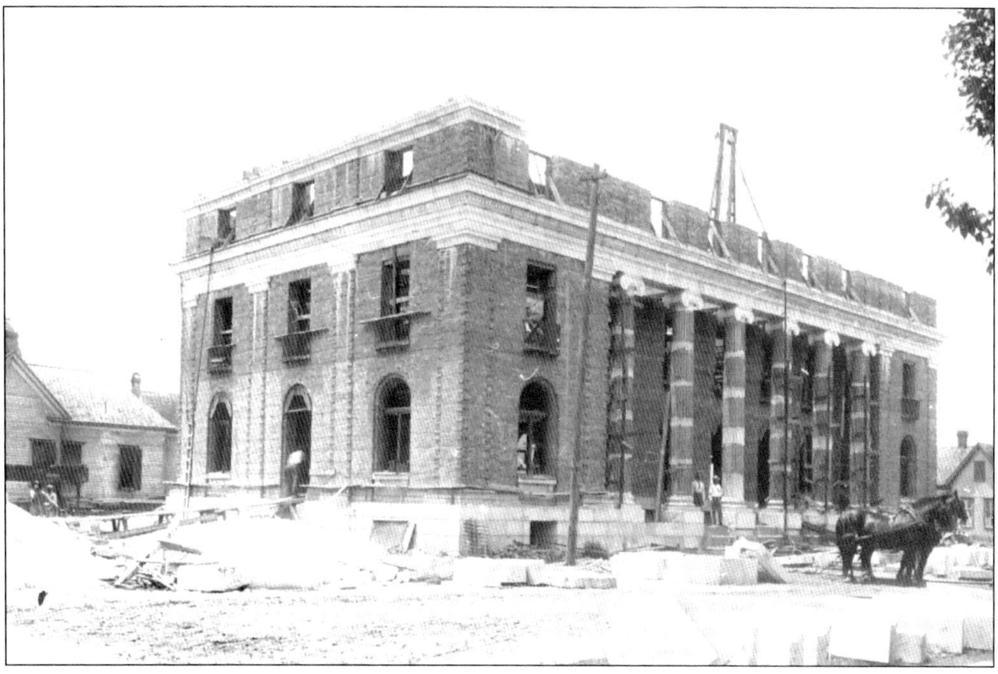

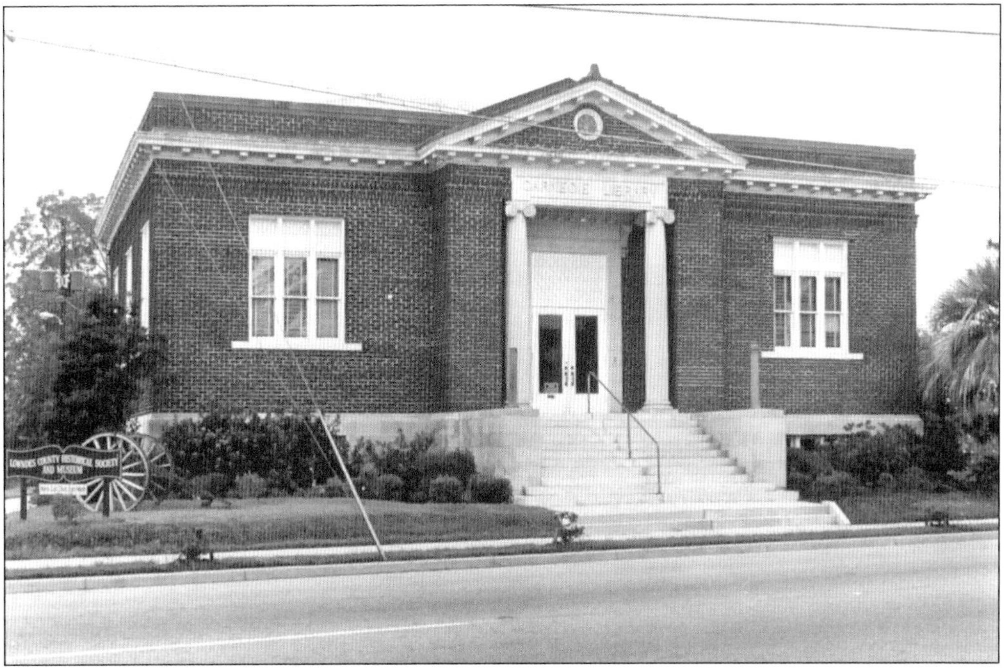

These images demonstrate the disparate fates of outdated public buildings. Above is the Valdosta Carnegie Library, constructed in 1913 at a cost of $40,000. Located at 305 West Central Avenue, it became the Lowndes County Historical Society's museum in 1977 after a new regional library was built on Woodrow Wilson Drive. The sad image below shows the old Valdosta City Hall when it was being torn down in the 1960s. The site became a parking lot, and it remains a parking lot today.

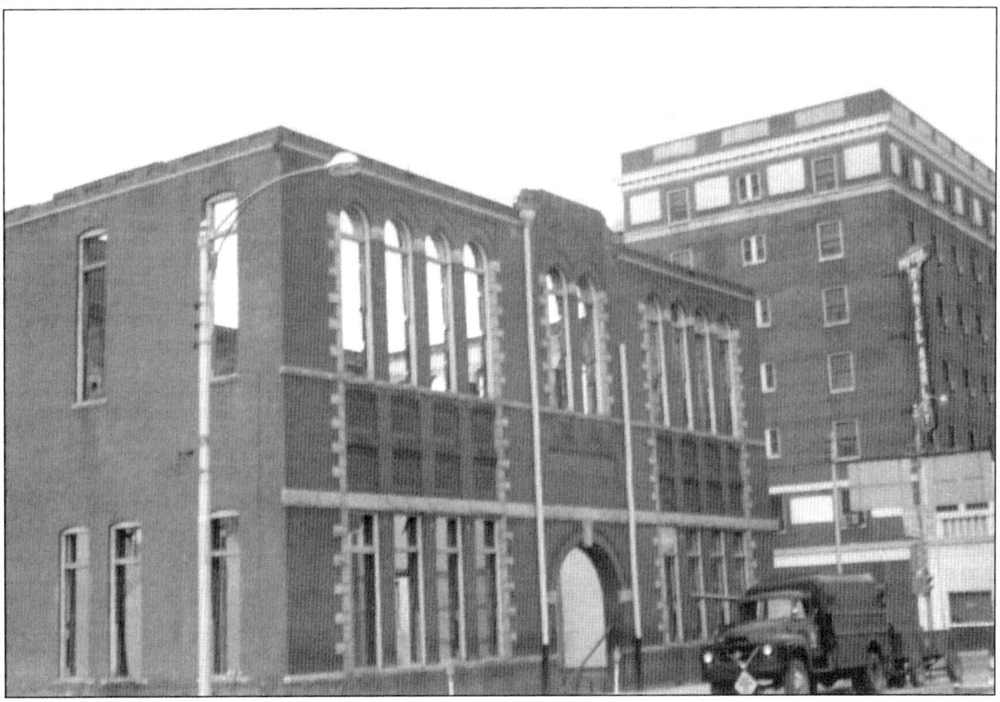

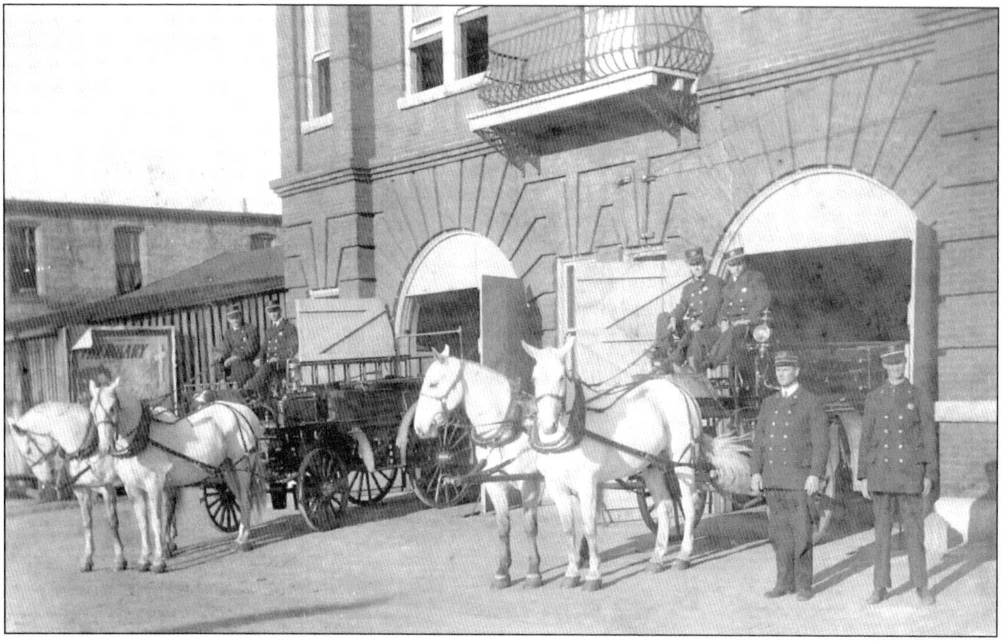

Both photographs show the Valdosta Fire Department's headquarters at 107 North Toombs Street at two different times years apart. At the top, in the 1890s or early 20th century, the fire engines are still powered by what appear to be white horses, possibly white mules. By the time of the lower picture, perhaps in the 1930s or 1940s, the internal combustion engine has taken over and much faster trucks are in use.

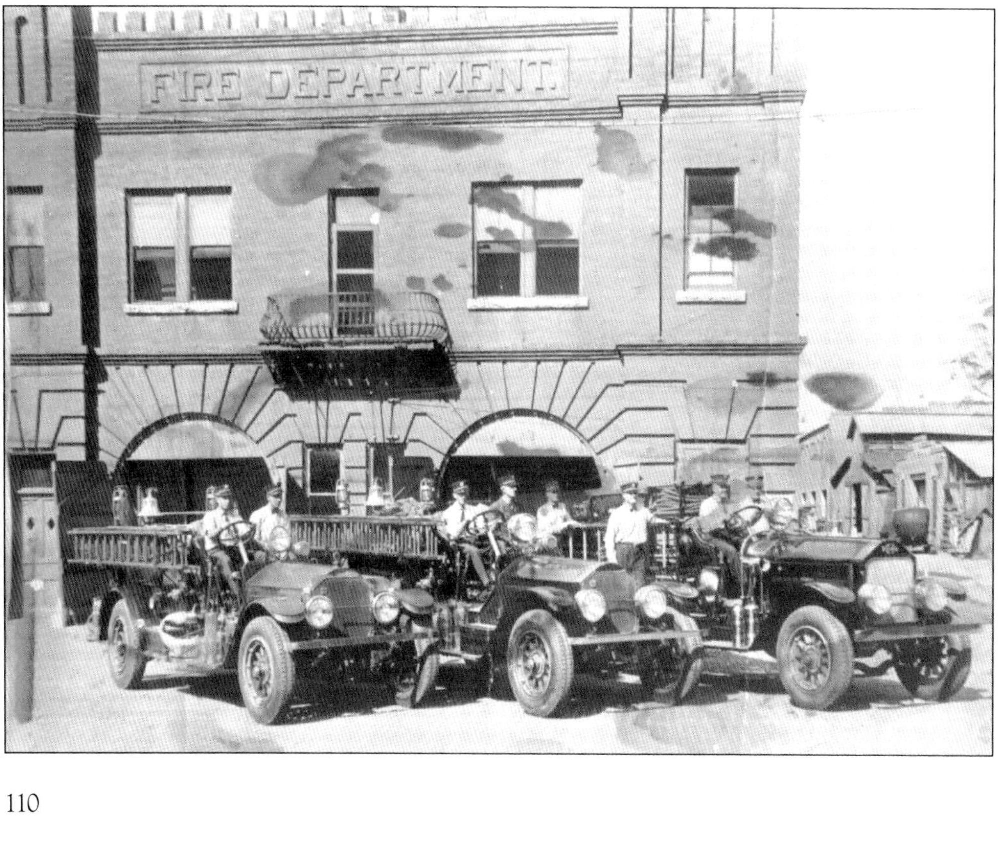

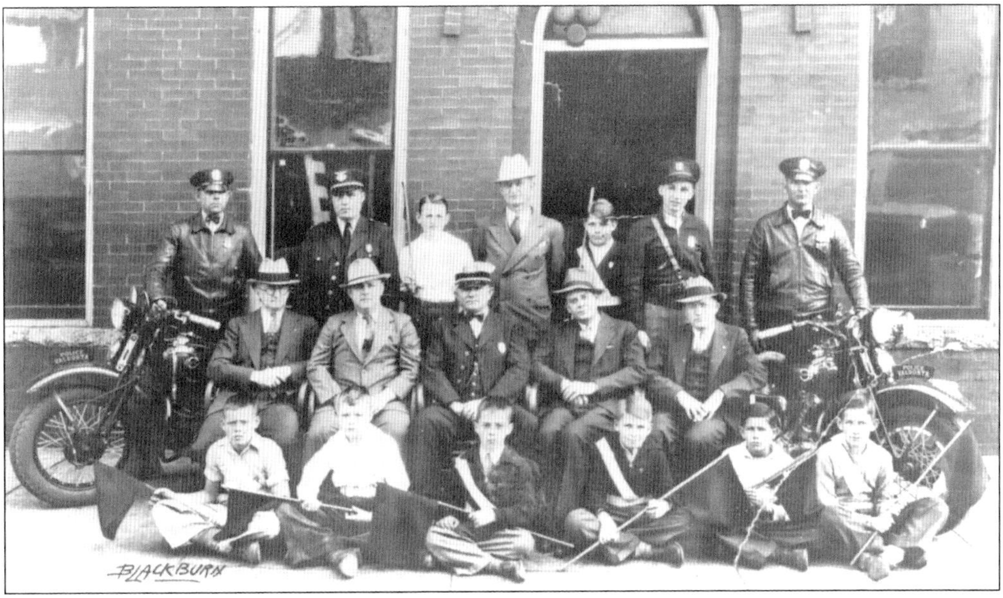

Shown here are members of the Valdosta Police Department in 1937 with school boys serving as Junior Police and prominent civilians. From left to right are (first row) unidentified, James Oliver, Billy Vallotton, Veran Blackburn, and two unidentified; (second row) Dr. Joyce F. Mixon, Nelse Holcombe, Chief R. L. Kemp, George L. Converse, and Dr. Joseph D. Durrenberger; (third row) E. K. Cooey, Lonnie Murphy, Jean Jenkins, Dr. T. Barron Gibson, Bill Briggs, Keepee Pitts, and Herman Carter.

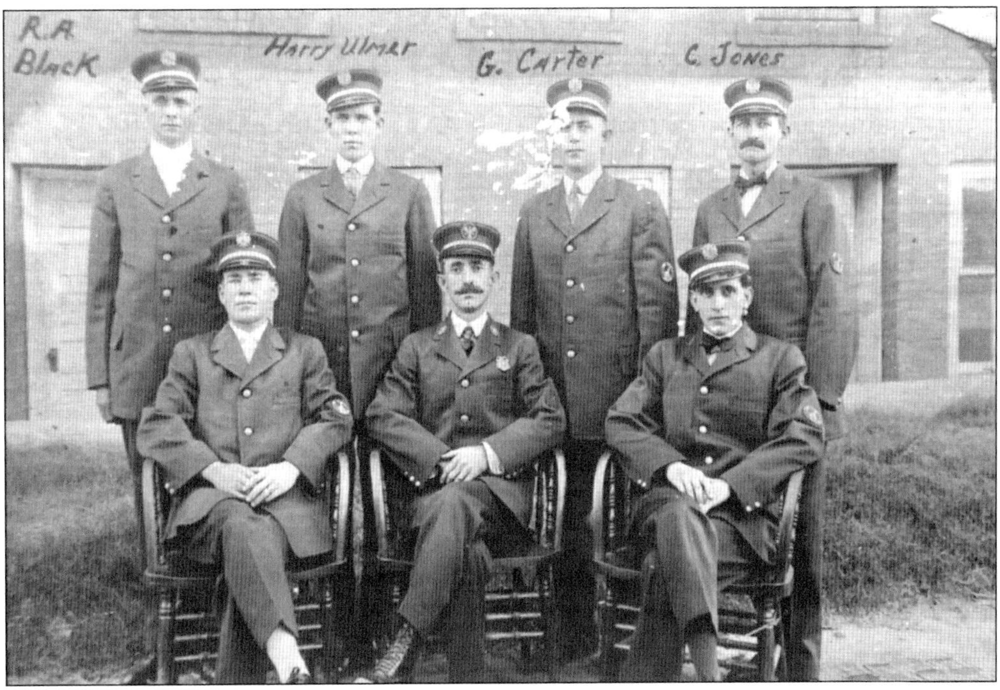

Valdosta firefighters pose for a formal portrait at the Toombs Street station in the 1920s. From left to right are (first row) Allen Touchton, Chief Tom Cook, and ? Ford; (second row) R. A. Black, Harry Ulmer, G. Carter, and C. Jones.

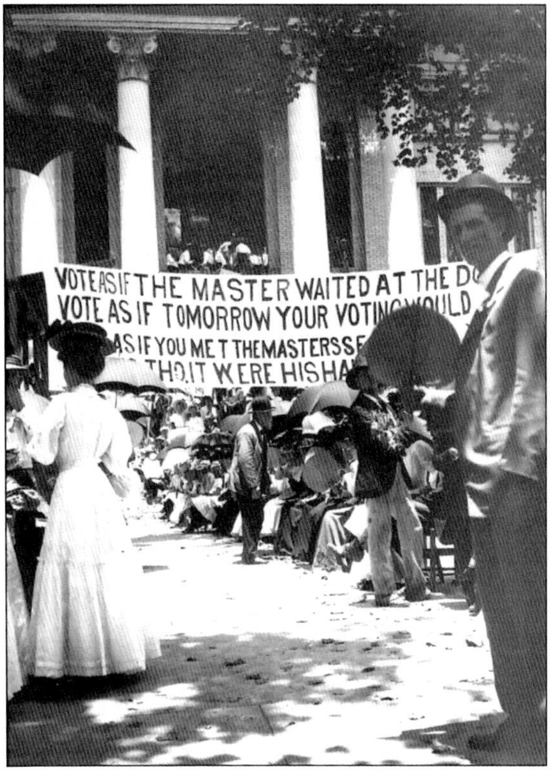

Shown here are two scenes at the Lowndes County Courthouse during the great Lowndes County Prohibition Referendum on June 24, 1907. Newspapers described the referendum as being "the most remarkable election ever held in Georgia." The top picture depicts the crowd, made up mostly of singing and praying female prohibitionists, through which a male voter had to walk to cast his ballot inside the courthouse, Note the banner overlooking the scene. The bottom image provides a close-up view of the crowd from the courthouse steps looking toward East Central Avenue. The figure in the foreground is Luther Rice Christie, a Baptist minister who led the Prohibition campaign in Lowndes County. Possibly it is superfluous to say that Lowndes County overwhelmingly voted to go "dry."

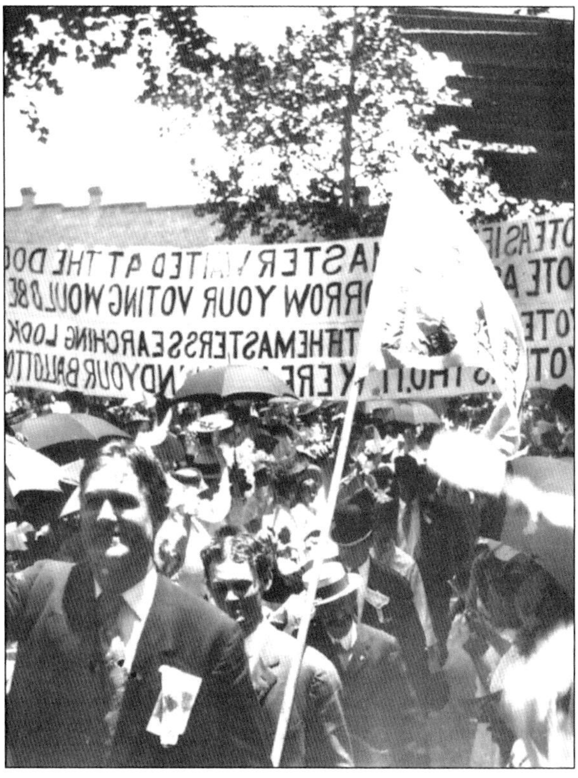

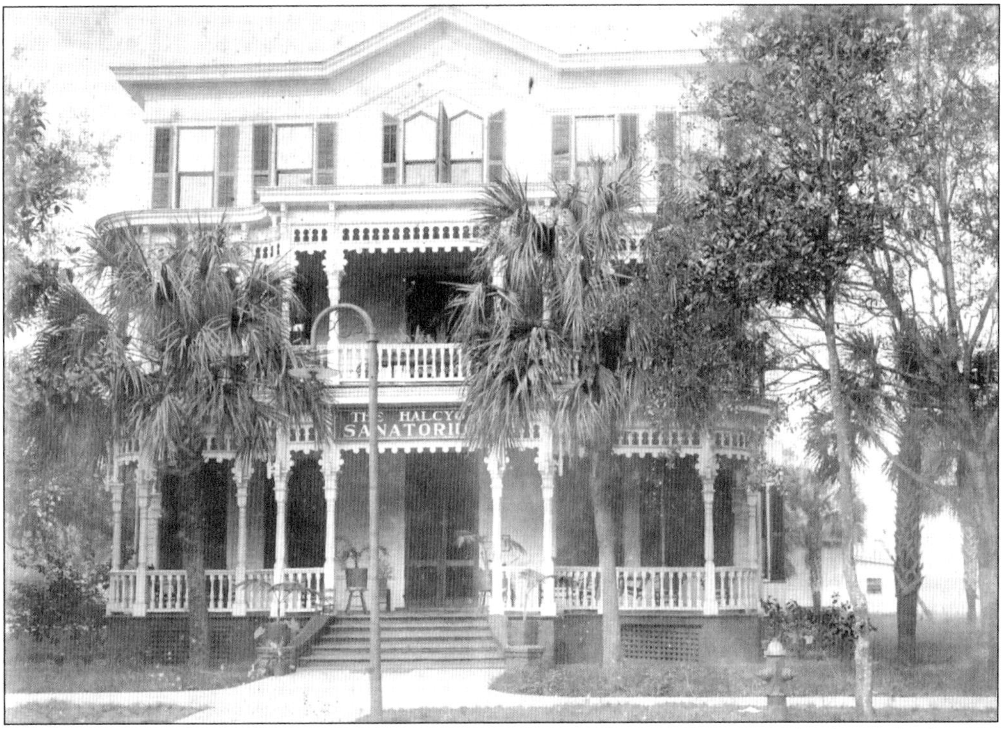

Pictured on this page are two of the earliest hospitals in Lowndes County, both of which were situated in Valdosta. At the top is the Halcyon Sanitarium, which was on North Troup Street. About 1917, Drs. Alex G. Little and Archie Griffin opened the Little-Griffin Private Hospital. The address originally was 1310 North Patterson Street, later 1306 North Patterson. The picture shows the original configuration of the facility, which changed over time with the additions made to the building. Little-Griffin continued as the major hospital in the county until 1955 and the opening of Pineview General Hospital as a public medical facility. In vastly expanded form, Pineview General has been South Georgia Medical Center for a number of years.

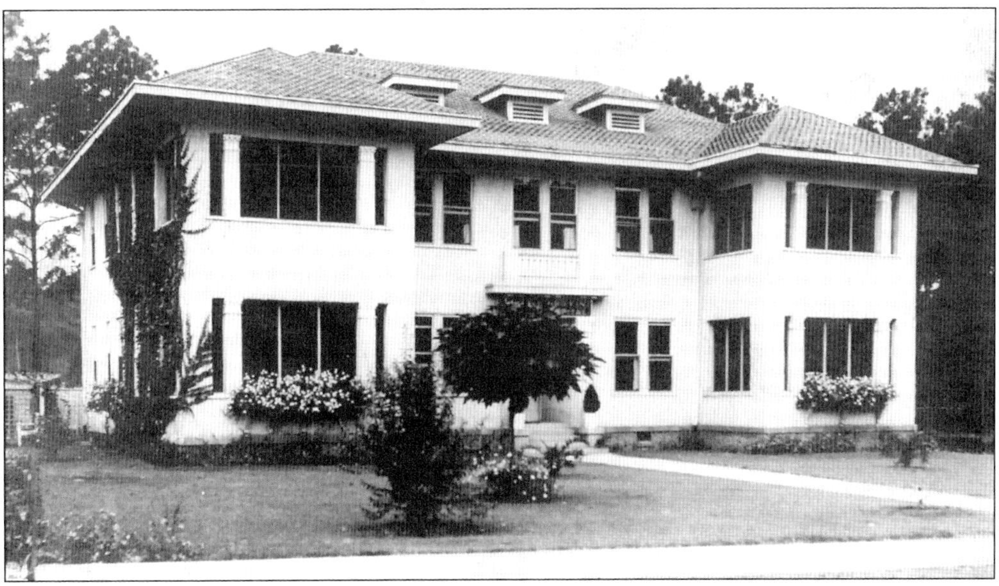

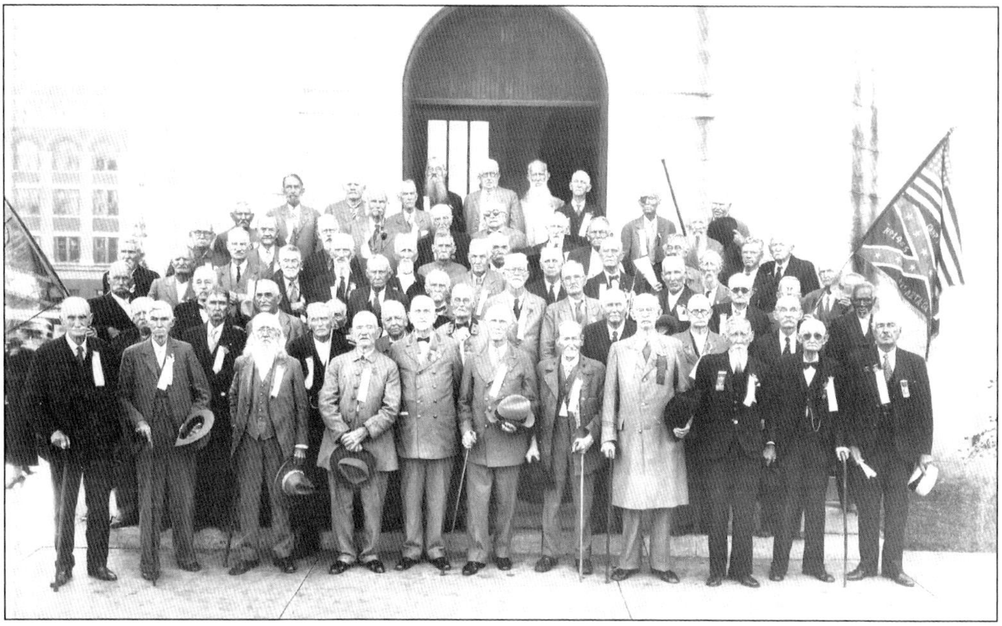

These two images are of events in Lowndes County involving veterans of military service. At the top is a group photograph of a Confederate veterans' reunion in Valdosta, date unknown. The site of the photograph is the steps to what was then the northeast door of the First Methodist Church on Patterson Street. In the background to the left is the McKey Building on the corner of North Patterson and East Central Avenue. At the bottom, the occasion is the groundbreaking for the American Legion Building on Williams Street, across from Valdosta High School, on September 3, 1931. The participants at the front are, from left to right, American Legion commander J. D. Everitts, Mrs. Nat Breedlove, Legion member E. N. Anderson, and Mrs. A. B. Clyatt, president of the Legion Auxiliary.

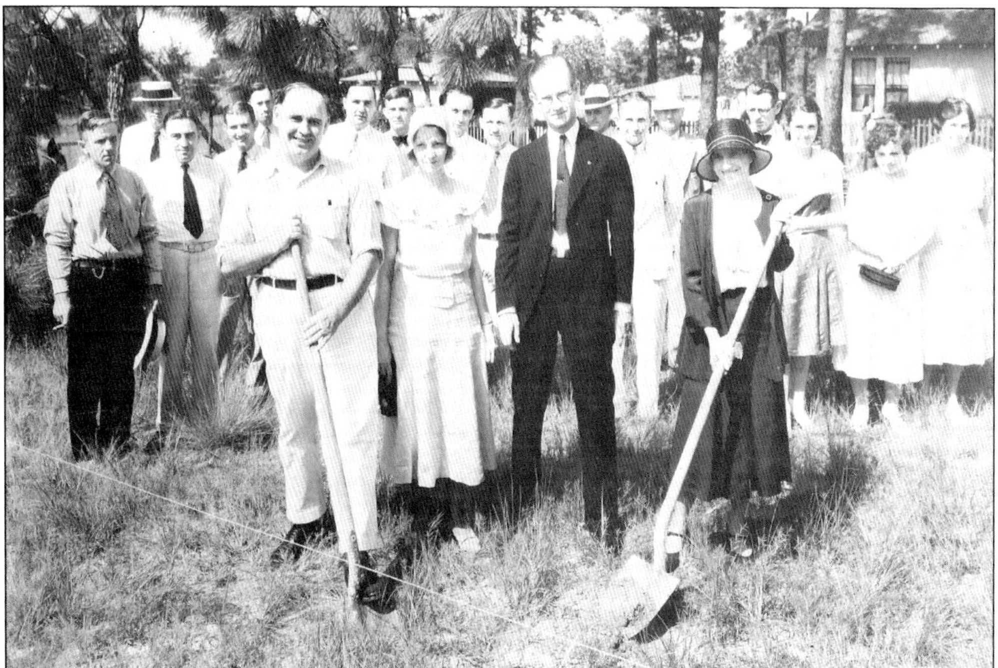

Shown here is the Harrell-Rogers house, built in 1938 at 1300 North Patterson Street. The image dates from 1972, when Lowndes County had an unusual snowfall. The house, as lovely as it was, was obliterated in 1976 to make way for a new building for the Southern Bell Telephone Company, now BellSouth. The replacement building currently is part of Valdosta State University.

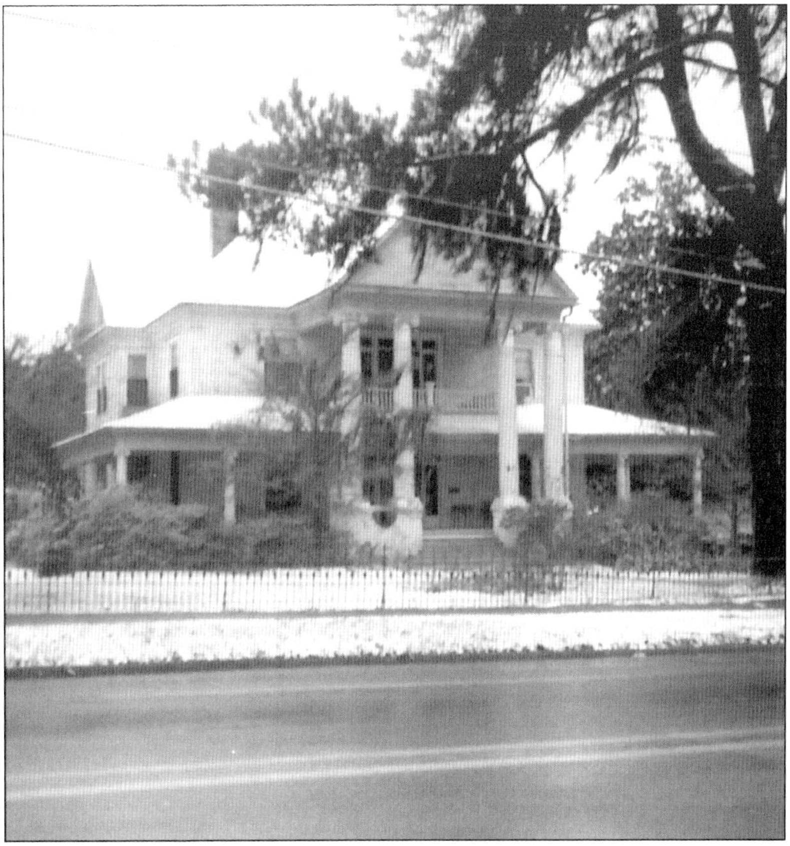

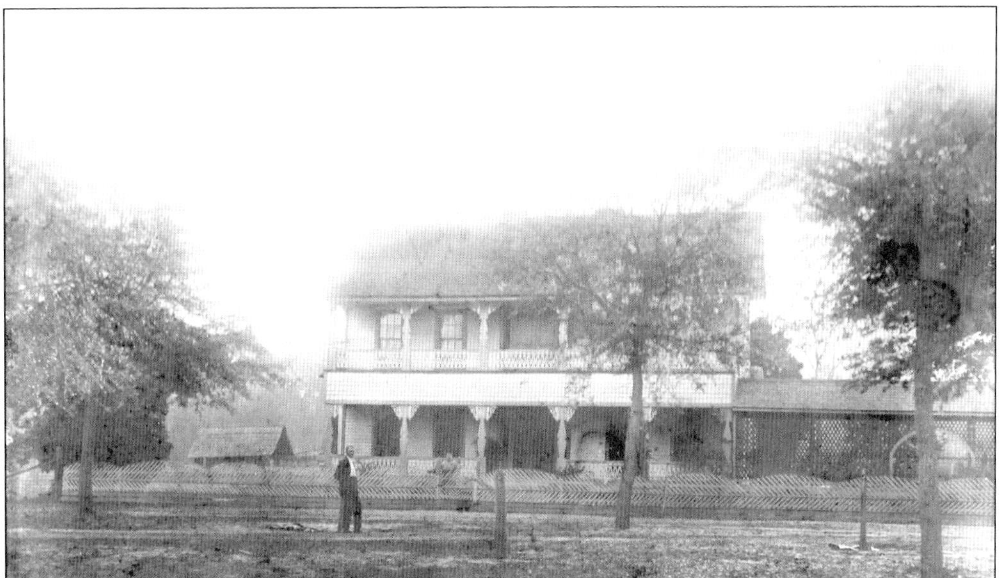

The home of Dr. Columbus Carter was at 203 Tomlinson Drive in Lake Park in the southern part of the county. The image appears to date from the 1880s–1890s. Dr. Carter died on November 11, 1893, and the house burned in 1992.

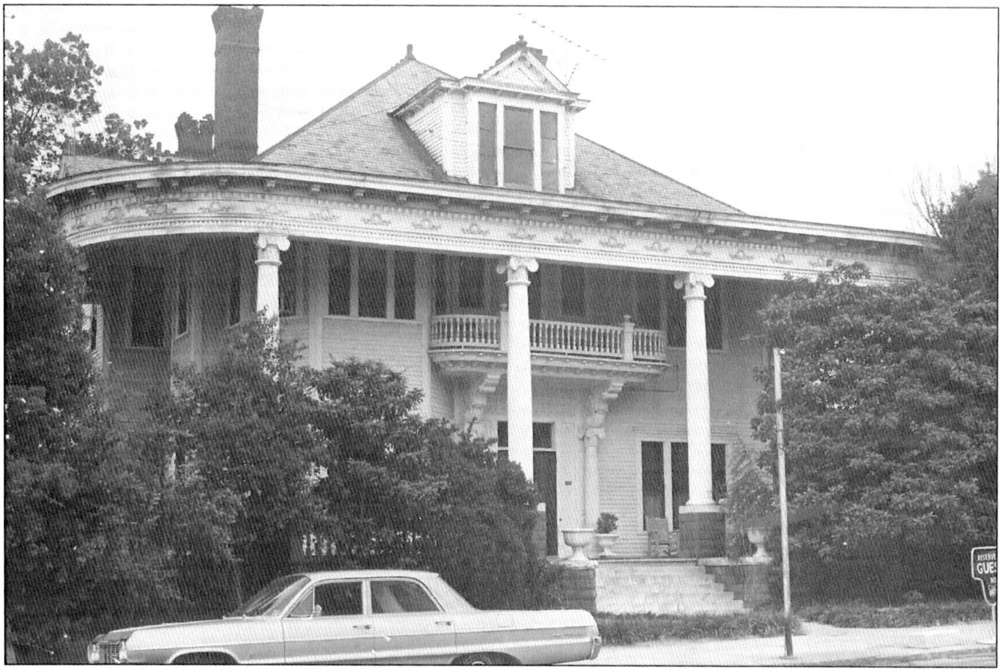

The Converse-Dalton house on North Patterson Street was one of Valdosta's stately homes and was affected by encroaching commercial buildings. However, it was saved from destruction when purchased by the Junior Service League, which restored the house and uses it for various purposes and occasions.

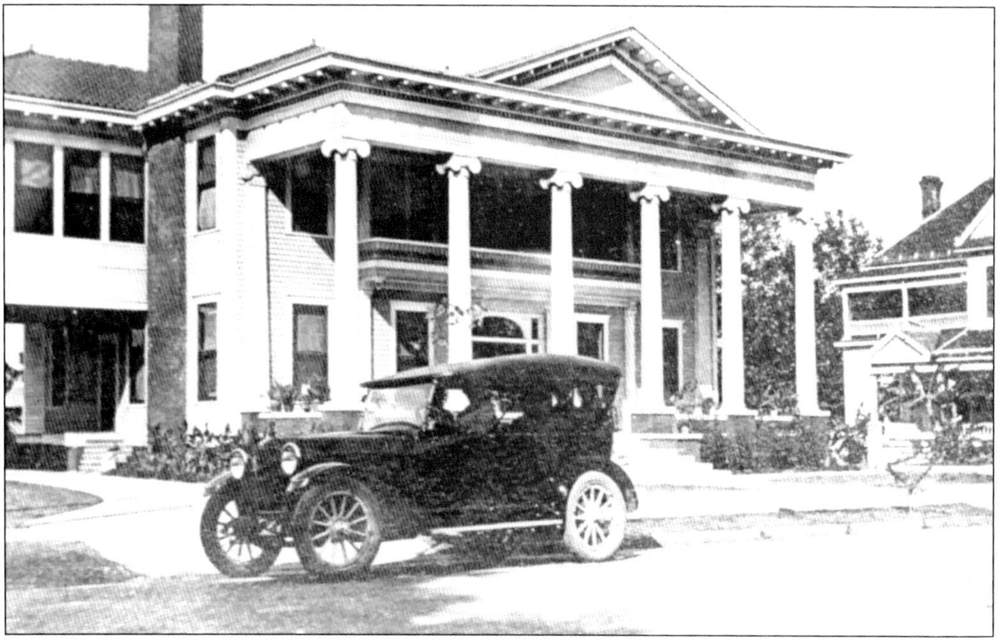

The E. R. Barber house, now known as the Barber-Pittman house, at 416 North Ashley Street was the home of Valdosta businessman E. R. Barber. The image is from the 1920s. Later the structure suffered considerable neglect, but more recently, it was preserved and restored and became the home of the Valdosta–Lowndes County Chamber of Commerce.

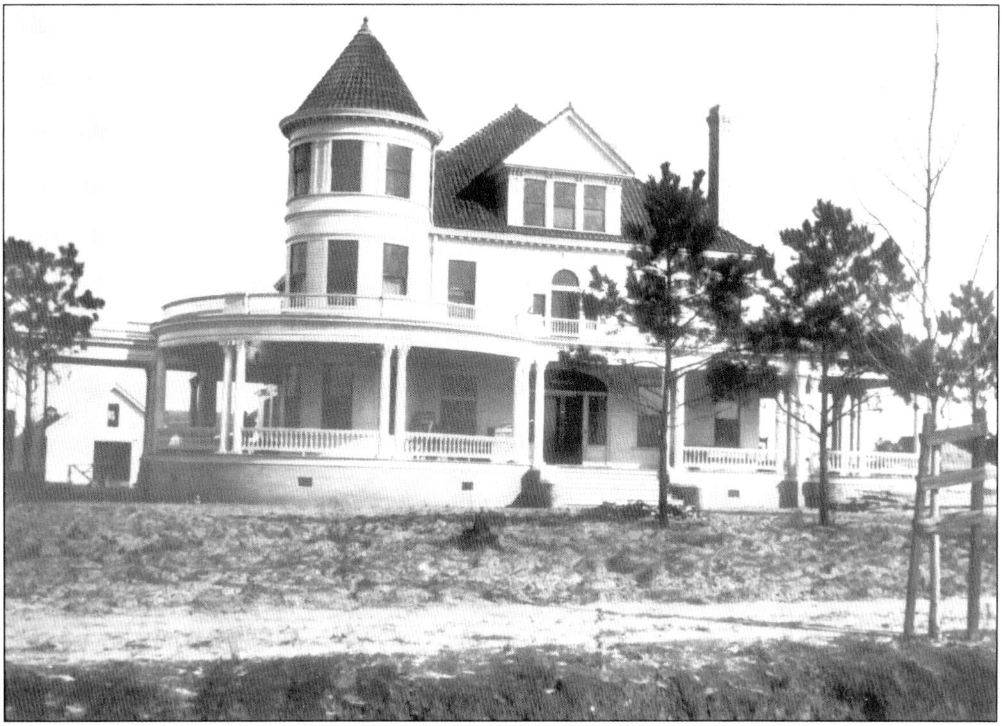

Here the John N. Bray house at 1203 North Patterson Street is seen soon after the completion of construction early in the 20th century. Located at the corner of Patterson and East Ann Streets, the house and several others were torn down in the early 1960s to make way for the construction of the Brookwood Plaza Shopping Center. The recently reconstructed shopping facility now is the University Center of Valdosta State University.

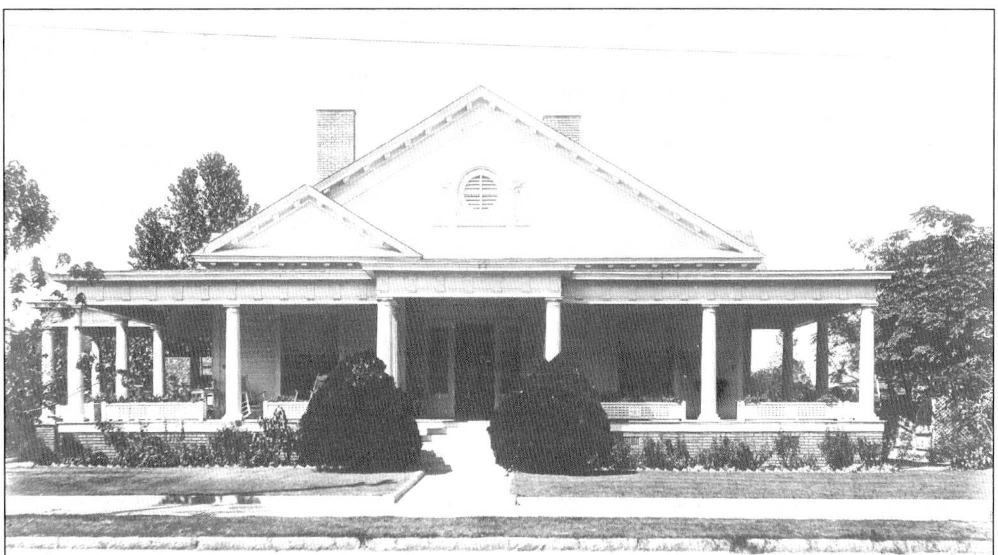

The George W. Varn house at 1002 North Patterson Street suffered the same fate as many other of the fine homes in the same area. It no longer exists. On the site of the Varn house, torn down in the 1970s, is now a small church and a book store.

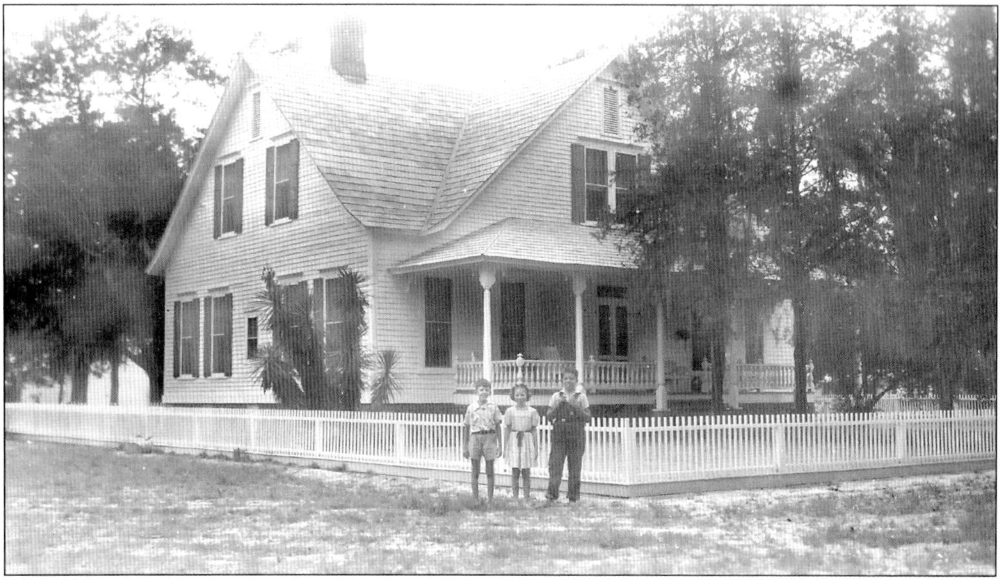

The J. B. Copeland house was originally in a rural area of Lowndes County bordering the northwest side of Valdosta. When Valdosta expanded, the house came within the city limits at 2114 Jerry Jones Road. Shown from left to right are Horace Hunt, Nell Fender, and Jimmy Copeland, son of J. B. Copeland. The Elder Mr. Copeland was a well-known attorney in Valdosta. His house was torn down at the beginning of the 1970s.

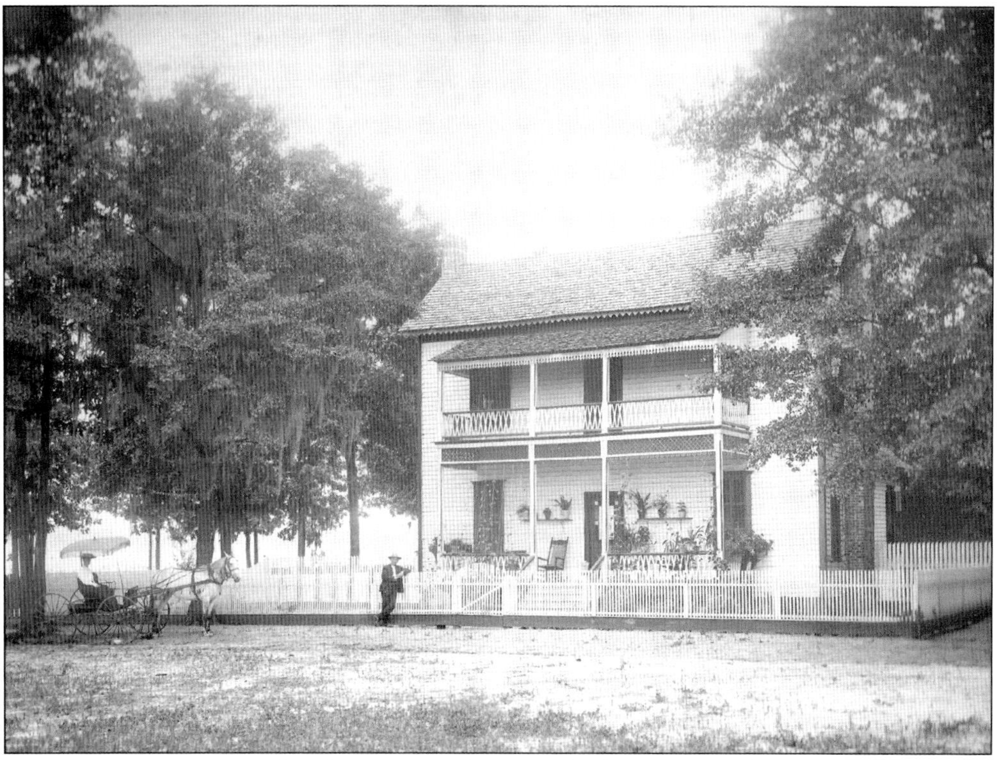

Shown above is a very good-looking country house at Naylor in eastern Lowndes County in the 1890s. The owner is unidentified.

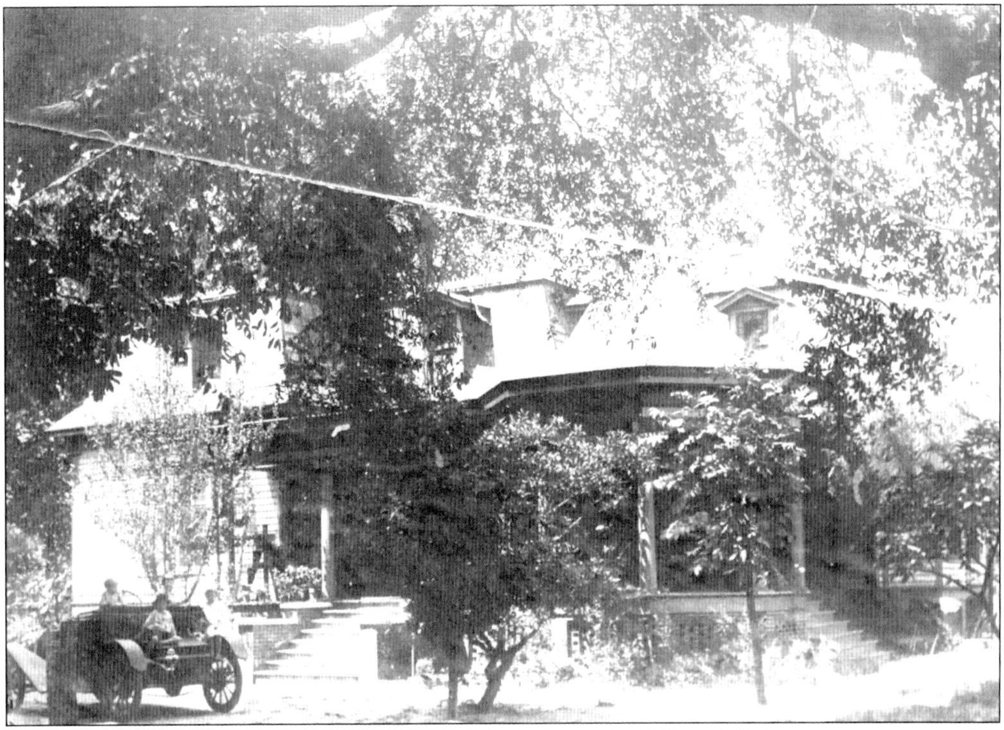

The W. M. Thomas house, located on a very shady lot at 706 West Hill Avenue, appears in this image from the 1920s.

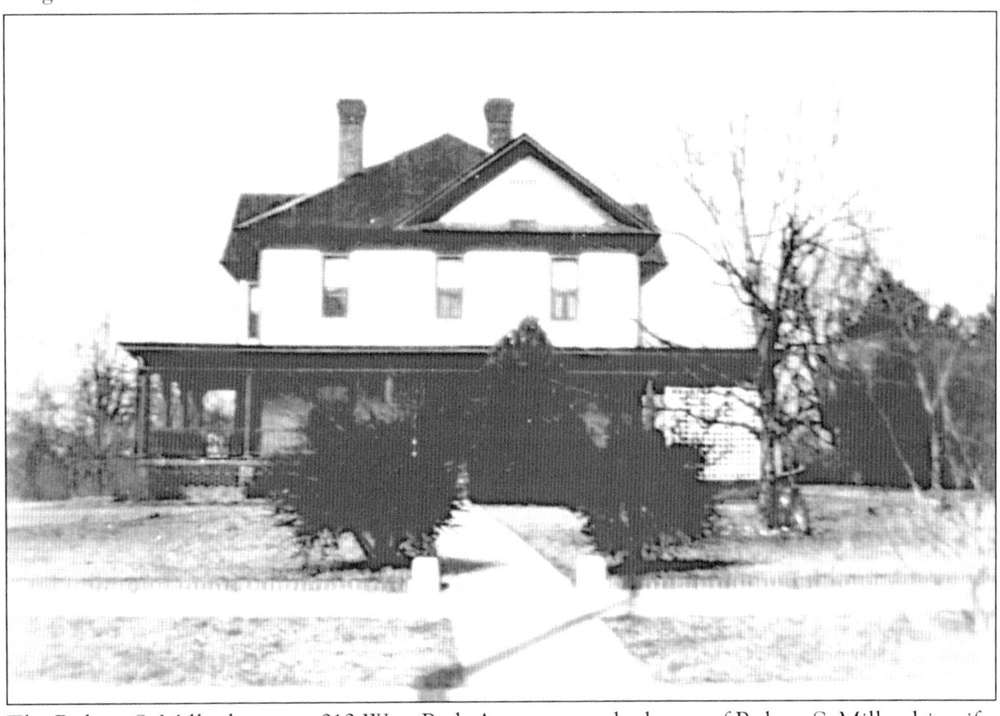

The Robert S. Miller house at 213 West Park Avenue was the home of Robert S. Miller, his wife, Uldine, and their five children from 1935 to 1950.

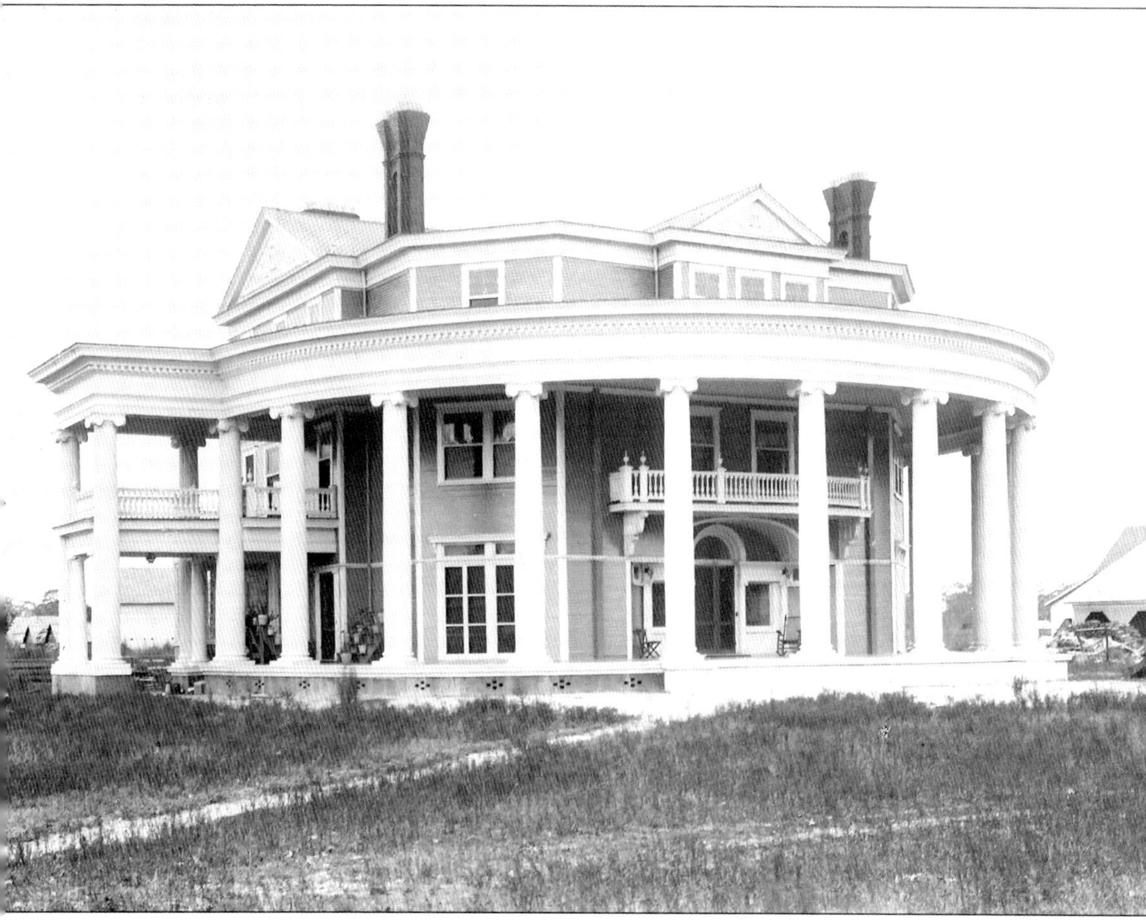

Construction on the Crescent, the home of W. S. West, began on North Patterson Street in 1897 and was completed in 1899. The picture is from 1899 or 1900, prior to the planting of any trees or shrubbery or the completion of any other landscaping work. In the 1950s, the Crescent was on the verge of destruction, but members of the Valdosta garden clubs mounted a successful campaign to save the house, which is now the headquarters of the garden clubs.

Shown right is Maj. George Putnam Moody, U.S. Army Air Corps, born in 1908 and a member of the U.S. Military Academy class of 1929. Major Moody died in the crash of an aircraft at Wichita, Kansas, on May 5, 1941. Moody Field in northern Lowndes County was named for him in 1942. In the picture below, a memorial plaque for Major Moody is dedicated at Moody Air Force Base of May 6, 1954. The Valdosta–Lowndes County Chamber of Commerce provided the plaque, and James Blanchard of the chamber is on the left with members of the Moody family.

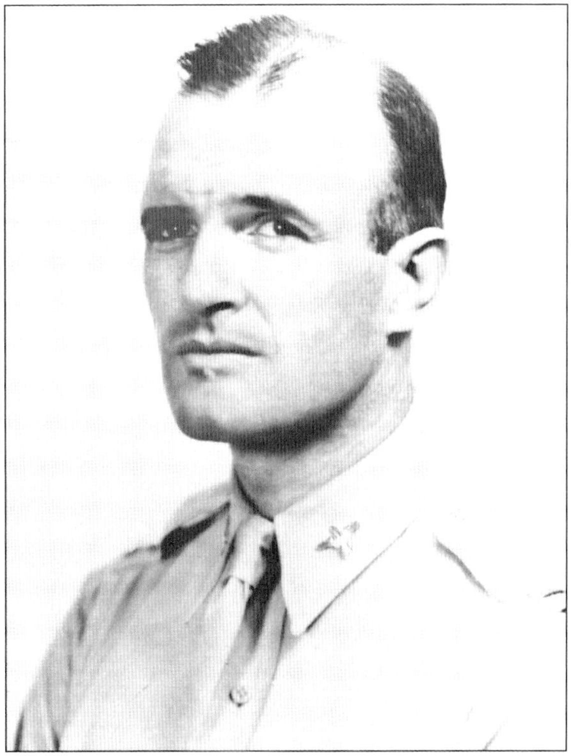

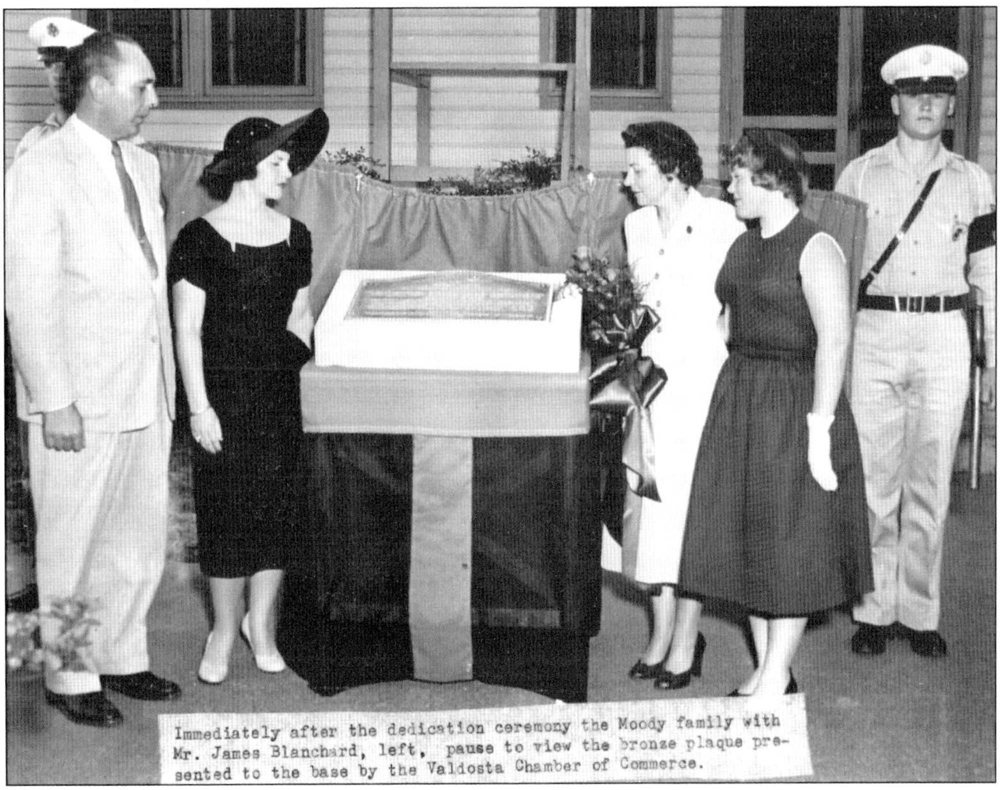

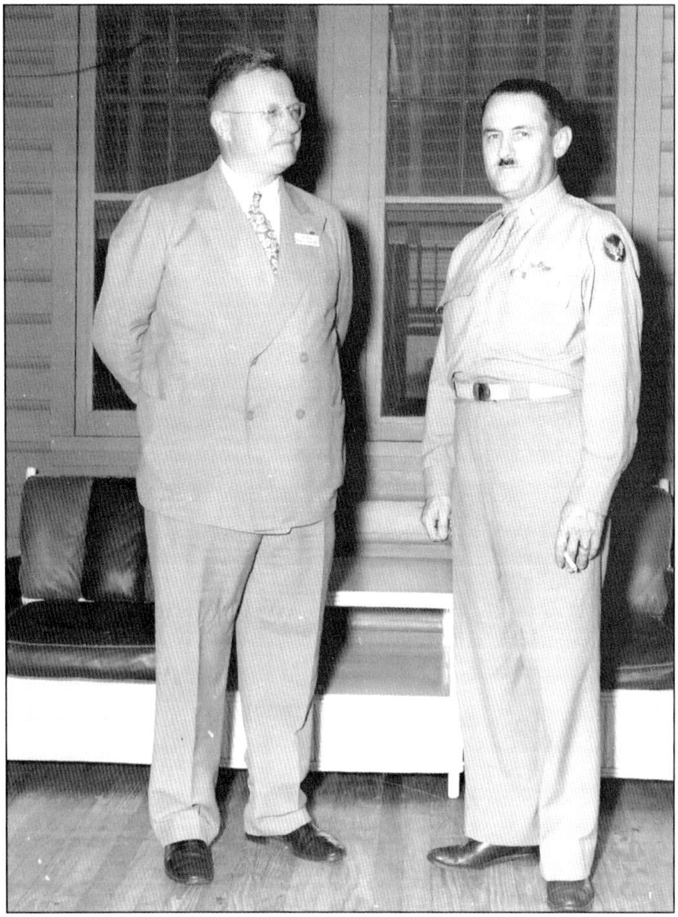

In this photograph, Frank L. Rose of Valdosta is shown with an Air Corps officer at Moody Field during World War II.

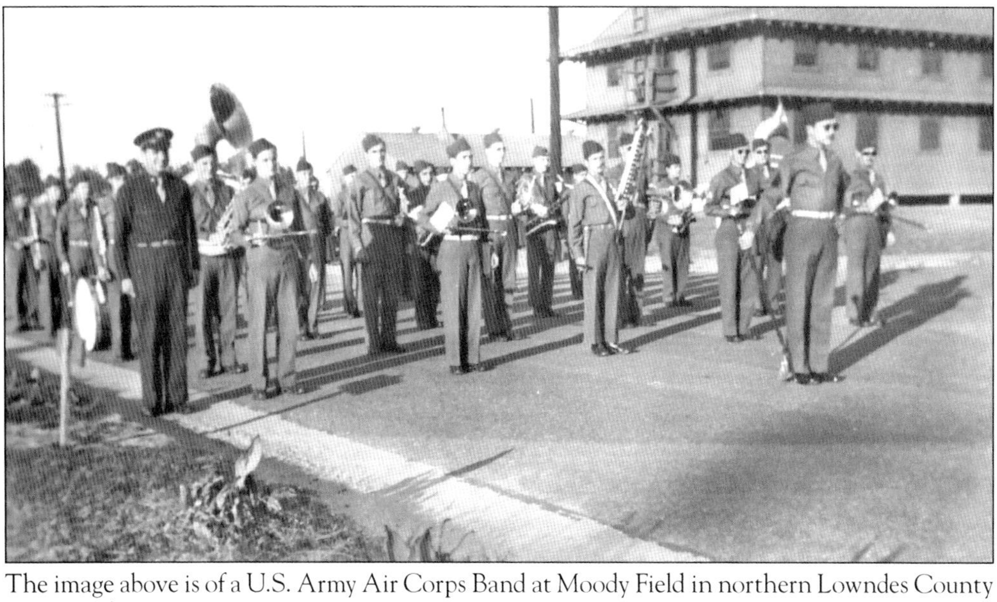

The image above is of a U.S. Army Air Corps Band at Moody Field in northern Lowndes County in November 1944.

Here a World War II war bond sale is underway in Valdosta. The booth's location was the entrance, next to the ticket booth, to the Ritz Theater on North Patterson Street. The exact date is unknown, but obviously it was between 1942 and 1945. The women in the sales booth cannot be identified.

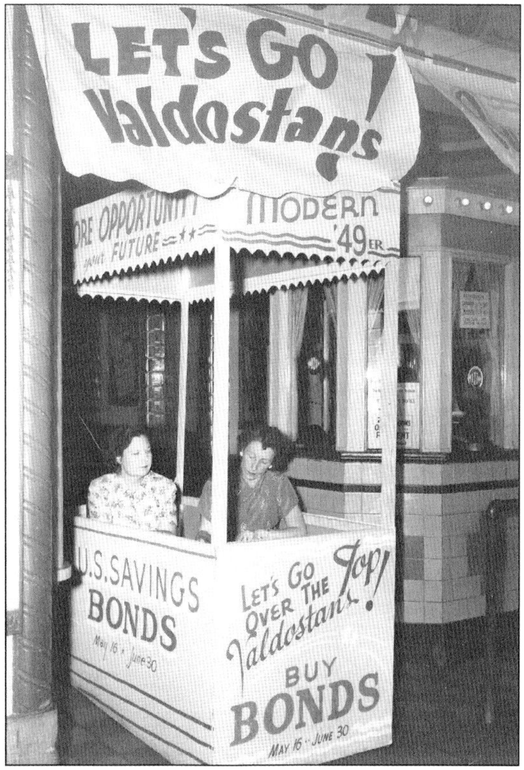

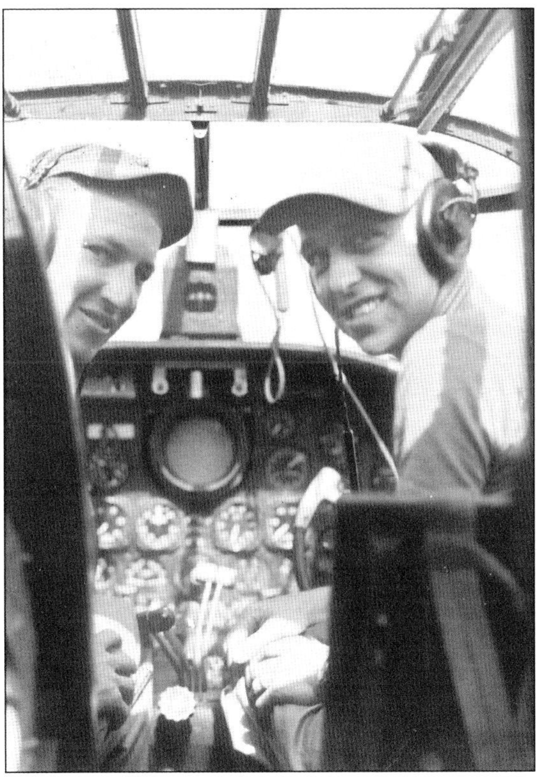

The two Valdostans in this photograph were in the Pacific theater of World War II in 1944. On the left is Lt. Frank Jarrell, U.S. Marine Corps, and on the right is Sgt. George "Bouncer" Smith. The location is the island of Saipan in the Marianas. Jarrell, by then a captain, was shot down and killed on May 3, 1945. Smith survived the war and afterward lived in Douglas, Georgia.

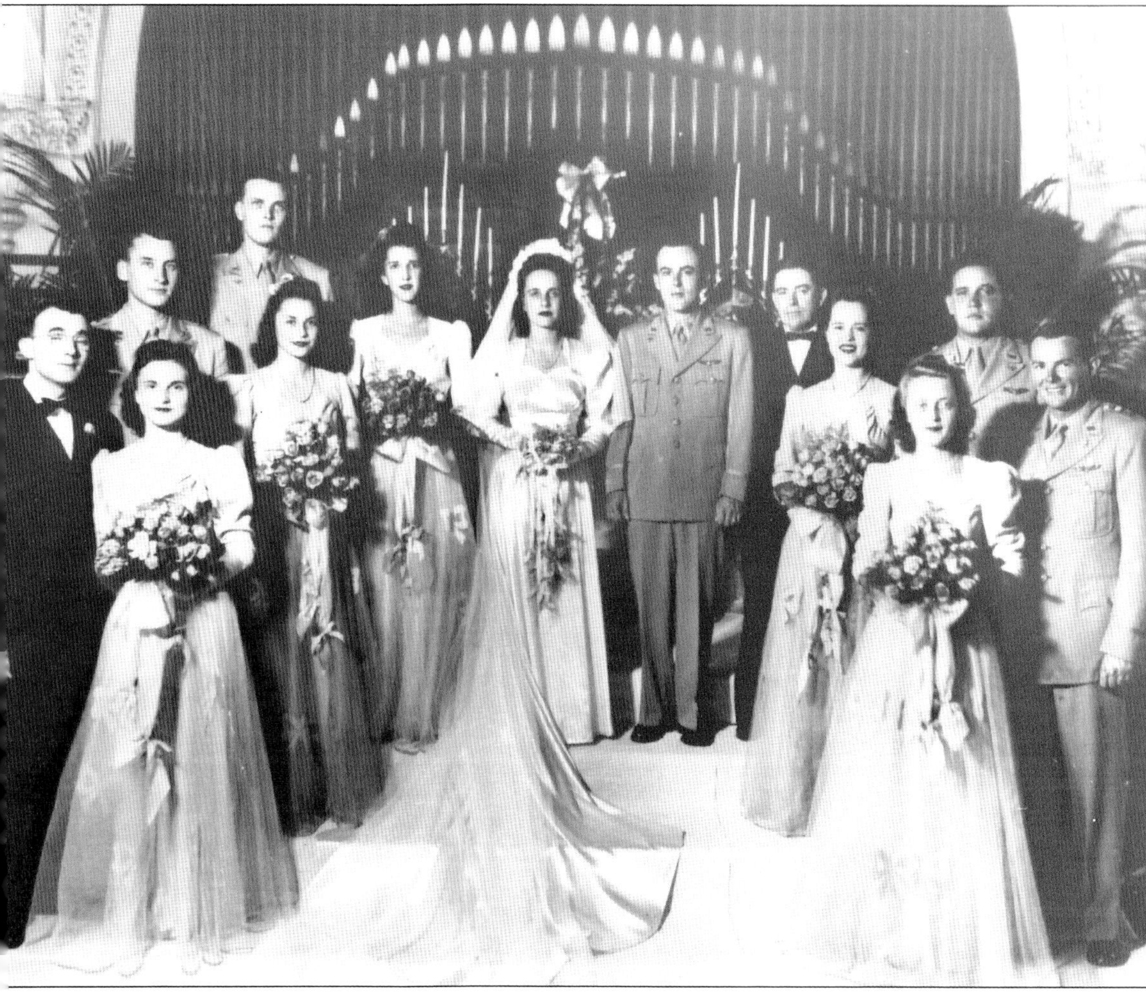

Pictured above is a wartime wedding on July 13, 1943, at the First Baptist Church of Valdosta. The bride and groom, in the center, are Mary Catherine Powell and Lt. Jim Williams. The bride's attendants, from left to right, are Fay Carroll, Mildred Griner, Evelyn Hewitt, Doris Terry, and Betty Sue Grant. The male members of the wedding, from left to right, are Frank Powell, Maj. Richard Lorenzen, Capt. Matthew Shannon, S. H. Williams, Capt. William R. Heck, and Maj. Henry "Buddy" Wills.

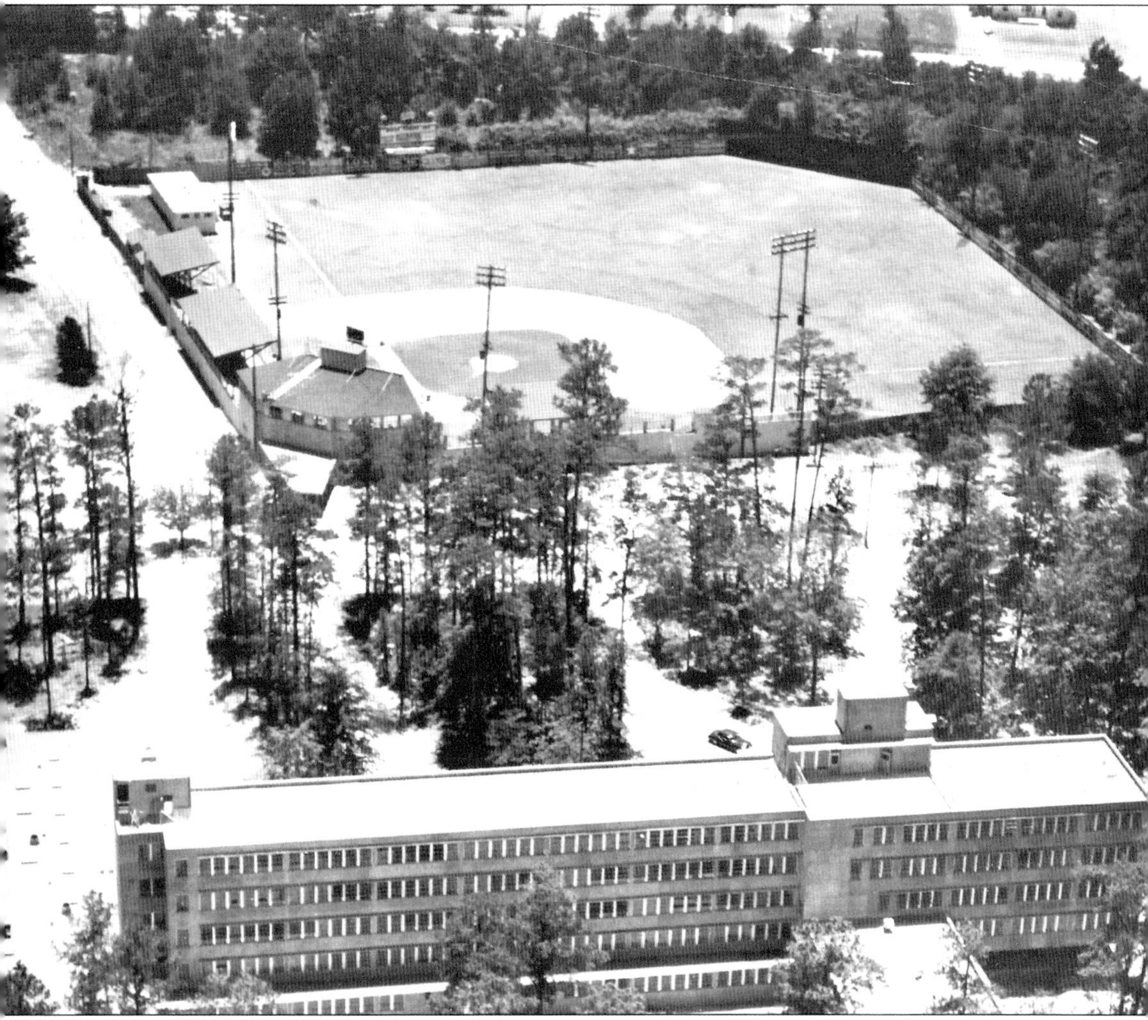

Pendleton Park, at the rear of this aerial photograph, was for many years the only stadium for a professional baseball team in Lowndes County. The picture, from the mid-1950s, shows in the foreground the new Pineview General Hospital, now South Georgia Medical Center. The ultimate fate of Pendelton Park was destruction; most of the site is now a parking lot for South Georgia Medical Center.

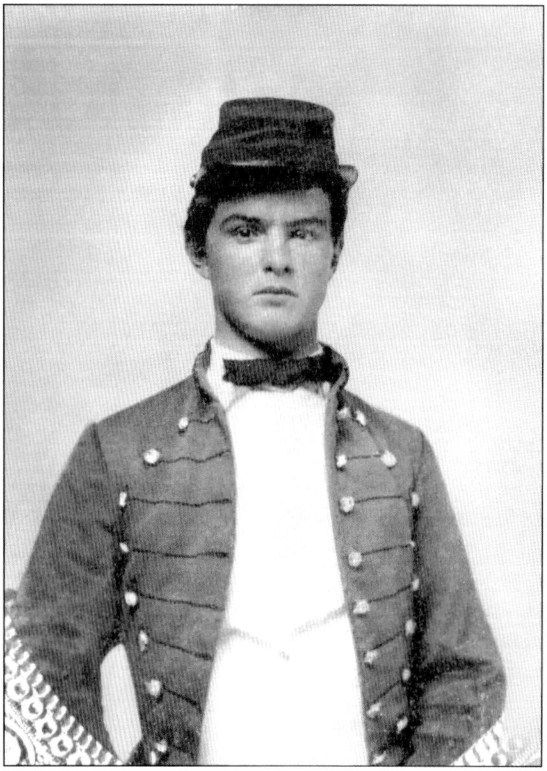

Reuben Roberds of Lowndes County here is pictured as a cadet at the Citadel in Charleston, South Carolina. At the age of 26, he was elected the first mayor of the new town of Valdosta, but when the Civil War erupted soon after, he volunteered. He was first a sergeant in the Valdosta Guard and advanced to the rank of major before being killed in a battle at Knoxville, Tennessee, in 1863.

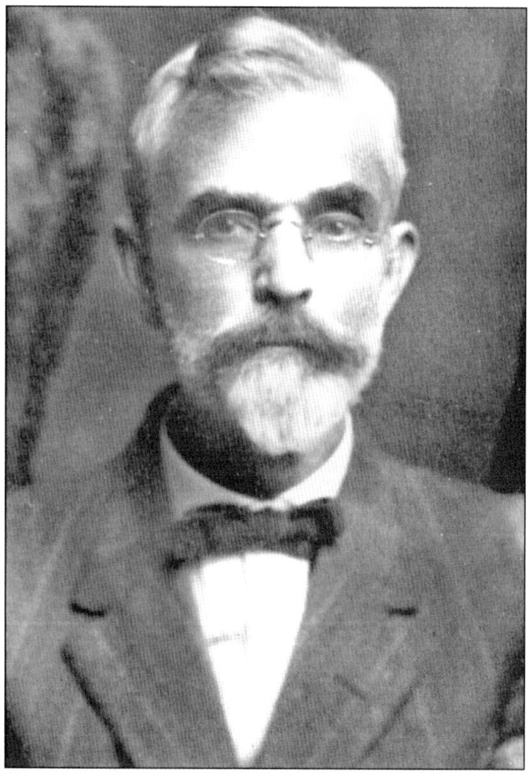

Willis D. Dunaway was a Valdosta pharmacist as far back as 1904, when his drug shop was located at 118 North Patterson Street. Later he moved to 109 South Patterson Street, and his shop was still there as late as the mid-1920s. During World War I, his son was a U.S. Army medical officer who served with the British Expeditionary Force in France.

E. L Turner was associated for decades with the *Valdosta Daily Times*, including service as both editor and publisher. Shown right at a very great age, he was still at work.

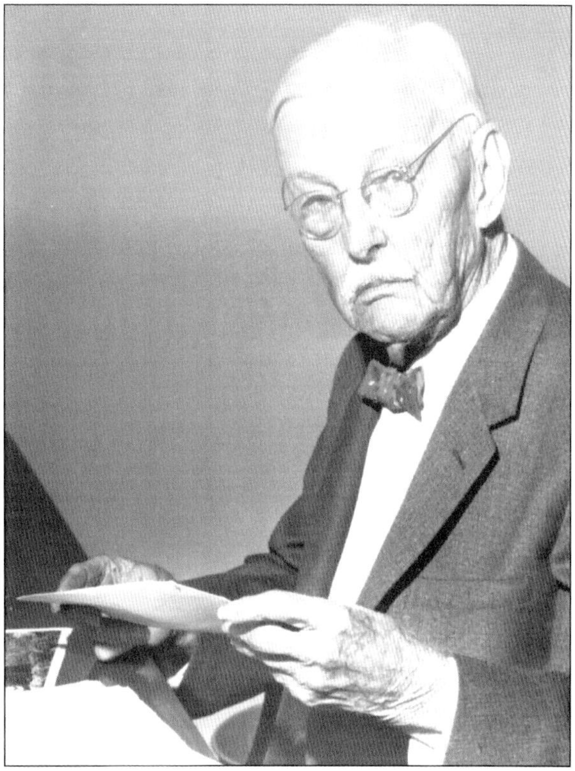

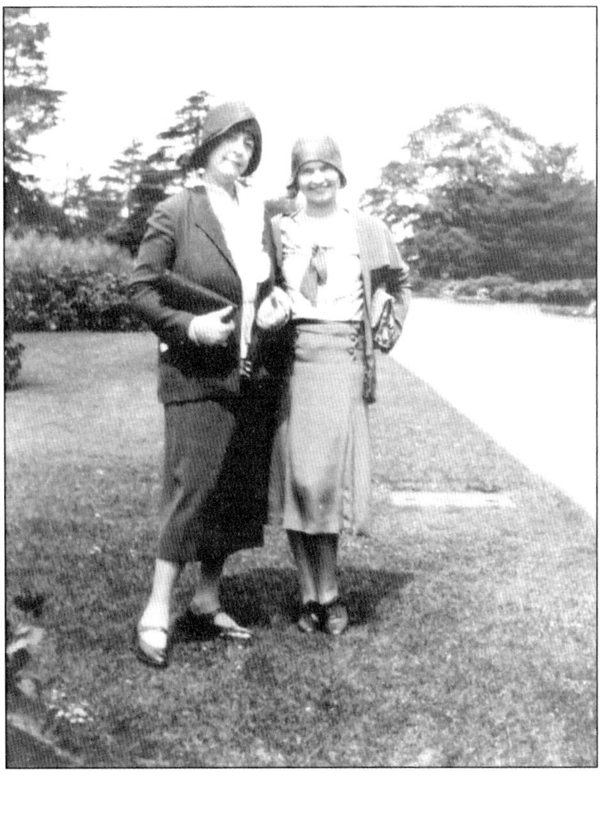

Two Lowndes County ladies pose for the camera on a lawn sometime in the 1920s. On the left is Maude Jenkins Peeples, and on the right is Elizabeth McRee Mencaccy.

Consistent with our mission to preserve history on a local level, this book was printed in South Carolina on American-made paper and manufactured entirely in the United States. Products carrying the accredited Forest Stewardship Council (FSC) label are printed on 100 percent FSC-certified paper.

MADE IN THE USA